Praise for Bhuvan Unhelkar's
Process Quality Assurance for UML-Based ▌

Although Unhelkar's approach to UML and Process Quality appears in ▌ far from "bookish." With some support from the author, the ideas outlin▐ have been of immense value to us in our large-scale CRMS implementation. This work is direct and practical.

Murray Heke
RMS Programme Director
Aon Risk Services

Using the UML in a project without due consideration to the various roles such as Business Analysts, System Designers, and Architects can be a major source of confusion, frustration, and, at worst, rejection. Unhelkar's practical exposition of modeling in the problem, solution, and background spaces addresses these issues. Worth applying in any project.

Andrew Powell
Chief Technology Officer
Merryl-Lynch Australia

In this extremely well-articulated view on software quality, Unhelkar has also proved the crucial role of UML in facilitating communications in project teams. The judicious combination of modeling, quality process, and quality management takes this book beyond just UML, and makes it applicable to all aspects of a software project. This work will be of tremendous interest to practitioners.

Prabhat (S D) Pradhan
CEO
iOpsis Software
San Francisco

We have run a series of successful two-day seminars in Mumbai, Bangalore, and Delhi, India, based on this exceptionally well-researched and well-presented work by Dr. Unhelkar. Our clients have found the ideas presented in this book extremely relevant to their effort in adopting process and modeling discipline, enabling them to climb up the CMM process maturity ladder. Well worth more than one read!!

Navyug Mohnot
CEO
QAIindia
Delhi, India

We started using UML along with the Quality Software Process for our consulting projects, as outlined here by Unhelkar, resulting in vastly improved communication with our clients and superior control of our projects. This book is a must read for practitioners.

Ashish Kumar
President and CEO
Jagat Technology, Inc.

Once in a long while does a manuscript come the reviewer's way that seems adequate in every respect. This is one of those instances. One does not have to be devoured by a tiger to realize one is present in the thicket; foot-prints shall suffice. The sample chapters were ample evidence that this book has every potential to succeed. This book is definitely for the professional, although I can see it used by academics and even as a supplemental textbook. The presence of end-of-chapter exercises certainly assists in this latter potential. To reach this wide array of audiences, again, one might add that the author has done well in striking a balance between depth and accessibility.

Prof. Houman Younessi
Rensselaer at Hartford
Hartford, Connecticut

Teaching and learning ìsoftware qualityî is always a challenge because of the elusive nature of quality. This book simplifies the task of teaching quality considerably. Each chapter is neatly outlined for a quality subtopic, followed by relevant FAQs and exercises. This work is an excellent blend of theory with practical examples that run consistently throughout the book.

Prof. Murat M. Tanik
University of Alabama at Birmingham
Birmingham, Alabama

Understanding and teaching quality requires a two-pronged approach. In the context of UML-based software development, first the UML-based models need to be subjected to rigorous quality checks of syntax, semantics, and aesthetics. Second, it is necessary to put in place the management and process aspect of development that would ensure creation of appropriate and good quality models in the first place. This second aspect is the focus of this book, as discussed in Chapters 2 through 4. While the introduction to the elusive nature of quality in Chapter 1 is extremely well-researched, Unhelkar has also demonstrated his practical experience in quality and UML in Chapter 5, "Estimates and Metrics." This is an excellent "accompanying" textbook for any course in quality, process, modeling, and management.

Prof. Athula Ginige
Head of School of Computing and Information Technology
University of Western Sydney
Australia

As the author of a commercial software process myself, I am pleased to see a book focus on process and quality rather than pure UML modeling. The focus on the process aspect of quality is the hallmark of this work. Certainly a process practitioner's material suitably interspersed with theory and anecdotes.

Dr Julian Edwards
Principal author of Process Mentor
Object Oriented Pty. Ltd.
Sydney, Australia

This work judiciously blends the crucial people aspect with software quality. Very practical, entertaining, and readable.

Ramin Marzbani
CEO
ACNielsen.consult
Australia

Process Quality Assurance
for UML-Based Projects

The Addison-Wesley Object Technology Series

Grady Booch, Ivar Jacobson, and James Rumbaugh, Series Editors
For more information, check out the series Web site [http://www.awprofessional.com/otseries/].

Ahmed/Umrysh, *Developing Enterprise Java Applications with J2EE™ and UML*

Arlow/Neustadt, *UML and the Unified Process: Practical Object-Oriented Analysis and Design*

Armour/Miller, *Advanced Use Case Modeling: Software Systems*

Bellin/Simone, *The CRC Card Book*

Binder, *Testing Object-Oriented Systems: Models, Patterns, and Tools*

Bittner/Spence, *Use Case Modeling*

Blakley, *CORBA Security: An Introduction to Safe Computing with Objects*

Booch, *Object Solutions: Managing the Object-Oriented Project*

Booch, *Object-Oriented Analysis and Design with Applications, Second Edition*

Booch/Bryan, *Software Engineering with ADA, Third Edition*

Booch/Rumbaugh/Jacobson, *The Unified Modeling Language User Guide*

Box/Brown/Ewald/Sells, *Effective COM: 50 Ways to Improve Your COM and MTS-based Applications*

Carlson, *Modeling XML Applications with UML: Practical e-Business Applications*

Cockburn, *Surviving Object-Oriented Projects: A Manager's Guide*

Collins, *Designing Object-Oriented User Interfaces*

Conallen, *Building Web Applications with UML, Second Edition*

D'Souza/Wills, *Objects, Components, and Frameworks with UML: The Catalysis Approach*

Douglass, *Doing Hard Time: Developing Real-Time Systems with UML, Objects, Frameworks, and Patterns*

Douglass, *Real-Time Design Patterns: Robust Scalable Architecture for Real-Time Systems*

Douglass, *Real-Time UML, Second Edition: Developing Efficient Objects for Embedded Systems*

Eeles/Houston/Kozaczynski, *Building J2EE™ Applications with the Rational Unified Process*

Fontoura/Pree/Rumpe, *The UML Profile for Framework Architectures*

Fowler, *Analysis Patterns: Reusable Object Models*

Fowler/Beck/Brant/Opdyke/Roberts, *Refactoring: Improving the Design of Existing Code*

Fowler/Scott, *UML Distilled, Second Edition: A Brief Guide to the Standard Object Modeling Language*

Gomaa, *Designing Concurrent, Distributed, and Real-Time Applications with UML*

Graham, *Object-Oriented Methods, Third Edition: Principles and Practice*

Heinckiens, *Building Scalable Database Applications: Object-Oriented Design, Architectures, and Implementations*

Hofmeister/Nord/Dilip, *Applied Software Architecture*

Jacobson/Booch/Rumbaugh, *The Unified Software Development Process*

Jordan, *C++ Object Databases: Programming with the ODMG Standard*

Kruchten, *The Rational Unified Process, An Introduction, Second Edition*

Lau, *The Art of Objects: Object-Oriented Design and Architecture*

Leffingwell/Widrig, *Managing Software Requirements: A Unified Approach*

Marshall, *Enterprise Modeling with UML: Designing Successful Software through Business Analysis*

McGregor/Sykes, *A Practical Guide to Testing Object-Oriented Software*

Mellor/Balcer, *Executable UML: A Foundation for Model-Driven Architecture*

Mowbray/Ruh, *Inside CORBA: Distributed Object Standards and Applications*

Naiburg/Maksimchuk, *UML for Database Design*

Oestereich, *Developing Software with UML: Object-Oriented Analysis and Design in Practice, Second Edition*

Page-Jones, *Fundamentals of Object-Oriented Design in UML*

Pohl, *Object-Oriented Programming Using C++, Second Edition*

Quatrani, *Visual Modeling with Rational Rose 2002 and UML*

Rector/Sells, *ATL Internals*

Reed, *Developing Applications with Visual Basic and UML*

Rosenberg/Scott, *Applying Use Case Driven Object Modeling with UML: An Annotated e-Commerce Example*

Rosenberg/Scott, *Use Case Driven Object Modeling with UML: A Practical Approach*

Royce, *Software Project Management: A Unified Framework*

Rumbaugh/Jacobson/Booch, *The Unified Modeling Language Reference Manual*

Schneider/Winters, *Applying Use Cases, Second Edition: A Practical Guide*

Shan/Earle, *Enterprise Computing with Objects: From Client/Server Environments to the Internet*

Smith/Williams, *Performance Solutions: A Practical Guide to Creating Responsive, Scalable Software*

Stevens/Pooley, *Using UML, Updated Edition: Software Engineering with Objects and Components*

Unhelkar, *Process Quality Assurance for UML-Based Projects*

van Harmelen, *Object Modeling and User Interface Design: Designing Interactive Systems*

Warmer/Kleppe, *The Object Constraint Language: Precise Modeling with UML*

White, *Software Configuration Management Strategies and Rational ClearCase®: A Practical Introduction*

The Component Software Series

Clemens Szyperski, Series Editor
For more information, check out the series Web site [http://www.awprofessional.com/csseries/].

Allen, *Realizing eBusiness with Components*

Atkinson/Bayer/Bunse/Kamsties/Laitenberger/Laqua/Muthig/Paech/Wust/Zettel, *Component-Based Product Line Engineering with UML*

Cheesman/Daniels, *UML Components: A Simple Process for Specifying Component-Based Software*

Szyperski, *Component Software, Second Edition: Beyond Object-Oriented Programming*

Whitehead, *Component-Based Development: Principles and Planning for Business Systems*

Process Quality Assurance for UML-Based Projects

Bhuvan Unhelkar

♠ Addison-Wesley

Boston • San Francisco • New York • Toronto
Montreal • London • Munich • Paris • Madrid
Capetown • Sydney • Tokyo • Singapore • Mexico City

The publisher offers discounts on this book when ordered in quantity for bulk purchases and special sales. For more information, please contact:

U.S. Corporate and Government Sales
(800) 382-3419
corpsales@pearsontechgroup.com

For sales outside of the U.S., please contact:

International Sales
(317) 581-3793
international@pearsontechgroup.com

Visit Addison-Wesley on the Web: www.awprofessional.com

Library of Congress Cataloging-in-Publication Data

Unhelkar, Bhuvan.
    Process quality assurance for UML-based projects / Bhuvan Unhelkar.
        p. cm.
    Includes bibliographical references and index.
    ISBN 0-201-75821-0 (pbk. : alk. paper)
     1. Computer software—Quality control. 2. UML (Computer science) I. Title.

    QA76.76.Q35 U54 2003
    005.1'068'5—dc21   2002027934

ISBN 0-201-75821-0
Text printed on recycled paper
1 2 3 4 5 6 7 8 9 10—MA—0605040302
First printing, October 2002

My Parents

My Parents

Contents

Foreword

When I agreed to write the foreword for this book, I expected to battle my way through a morass of technical jargon. I was willing to do this because the Unified Modeling Language (UML) is an approach widely used at the Raytheon Garland, Texas, site and I wanted to expand my knowledge of it. I must honestly admit that I started reading the text with dread and with a rather basic (and somewhat cynical) question: Other than a general understanding of what UML is, why should I care about it?

In my position as Director of Software Engineering, I rarely need detailed knowledge of development languages and tools, not to mention the fact that these development aids are constantly changing. UML, however, seems to have caught the attention of my software engineers, so I marched forward into *Process Quality Assurance for UML-Based Projects.* I convinced myself that quality assurance and process were at least familiar words and an integral part of my job.

Then something amazing happened: I couldn't put the book down. The introduction to the elusive nature of quality is consistent with my own views, and these views are well expressed (and frequently humorous). The historical facts behind UML (Booch, Jacobson, and Rumbaugh creating UML), the definition of UML (a means of visualizing, constructing, and documenting object-oriented software artifacts through a standard set of notations, diagrams, and specifications), and the relevance of UML to practical modeling are stated succinctly. The text deepens the reader's understanding of the direct and practical aspects of modeling with UML through the discussion of UML-based CASE tools and processes, which can contribute to requirements modeling and testing as well as system, database, and architectural design. As I read through the text, I condensed the information into the following major concepts:

- UML standardization is a good thing for large programs.
- UML supports major program activities associated with requirements, testing, design, and implementation.
- UML is effective in reducing the complexity of and enhancing the ability to test reality.
- UML addresses some of the most serious problems in system development, especially satisfaction of user expectations.
- UML helps mitigate the long-standing problems related to the intangibility of software.
- UML helps clarify interdependencies, which are common problem points in system integration.
- UML is not a monolithic construct—it has a different relevance and application in each of the three modeling spaces of problem, solution, and background (architecture).
- UML transition should be planned and handled carefully, particularly in separating UML techniques from its CASE tools and processes.

By the end of the first reading session, I became a fan of UML and Bhuvan Unhelkar's writing style. Instead of seeing UML as a software mystery understood by only the most esoteric guru or hard-core programmer, the reader begins to see UML as a value-added tool. In the quest for quality, UML supports system development through reduction of complexity, clarification of requirements, and addition of structure to the design and integration process.

One of the strong points of the text is the "big-picture" view of an entire program-development cycle. Unhelkar approaches the discussion of UML in the context of each modeling space and the process support required in each of these modeling spaces. The text is distinguished through the emphasis on definition of roles required to perform each process activity.

Many technical texts focus on the *what, when,* and *how,* but neglect the *who.* In this work, Unhelkar recognizes the importance of the sociological aspect of system development. In my own experience, I have seen system-integration program managers begin to recognize the psychological traits and attitudes of the program developers as valid parameters in determining and managing the program constraints of cost, schedule, and quality.

Traditionally, system development has been organized around technology and methodology. Nonquantifiable aspects of program success such as communication have been overlooked, despite the fact that poor communication accounts for a large percentage of project failures. Program managers focus on the triple constraints—quality, schedule, and cost. Unhelkar inspires the reader to also look at the second tier beneath each of these constraints—people, technology, and process. While making it clear that UML is not a process, the text addresses process-components with their respective roles, responsibilities, activities, tasks, and deliverables that produce UML-based artifacts.

Unhelkar has validly recognized that people are the key to building quality systems, and that training, organizing, empowering, and managing people are essential to producing a quality product. Emphasis on the human factors related to system developers and system users is found throughout the text. For example, Unhelkar states, "Proper study of quality would have to delve into other branches of science such as psychology, sociology, and social sciences."

To develop a system, many competencies—both engineering and nonengineering—are required. Some of the less-technical competencies addressed include understanding the user, establishing trust relationships, evaluating and selecting component suppliers, developing cost estimations, preparing test plans, balancing cost and quality, balancing reuse against customer requirements and system quality/cost/schedule, creating and managing schedules, managing system configuration, developing flexible designs, and selecting and using appropriate metrics.

Obviously, finding individual engineers capable of fulfilling all the required roles in system development is a difficult task, if not an impossible one. The solution lies in the ability to form teams composed of members whose skills are complementary and cover the gamut of necessary roles. Issues that affect the ability to form such complementary and effective teams include project size, geographical distribution of team members, and inherent communication issues arising from the possible lack of face-to-face interactions.

The text addresses ways to assemble teams, the value of diversity, and issues arising in a virtual environment. Unhelkar also touches on profiling team members to help each one determine roles best aligned with their skills and interests. Domain expertise and mentoring are addressed and presented as tools to aid in team coalescence.

Unhelkar's belief in the value of mentoring is demonstrated in his approach to writing this text. He does not seem interested in impressing the reader with his technical jargon, but rather, he sets the stage for learning about the UML and its relation to quality by virtue of its application within the framework of a process. His analogies and examples are entertaining as well as instructive as he steps logically through the text material.

As a mentor to system-development professionals, he clarifies who should develop or review UML models of the problem space, the solution space, and the background space (architecture) of the system. He provides commonsense suggestions for determining the applicability of UML to a project, and for planning UML training and mentoring. His instruction is encapsulated in FAQs and exercises at the end of each chapter. As a result, the text can serve as an excellent seminal reference for practitioners, academics, and researchers. The text might also be selected as an excellent basis for a class or a self-study group as well as an ideal textbook used in a transdisciplinary or interdisciplinary engineering curriculum.

Unhelkar's practical understanding of issues that confront those who build systems adds a dimension to the text that is lacking in many technical writings. I applaud this unique blend of theory and practice and highly recommend this text as a reference for software-system projects, software engineering courses, and research in the areas of quality, modeling, and process. My best wishes are with the author for this influential work, and I offer encouragement for him to pursue future projects, especially in the areas of product integration, metrics, cost estimation, and sociological/psychological factors affecting project success. I believe that my enthusiasm for *Process Quality Assurance for UML-Based Projects* will be shared by all who read it.

Vicki P. Rainey, Ph.D.
Director, Software Engineering
Raytheon—Garland Texas Site

Preface

Quality is subjective[1]

Purpose of This Book

This book is about the *process* aspect of quality assurance in UML-based projects. Process is one of the two major aspects of software quality assurance—the other being *modeling*. This book is written with an aim of directly addressing the paucity of literature in the area of quality assurance for UML-based projects—with a specific focus on process.

This is because despite its popularity, the UML literature needs discussion on and application of quality *with* UML. While we have some excellent literature on the processes of software development (most notably *The Unified Process* by Jacobson et al. and *The OPEN Process Specification* by Ian Graham et al.) it seems to fall short of separate and detailed discussions on quality.

On the other hand, works like Binder's *Testing Object Oriented Software* focus on the technical aspects of testing using the UML notations, but they do not provide the process aspect of improving the quality of software development. Indeed, none of this literature deserves any criticism for the lack of "quality" discussion—because these literary works do not purport to be discussing quality. The focus of these respectable and popular works

---

[1] This is such a universal statement, it must have come from you!

is either development or testing. This book in your hand complements the current literature in the UML arena.

Good quality is all about satisfying the needs of the user. However, "good" is a highly subjective term. The reference point against which quality is judged depends on time, place, and situation—all of which can change! Hence, the essential ingredients in producing good quality are:

- A product that satisfies the changing needs of the user
- A process that enables the creation, verification, and validation of such a product
- A common mechanism to establish communication
- Continuous improvement of the process of producing product

When applied to software development, these quality requirements translate into producing a software product that evolves, scales, and changes according to the needs of its users—primarily the business. We not only need a process for developing such a software product, but we also need significant checking and cross checking of the models and processes that have been used to construct the software product. There is a need to create, follow, and check all necessary process steps in order to achieve maturity of processes that result in good quality software products. These process steps must be executed iteratively, incrementally, and sufficiently.

Process steps should also be malleable enough to suit various development environments and various types and sizes of projects. These are some of the specific and significant areas of process-quality-related work required in a project incorporating the UML that are addressed in this book. Some of this quality work includes how to organize the overall quality function, the process steps to be followed in the creation of UML diagrams, the steps in the verification and validation of these diagrams, when to conduct such verification, how to interpret the results of quality activities, who should create and validate the UML diagrams, and how to create a quality control (testing) strategy.

These process steps eventually result in good quality models. Quality, however, is further enhanced by applying quality checks to the software models—ensuring their syntactical correctness, semantic consistency, and aesthetic symmetry. For detailed analysis and discussion of the model quality of UML diagrams, readers are encouraged to peruse *Model Quality Assurance of UML-Based Projects* (due 2003).

Summary of the Book

This book is divided into six chapters as summarized in the table below.

Chapter	Description
1. The Quality Game	Builds the background theory and arguments for quality
2. Quality Environment: Managing the Quality Function	Quality management, team formation, sociology, and psychology of quality teams; importance of process
3. The Quality Process Architecture	Process-components encompassing activities, tasks, deliverables, and roles that make up a Quality Software Process
4. Enacting the Quality Software Process	Quality process in practice; iterations, increments, and parallel development
5. Estimates and Metrics for UML-Based Projects	Some suggestions on practical estimation of time, budgets, and people for UML-based projects
6. Quality Control of Software Products	Detailed discussion on strategies for quality control and testing

Chapter 1: The Quality Game

In this background chapter on quality assurance we discuss the elusive nature of quality in the context of software. Modeling, particularly with the UML, is shown as a means to improve communication and quality and is conducted in the three distinct yet related modeling spaces of problem, solution, and background. We discuss process in the context of its three dimensions of technology (what), methodology (how), and sociology (who). This is followed by a discussion on the various checks (syntax, semantics, and aesthetics) needed to validate and verify UML-based models and the checks of necessity, sufficiency, and malleability needed for a good quality process. Chapter 1 also discusses the organization of the quality function and its application to various types of projects (development, integration, package implementation, outsourcing, data warehousing, and educational) as well as various sizes of projects (small, medium, and large).

Chapter 2: Quality Environment: Managing the Quality Function

The process aspect of quality encompasses the management functions of creating and managing a quality environment. This is because software quality is not just about verifying and validating what has been produced; it's also about sustaining an effort to follow the discipline of producing models and software. This discipline encompasses the process or the steps involved to produce good models and good software. This part of the book comprehensively considers the organization and execution of the quality function, with a detailed emphasis on the process of developing UML-based software. In other words, we discuss "how" the quality function is organized and carried out in UML-based projects. The people issues ("who") are also given due relevance in Chapter 2.

Chapter 3: The Quality Process Architecture

This chapter discusses what constitutes such a process and how it is helpful in enhancing quality in a UML-based project. This chapter does not propose a new process, but discusses a most generic process including the technological, methodological, and sociological dimensions—what constitutes a process, and its major dimensions. The technological dimension of a process deals with the "what," the methodological dimension with the "how," and the sociological dimension with the "who" of an overall process. These dimensions are described with common workday examples. Furthermore, the generic process also describes the most commonly used activities and tasks that should be present in any process. These activities and tasks and their related roles and deliverables are described with the aim of improving the discipline in a process, resulting in the enhanced quality of UML-based deliverables, and eventually the software product.

Chapter 4: Enacting the Quality Software Process

In this chapter we discuss the enactment of an example process including the practical issues of configuring an Iterative, Incremental, and Parallel (IIP) project plan, based on the process-components discussed in the previous chapter. We also discuss practical issues of tracking the progress of a project as well as modifying the project plan based on that tracking. An iterative and incremental project plan facilitates better absorption of changes than a sequential project plan. The creation and management of such a changing plan, derived from the malleability aspect of the process, is also discussed. This chapter discusses what happens when the "rubber hits the road" in terms of application of a process.

Chapter 5: Estimates and Metrics for UML-Based Projects

This chapter discusses the important issues of measurements and estimates in UML-based software projects. Starting with an argument for the need to make good estimates and how good metrics help to make good estimates, this chapter delves into the importance of these measures and estimates in improving the quality of models and processes in the project. Technical measures related to sizes and complexities of the UML artifacts and diagrams are also discussed. Estimates for an example implementation project using the UML are shown with a view to demonstrate the application and significance of metrics in a practical project.

Chapter 6: Quality Control of Software Products

This chapter discusses in detail the quality control and testing aspect of a quality lifecycle. While we discuss process quality in the previous chapters, quality control (testing) is a major process-component dedicated to verifying and validating the results of our efforts thus far in creating models and following a process. Good quality control is inherently negative, as it is aimed at breaking everything in a system—its logic, its execution, and its performance. Thus, although quality control is an integral part of quality assurance, it is not synonymous with it. This separation is given its due importance in this separate part of the book.

CD-ROM and Potential Web Support

The CD-ROM contains details of the chapters, diagrams, and a set of templates (deliverables, project plan, and so forth) that can be customized for use in projects. Suggested metrics for improving quality (for example, size of use cases and effort in creating classes) are also incorporated on the CD-ROM. With permission, evaluation copies of relevant process tools that deal with quality process are also provided.

Literary Audience

There are numerous books written on the UML and on processes. Their scope encompasses both academic research and practical applications. This book attempts to synergize the application of quality processes in UML-based projects. With the process focus, the reader is expected to be familiar with the UML and its modeling technique, as the book does not purport to discuss the modeling techniques of the UML.[2] However, a person responsible for quality assurance will find this work self-sufficient and may even be encouraged after reading this material to extend their

Chapters	Quality Manager	Project Manager	Tester	Process Engineer	System Designer	Developer	Business Analyst	System Architect	Academic	Director
1. The Quality Game	**	**		**					**	**
2. Quality Environment: Managing the Quality Function	**	*		*	*		*	*	**	*
3. The Quality Process Architecture	**		*	**		*	*	*	**	
4. Enacting the Quality Software Process	**		*	**	*	*	*	*	*	
5. Estimates and Metrics for UML-Based Projects	**	*		*					**	*
6. Quality Control of Software Products	**		**		*	*	*	*	*	**

[2] This is discussed in my forthcoming book *Model Quality Assurance of UML-Based Projects,* to be published by Addison-Wesley.

UML understanding. Following is a cross-reference of the book categories and the extent to which readers will find each chapter interesting. The intensity of potential interest is designated by the number of "*" (maximum three for highest intensity).

Semantics

I firmly believe in gender-neutral language. *Person* is therefore used wherever possible. However, in order to maintain reading simplicity *he* has been used as freely and has been balanced by equal, if not more, use of *she*.

Terms like *programmer* and *quality manager,* unless otherwise mentioned, represent roles performed by actors. These terms don't tie down real people like you and me who, in a short span of time, can jump from the role of a programmer to a quality manager to a director and back. It is also recognized that people may be playing more than one role at a time. For example, a business analyst may also be a part-time academic or a researcher.

Throughout the text, *we* primarily refers to the reader and the author— you and me. Occasionally, *we* refers to the general information technology (IT) community, of which the author is a member. *We* also refers to the teams in which the author has worked. Therefore, although this is a single-author book, you may encounter *we* as a reference by the author to himself, as well as to the IT community. Real conversations, as you and I are having through this work, cannot be statically typed.

Mapping to a Workshop

The practical aspects of UML and quality, displayed in this book, have been popular in seminars and conferences. Among many presentations based on this book, particularly noteworthy are its acceptance as a tutorial at the UML 2001 Conference in Toronto, Canada, and the two-day seminar series[3] in Mumbai, Bangalore, and Delhi, India. Many additional workshops and seminars are scheduled at the time of this writing. The following table is a generic outline of one day of a possible two-day workshop based on the topic of this book. For the education and academic

---

[3] See *www.qaiindia.com* for more details.

community, each chapter in this book corresponds to a three-hour lecture topic, with the early part of the semester concentrating on creating the UML-based models based on the case study.

Mapping of the chapters in this book to one day of a two-day workshop

Day	Session	Presentation and discussion workshop topic	Relevant chapters	Comments
1	9:00–10:30	Pressures on quality; relevance in UML projects	1, 2	Outline the elusive nature of quality; argue for the need and approach to quality
	11:00–12:30	Quality management; quality process architecture	3, 4	How to organize the quality function; quality management and quality process
	1:30–3:00	Process enactment; project estimation and metrics; quality control (testing) of UML artifacts	5, 6	Practical session on numbers. People, time, and budgets for UML-based projects
	3:30–5:00	Case studies	CD	Example discussions; utilizing the checklists provided in practice

Acknowledgments

Encouragement and support take various forms—a word of encouragement here, a hint of a smile there! And then there are those detailed discussions and arguments with honest reviewers of the manuscript on what should be included and how it should be presented. This is interspersed with the arduous task of typing the manuscript, drawing the figures, and the rather trying job of proofreading someone else's writing. All this has come to me through many wonderful people, whom I acknowledge here gratefully:

Anurag Agarwal
Harpreet Alag
Rajeev Arora
Craig Bates
Paul Becker
Vikram Bhalla
Christopher Biltoft
Bhargav Bhatt
Ilona Box
Graham Churchley
Kamlesh Chaudhary
Sandra Cormack
Joanne Curry
Sanjeev Dandekar
Edward D'Souza

Con DiMeglio
Julian Edwards
Jeffrey Ferguson
Nandu Gangal
Athula Ginige
David Glanville
Mark Glikson
Nitin Gupta
Brian Henderson-Sellers
Murray Heke
Ivar Jacobson
Sudhir Joshi
Ashish Kumar
Vijay Khandelwal
Akshay Kriplani

Yi-chen Lan
Girish Mamdapur
Bahman Marzbani
Ramin Marzbani
Javed Matin
Sid Mishra
Rahul Mohod
Navyug Mohnot
Narayana Munagala
Karin Ovari
Les Parcell
Chris Payne
Andrew Powell
Abhay Pradhan
Amit Pradhan

Anand Pradhan	*Bran Selic*	*Asha Unhelkar*
Prabhat Pradhan	*Ashish Shah*	*Sunil Vadnerkar*
Rajesh Pradhan	*Paresh Shah*	*Ketan Vanjara*
Tim Redrup	*Prince and Nithya*	*Suresh Velgapudi*
Tracey Reeve	*Soundararajan*	*John Warner*
Prashant Risbud	*Pinku Talati*	*Houman Younessi*
James Ross	*Amit Tiwary*	
Magdy Serour	*Murat Tanik*	

Paul Becker, my editor at Addison-Wesley, has provided invaluable support in this work and deserves special recognition. Bearing with my delayed submissions, passing encouraging comments when the progress was slow, and accommodating my changes up to the last minute are some of the traits of this considerate editor that I gratefully acknowledge.

Finally, my family makes all this possible by just being around me—even, and especially, when I am mentally lost. I am grateful to my wife Asha, my daughter Sonki Priyadarshini (whose view on quality took a jagged turn as she stepped into her teens), and my son Keshav Raja, who appreciates quality in cars, bikes, and planes—the ability of these "tools of the kindergarten" trade to withstand punishment meted out by rather tough six year olds.

Finally, this work acknowledges all trademarks of respective organizations, whose names and/or tools have been mentioned in this book. Specifically, I acknowledge the trademarks of Rational (for ROSE), TogetherSoft (for TogetherControlCenter), Object-Oriented Pty. Ltd. (for ProcessMentor), and eTrack.

Critiques

It reflects a healthy state of affairs within the IT world, and especially the UML and process community, if work of this nature receives its due share of criticism. All criticisms have an underlying rationale and they should all be accepted in a positive and constructive vein. All comments on this work, both positive and negative, *will* be accepted positively. Thus, to all my prospective critics, whose criticisms will not only enrich my own knowledge and understanding of the "quality" topics discussed in this book, but will also add to the general wealth of knowledge available to the IT community, I wish to say a big *thank you* in advance.

Bhuvan Unhelkar
Sydney, July 2001
Revised, May 2002

part

Setting the Scene for Software Quality Assurance

Part I is a relatively philosophical chapter that discusses the issues of quality from a general perspective. By discussing quality separately, we can proceed to apply our discussion to various important aspects of a project—such as management, modeling, programming, or process. This chapter provides important background reading, followed by a discussion on the process aspect of quality in the remaining parts of the book.

The Quality Game

The Golden Rule: The one who owns the Gold, makes the Rules.[1]

Putting This Chapter in Perspective

The final word on any quality initiative comes from the one who pays for the product or service whose quality is being judged. More often than not, this final word is a subjective interpretation of the product or service by its user. Instead of arguing against this subjective judgment, it is vital to develop a good understanding of the subjective nature of quality itself. This is akin to understanding the canvas before painting the picture; it is the main topic of discussion in this chapter. In this chapter on quality assurance we discuss the elusive nature of quality in the context of software.

Modeling, particularly with the UML, is shown as a means to improve communication, in the three distinct yet related modeling areas supported by specific quality activities: Problem Space, Solution Space, and Background Space. Process is discussed in the context of its three dimensions of technology (what), methodology (how), and sociology (who). This is followed by a discussion on the various checks (syntax, semantics, and aesthetics) needed to validate and verify UML-based models and the

---

[1] While I am sure we have all heard this many times, I came across it first in Retd. Major John Phippen's extensive 10-day Software Quality Assurance course in 1993, conducted under the auspices of the Australian Computer Society.

necessity, sufficiency, and malleability checks needed for a good quality process. The chapter also covers organization of the quality function and its application to various types of projects (development, integration, package implementation, outsourcing, data warehousing, and educational) and the various project sizes (small, medium, and large).

The Prime Reader: User, Business Analyst, System Designer, Architect, Project Manager, Quality Manager, and variations of these roles

1.1   Elusive Software Quality

1.1.1   Defining Quality

Good Quality is all about satisfying the needs of the user. However, "quality," and especially "good," are highly subjective terms. The reference point against which quality is judged depends on time, place, and situation. For example, my high-quality Cross pen may be used to sign a check, but it is not convenient when scribbling long, winding crib notes for this book. My needs as a user change, and change rapidly! However, it is unfair to label users capricious in terms of determining their quality needs. The information technology (IT) community, who *uses* databases, language compilers, and Web application servers to produce software, is also subjected to the same needs for, and judgments of, quality. Despite the subjectivity of its definition, quality is dear to everyone's heart. Basing a quality approach entirely on "head" or logic, without giving due credence to the emotional nature of quality, is likely to fail. Therefore, we need a definition of quality, but with the understanding that the issue of quality in practice is invariably going to transgress that definition. So how do we define quality?

Coplien [1994] quotes Christopher Alexander in order to come close to what is meant by quality. Mathematician Alexander is well known in the architectural world, especially for applying his measures of quality to building and extending them further to any creative process. During his keynote address at OOPSLA 96,[2] Alexander described quality in broad

---

[2] OOPSLA, a popular conference on object technology, stands for Object Oriented Programming, Systems, Languages, and Applications. According to his own admission, Christopher Alexander was perhaps the only nontechnical person at the conference in San Jose, when he delivered his keynote address in 1996.

terms as a system's[3] ability to be alive; to be a part of, and to support, our lives. He also referred to coherence, as well as another subjective term—happiness. At a lower level, this quality is utilitarian, aesthetically pleasing, robust, and whole. But Alexander notes that any attempt to name or measure the quality is futile: words can confuse more than they explain. Gabriel [1993] also discusses Alexander's definition of "quality without a name":

> A system has this quality when it is at peace with itself, when there are no internal contradictions, when it is not divided against itself, and when it is true to its own inner forces. Alexander's words to define this quality are— *alive, whole, comfortable, free, exact, egoless,* and *eternal.*

Thus, it appears that quality cannot be named or pointed to. Perhaps, quality comes philosophically closer to the definition of the Tao: "The Tao which can be named is not the true Tao" [Cheng 1981].

One of the most well-known authors in the field of quality assurance is William Perry. In his classic work *Quality Assurance for Information Systems* [1991], Perry begins the discussion on "what is quality" with a dictionary definition:

> The dictionary defines quality as an attribute or characteristic that is associated with something. Thus, quality cannot be universally defined but rather must be defined for the item in question.

My dictionary (*Oxford*) also makes a fervid attempt to define quality:

> The degree of excellence of a thing; general excellence; a distinctive attribute or faculty; the relative nature of kind or character of a thing.

Based on the above "formal" definitions of quality it becomes obvious that coming up with a *precise* definition of quality is not easy, if not impossible. We can continue to forage in the *Webster's* and the *Oxfords* of the world and still be short of a formal and acceptable definition of quality. The closest we can get to the real meaning of quality, the meaning that can help us in our quest for quality, is the one interpreted by Perry, above. *It depends on the context.*

Therefore, a good starting point in understanding quality is to understand as much as we can about the context in which quality is judged. The users operate in an environment given to them and they want the product (tool) they use to help them achieve their objectives. Those who are

---

[3] Not necessarily a software system.

responsible for the production of such products should follow a discipline and a set of standards that facilitate creating such products. And the entire approach of the producers and consumers should be based on the ever-changing context. Thus, the essential ingredients in creating good quality can be described as:

- A product: The product with which users perform their functions and the manner and extent to which the product helps them achieve their objectives is a primary criterion for quality. However, these objectives or needs are continually changing. Hence, product quality is judged by the ability of the product to satisfy the changing needs of the users.

- A production process: The process or method used in the creation of the product is as important as the product itself. The manner in which a particular product is created reflects the thinking behind the product, the discipline of the people and teams behind the product, and the commitment of the producers. Producers of products such as cars and laptops not only advertise their products, but also promote their production process as a key ingredient of their commitment to quality. The production process plays a crucial role in quality by not only enabling the creation of the right product, but also ensuring its verification and validation *as it is being produced.*

- A communication mechanism: A formal mechanism to communicate within the development domain and across the industry is a vital ingredient in creating quality. A process discipline that lies buried in reams of pages, and which is itself subject to different interpretations, is not helpful in providing the detailed and instantaneous communication expected in modern-day software projects. A good common communication mechanism provides a rigorous set of standard visual means for thinking, creating, recording, and sharing the deliverables of the process. It establishes communication between the users and the producers of the product.

- A continuous improvement of the above three ingredients (the product, the production process, and the communication mechanism): It takes effort to produce a good quality product. A good process enables repetition of the steps that are crucial for mass production. Finally, a good process can become a bureaucratic nightmare unless it is supported by a robust, industry-standard communication mechanism.

This book focuses on the quality aspect of the process of creating a product (in this case, a software product), and the continuous improvement of the process itself.

1.1.2 Quality and Objective Effort

Understanding *and* establishing the context in which the end user of our product operates is a good starting point in understanding how to approach quality. Once we accept that we *will* be confronted by users who continue to vacillate between wanting exactly the same product and wanting something different, we start planning *beyond* simply producing the product. We bring in broader concepts—such as domain-level requirements, extensive prototyping, user training, and usability—that add substantial quality to the product but are not the product themselves.

The issue of quality remains so vital to every user of every product, that even without a precise definition, we still need to put in as much objective effort as possible to improve the quality of our products, processes, and communication mechanisms. This effort encompasses (but is not limited to) using detailed checklists for quality verification, following a formal process for development, and attempting to measure and improve quality. Vacillating quality requirements causes frustration for well-meaning developers. But that should not deter us from thinking, debating, and implementing quality concepts, checks, and processes in every development environment.

In other words, even if we are faced with a moving target, we should endeavor to aim in a general direction and fire. Precision will come in due course, but we cannot wait for it. We must put forward our best effort and hope for the best. And the more product and process failures we see—both the colossal (as described by Glass [1997]) and the day-to-day frustrations of users saying, "This is not what we wanted"—the more we should be encouraged to try to improve quality. The underlying motto can be:

> Even with extra effort at improving quality of my products, my users still say, "This is not a quality product." Imagine what they will say if no effort is put into quality at all!

Effort in the realm of quality is an ongoing objective effort to achieve something that is still subjective. It needs a lot of common sense, and then it needs more common sense. Quality, as seen in the dictionary definitions, is an *adjective*. It is thus an attribute of something. We can't produce quality on its own. We still have the responsibility to produce the product, and quality remains a characteristic of that product.

Brooks [1995] has quoted Boehm, pointing out that productivity drops again as one pursues extreme quality, as in IBM's space shuttle program. Therefore, we continuously have to keep the relevance for the end user in mind when we produce the product. This is especially true with third-party products, such as Enterprise Resource Planning (ERP) packages or reusable component libraries, where we cannot confer with the user during the development phase.

Our objective effort in producing quality products should lead us to a scalable, changeable, and maintainable product—in our case, software. Concepts of requirements, architecture, design, development, testing, and deployment will all have to be prefixed with quality. Therefore, we will aim for quality requirements, quality architecture, quality design, quality development, quality testing, and quality deployment in whatever we produce. And despite all our senses and sensibilities, we should also be prepared for what may appear at first to be "nonsense." As my quality boss in my first job used to say: "It is not that the request from the user is nonsense; it just *appears* like that to you."

1.1.3 Nature of Software

To make matters more interesting, the product we are talking about is also effusive, to say the least! It's software. Can't touch it, can't feel it, can't smell it. We all agree that it's there, but unlike a car or a house, it's not an object.[4] In fact, it is not even like a painting. A good Van Gogh cannot be easily executed in two different ways by two different observers, but a piece of software certainly can—and usually is.

Lanier [1997], discussing "the frontier between us," on the first 50 years of computing in the commemorative issue of *Communications of the ACM*, states:

> The easiest predictions to make about the next 50 years of computer science are those centering on the computers, not the people. It's when people are brought into the equation, however, that the business of prediction becomes difficult. . . . The biggest surprise from the first 50 years of computers is that

---

[4] Yeah, even object-oriented software is not an object in the same sense that a car or a house is.

computation turns out to be a cultural object in its own right, with all its warts and semicolons.

This consideration of the human factor in computing permeates all aspects of software development, especially quality assurance. A piece of software may succeed or fail based on apparently flimsy reasons like the background colors or position of the Help buttons. Except for the high-tech end users, many users tend to judge the quality of software by what is presented to them, rather than what is underneath the presentation. The graphical user interface is their means of interacting with the system, and it is the interface that will enable them to satisfy their own objectives.

The system's interface is not just its pretty face, but also its speed, performance, and reliability. Furthermore, the ever-changing needs of modern-day software means that even the producers of the software, who have to keep up with these changes, have quality needs that must be satisfied.

The nature of software is such that it is difficult to judge its quality objectively. Add to that the quality needs of the end user and the producer of such software. The subjective needs of such a diverse group of people demand a broader contextual study to understand software quality, much more than a mere definition and a checklist provides (although definitions and checklists are essential ingredients of quality approach). The proper study of quality will delve into other branches of science such as psychology, sociology, and social sciences. In this work, too, we will bring in the relevant soft factors as necessary, in describing the quality approach.

Given the above discussion, the best view we can form on software quality is that it is elusive and that more than just software engineering is needed to properly address it. However, we cannot wait for such a comprehensive approach to be developed or for a more objective definition of software quality before we start producing quality software. While the thinkers and the researchers can continue to investigate, understand, and objectify the concepts behind quality, the practitioners have the job of producing software with as many quality attributes attached to it as possible. The nature of software is such that it needs an intertwining of both of these groups of people, all the time.

1.1.4   Assuring Quality: A Distinct Activity

Is assuring the quality of a product—especially a software product—a part of the overall process of development? Or is it a distinct activity in its own right? And here, I am not talking about just controlling the quality of software—which is a separate topic of testing, discussed in Chapter 6.

Many proponents of software processes say that by following a process, quality will eventually result.[5] "If everyone in the project is responsible for quality, and if every activity is performed as it is meant to be performed," they argue, "quality will result." I have my doubts about this approach. Unless quality assurance is made an ongoing and *distinct* activity, quality for both producers and consumers of software will not result from the benefit of sustained objective effort. The people responsible for production and the process of production can be made "quality aware," but that is not the same as performing independent quality activities. It is important to keep the activities related to quality assurance distinct from the activities of production and quality control.

And there is a good reason why this should be the case. Take, for example, a top athlete who knows all about her sport, participating in an Olympic event. Why does she still need a trainer? Take an even simpler example: We all need to go to a barber, although the process of cutting hair is relatively simple.[6] My request to the barber is simple: "A little trim please," and yet I have never been able to do it myself. Forget about my hair or yours, even the skilled barber is unable to give *himself* a haircut. And the simple reason is that the barber (or the athletic trainer) is able to do something that you cannot do—to *see* the product that is on your head, or the process the athlete is following.

A trainer can *see* what an athlete is doing, how she takes a start, sprints, or dives into a pool. Similarly, a barber is able to *see* the hair on my head that I cannot (if I use a mirror to cut my own hair, the results are embarrassing to say the least). Thus, one of the primary roles performed by quality assurance and quality control is to see what is being done by others, evaluate it, criticize it, and improve on it. In order to achieve this

---

[5] Advanced readers familiar with Rational's Unified Process will recall that there is no separate discipline (workflow) in RUP for quality assurance; there is only a test discipline (www.rational.com).

[6] I am sensitive to people with fine, long, black hair, but then again I am not balding either (yet)!

properly, a quality person must be independent from the modelers and the developers, as should the activities and tasks performed by this person. This independence ensures that the quality activity continues to observe other normal development activities, and the quality person continues to see what others, who have produced the artifacts, cannot.

1.2   Pressures on Quality

Because of the elusive nature of quality, it is easily dispensed with under pressure. Once the basic necessities of a product are satisfied, there is always a desire to push the product out the door. Being a practitioner, I am occasionally guilty of this indulgence. "It does the job, so let it pass—we'll fix the rest later on." This attitude results in the concept of "good enough software," described as early as a decade ago by Ed Yourdon in *The Rise and Resurrection of the American Programmer* [1998].

However, if we understand from the beginning the kinds of pressure that quality is subjected to, it will help us plan a product's release with full knowledge of which functionalities are available and which are not. We can also make our potential users and product sponsors aware of these functionalities. In my experience, the four interests depicted in Figure 1.1

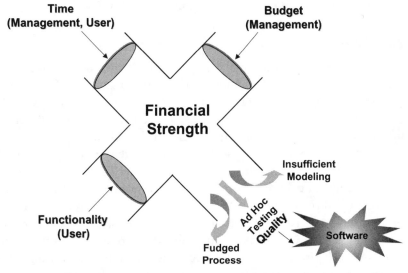

Figure 1.1 *Quality priorities*

vie against each other during a project. Also, as shown in Figure 1.1, quality is the *least* objective of them, and therefore the most likely to be ignored whenever the project is under pressure.

1.2.1   Budget

The budget is, of course, the prime interest of any astute project sponsor and project manager. All projects have a budget—officially stated or not. Although completing a project within budget is not the sole criterion of its success, budgets and associated costs are the easiest things to measure. Costs play an important role in projects, not only because they fund the product, but also because the first thing that a project manager does is to count these figures, even if using an elementary spreadsheet.

Furthermore, in almost all budgeting exercises, the basic figures relate to the costs associated with the development or integration of the software. What is not usually considered is the cost of software maintenance over its lifetime. The cost of software maintenance is likely to be as much as its development costs, if not more. But because the maintenance costs are not easy to compute, they are not included in the initial budgeting exercises. If total costs of enhancements and fixes were to be considered over the life of a system, then the upfront costs associated with quality would be easier to justify. In the absence of such justifications, however, budget constraints exert enormous pressure on quality.

1.2.2   Time

Senior management is continually worried about time. Having received the budget for a project, the entire attention of management focuses on time. Not only is time slightly more difficult to estimate as compared with budgets, but it's also difficult to *track*. Indeed, meeting the timeline roughly correlates with meeting the budget, but not always.

Contrary to popular belief, it is worth noting that time, especially in software projects, is many times *nonlinear*. One day is not the same as another, and meeting or missing a deadline has far more implications than just good or bad project management. The context in which time is available and/or lost is more important than the loss of a particular hour. Modern-day software projects are interconnected to many aspects of the business, which, in turn, is connected with other businesses and the industry. A missed deadline can have a snowball effect that cannot be estimated or anticipated upfront.

1.2.3 Functionality

"Just this one small extra functionality" is a commonly heard phrase in the corridors of software projects. It usually comes from well-meaning, sincere users who genuinely believe that the extra functionality they ask for will make their life much easier and will enable the business to make more money. However, adding what appears to be a small functionality (from the user's viewpoint) sometimes becomes a fairly complex operation requiring a suite of changes to the application, GUI, database, security, and so on.

While it is important for software developers to be sensitive to the needs of the user, these additional functionalities tend to creep in, and before long the overall scope of the system has increased substantially. Furthermore, additional functionalities are not always subject to even a simple cost-benefit or time-benefit analysis, resulting in functionalities receiving wrong priorities. Finally, functionalities are allowed to creep in to please a project sponsor or a key business stakeholder. Vested interests and related political issues[7] have the potential to pull the project goals sideways to unrelated or ulterior goals, resulting in a negative impact on quality.

1.2.4 Quality

The aforementioned pressures on quality are experienced by project managers regularly. No wonder they are echoed by many authors, including Bill Gates [1999] in *Business @ The Speed of Thought*:

> Customers want high-quality products at low prices, and they want them now. Every business, whether it's a producer of products and services or a supplier to that producer, has to deal with a shrinking time to market while keeping quality high and price low. Information Technology has become a major contributor to the faster turnaround, the higher quality, and the low inflation that have characterized business in the last decade.

What is also important to us in this discussion is the fact that information technologists (software developers) are themselves customers of some sort—looking for quality ways to develop software that satisfies the needs of their users, who can then provide the necessary products and services

---

[7] This is discussed in greater detail in Chapter 2, particularly Section 2.4 on project sociology and Section 2.5 on transactional analysis and games.

to satisfy the end users. However, by its very nature, quality remains subjective; therefore, once the pressure is exerted by *measurable* entities like budgets, time, and functionality, the effort to meet quality requirements starts to dwindle.

In this book, we attempt to understand as much as possible about the nature of software quality, what affects it, and how it can be improved. Application of quality is not restricted to a particular piece of code or data. It can and should be applied to a variety of levels within the software environment, as seen in the next section.

1.3   Quality Levels

Perry [1991] highlights goals, methods, and performance as three major aspects of quality. The quality context triangle, shown in Figure 1.2, further expands on Perry's basic definition. Understanding and appreciating quality, especially in the context of software, can be developed if we consider the various levels at which quality criteria can be applied.

For example, the goals of quality at the process level are established to ensure that all necessary steps in the process have been followed—and repeated a sufficient number of times. Model quality, on the other hand, may focus on the most efficient design that results in high performance and/or easier maintenance. These various focuses of quality are highlighted in the layers of the quality context triangle of Figure 1.2. These divisions facilitate easier understanding and concentration of quality effort in the area most needed. The following quality levels deserve our attention when we consider software quality:

- Data Quality
- Code Quality
- Model/Architecture Quality
- Process Quality
- Management Quality
- The Quality Environment

There are times when the distinctions shown here might blur, but they are important in providing a background for a project's quality needs.

Furthermore, each of these quality needs can have two aspects to it: quality control, which deals with ensuring the quality of whatever is

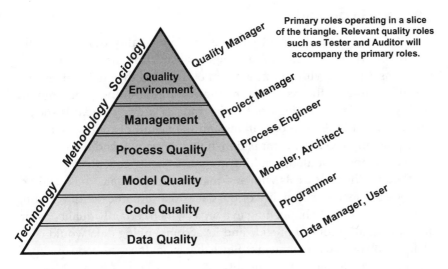

Figure 1.2 *The quality context triangle*

produced within these areas, and quality assurance, which deals with the quality of process that produces artifacts within these areas.

The following sections discuss these elements of the quality context triangle in further detail.

1.3.1   Data Quality

In Figure 1.2, the basic layer of quality is the data quality, which is the widest layer of the triangle. Data in any modern industrial application (including Web applications), or in any multidimensional data warehouse application can span from gigabytes to terabytes and more. Ensuring the quality of this data is a major part of both quality control and quality assurance. The quality manager must be aware of techniques of equivalence partitioning, boundary values, and so on, in sampling, checking, and correcting the data that goes into a system. Data quality is an important aspect of quality to be considered, especially in large-scale conversion projects. Detailed description of techniques to ensure data quality and related testing is discussed in Chapter 6.

1.3.2   Code Quality

The next layer of the context triangle is the code quality, or quality of the programs written. This layer is at a higher abstraction than the data level. Programs can deal with a large amount of data, but they themselves may not be as large as the data they manipulate. In assuring programming quality, we consider the logic of the program, as well as standards such as naming of attributes and operations and the layout of code specific to a particular language. The compilation, link, integration, and build of code are verified and validated, resulting in a good quality code.

Because the code deals with and manipulates the data, the quality of the code influences the quality of the data (to a certain extent). If coding were the only activity happening in a project, then certainly quality assurance and quality control of code and its accompanying data would complete the job of a quality manager. Since that is not the case, code quality is separate from data and model quality.

1.3.3   Model Quality

In a UML-based project, we do not code directly from what the developers or the users have in their heads (thankfully). First the problem is modeled in detail, and then the solution is modeled. The problem and the solution models are influenced by models of the architecture, which stay in the background. All UML-based projects undertake a detailed amount of modeling, which is neither the actual data nor the actual code. These models go on to improve the quality of the code produced.

However, it is not just their influence on the implemented code that interests us, but also their own quality—that is, the quality of the models themselves. We want the models we have produced to be subjected to the quality assurance process. It is important that these models adhere to known standards and are also subjected to stringent quality control, because models play a crucial role in improving the quality—by improving the communication among project team members and among projects. This detailed quality aspect of the UML-based models themselves is a topic outside the scope of this book, and is covered separately in another book [Unhelkar 2003].

1.3.4 Process Quality

One way to ensure production of good models is to produce them by following a quality-conscious process. Models in UML-based projects are outputs or deliverables that are produced by following certain steps. Once these steps are researched and organized (and possibly supported by a process-tool), they become a full process. The process plays a crucial role in what gets produced as a model. Therefore, it is absolutely vital to consider the process aspect of quality within the context triangle.

Furthermore, as Fowler [2000] correctly states, without having at least some semblance of a process, it is difficult to discuss modeling. This also implies that it is difficult to disregard process in a serious discussion of quality of the models produced. A set of well-thought-out activities and tasks, as available in a process, is likely to result in more accurate and higher quality models than a random attempt. This level of the quality context triangle finds a separate, serious, and sustained workout in Chapters 3 and 4.

1.3.5 Management Quality

"Management of Quality" or "Quality of Management"? While most of the time these two phrases are used interchangeably, they are two separate aspects of quality, albeit heavily dependent on each other.

"Quality of Management" delves into the quality of everything that needs to be managed in a project and that is represented by "Management Quality" in the quality context triangle. This includes the need to organize resources, form teams, set objectives, prioritize scope, manage risks, and enable communication, to name a few. These are standard project management tasks. The manner in which they are performed has a direct bearing on the success or failure of a project. These tasks need to be performed in a quality way, leading us to the discussion on quality of management. It is important to perform all management tasks with quality consciousness, because more projects fail because of a lack of proper project management considerations than because of technical issues.

This viewpoint is ratified by a KPMG report presented by Greatrex [1996] at the IT Project Management conference in Auckland in April 1996. More than 250 companies whose IT projects failed were surveyed. The results indicate that in 32 percent of the cases inadequate project management led to project failure. Other major factors were inadequate communication (20 percent) and failure to define objectives (17 percent). These factors can all be categorized into what Constantine [1995] calls *soft factors* and what DeMarco and Lister [1987] call *sociological factors*.

When we talk about quality of management we are talking about the manner in which these soft factors are handled by management. The quality of management is discussed and highlighted, as are the related process aspects, deliverables produced, and the application of quality techniques to the management approach. An improvement in quality of management leads to an overall improvement in the way in which risks are managed, objectives are scoped, and teams are motivated, for example.

Management of quality, on the other hand, is different. It deals with applying the principles of management to the quality work itself. For example, managing the quality assurance personnel, organizing the quality meetings, procuring the quality control tools, and managing the risks associated with quality (as well as extreme quality) are some of the things that fall under the category of management of quality. One of the primary responsibilities of a quality manager in managing quality is creating a complete quality environment.

1.3.6   Quality Environment

This is a separate and focused attempt at quality; it can also be described as quality management that deals with the creation and management of quality environment, as shown in Figure 1.2. Planning for quality, organizing the resources, and providing an approach with associated quality tools is part of creating and managing the quality environment.

Placed on top of the quality triangle, the quality environment deals with all aspects of quality underneath it. The quality environment is responsible for data quality, code quality, model quality, process quality, and management quality. Furthermore, it is also responsible for itself—that is, organizing the quality management functions itself is subject to the quality criteria setup in the quality environment.

Specifically, in terms of a process, the quality environment deals with the tools and techniques of the process itself. It deals with process transition issues, training issues, pilot project selection, process deployment with a case tool, and quality control organization. It provides an overall environment in which good process, followed by good models, followed by good programming, followed by good data is made possible. A software process can deal with a project, but the questions of whether to create an in-house process or buy an "off-the-shelf" one, how to ascertain a suitable process if buying one, how to customize it, and how to deploy it should fall outside the process. For example, if I am deciding to use a particular process, such as eXtreme Programming (XP) or RUP, that decision-making process should not be a part of XP or RUP. That decision is taken by or suggested by a quality process—which in turn is within the full quality environment. A quality environment, therefore, is made up of not only a software development process, but also a quality process.

1.4   Quality Software Process

Most of the work that goes on in the quality environment (as shown in the quality context triangle in Figure 1.2) is process based. Note also that in discussing the various levels of quality and how they relate to each other, the process quality level is important. Processes play a crucial role in producing quality. Processes also help management reduce development time, control the scope of the project, and provide potential checkpoints to ensure validation and verification of what is being produced.

1.4.1   What Constitutes a Process?

The dictionary defines process as:

> A course of action or proceeding, especially a series of stages in manufacture or some other operation; the progress or course of something (*in the process of construction*).

From this definition we infer that a process involves a course of action that is performed by a series of steps. The definition also indicates *fluidity*—it indicates that a process represents some sort of behavior. A process, by this definition, is essentially a set of activities that is performed in a given sequence. It is a dynamic behavior plan rather than a static or hierarchical organization of work that used to be based on the old concept of work breakdown structure. Furthermore, this sequence of steps itself should be malleable and can be created based on the given situation in which the process is performed.

Other characteristics of these activities or steps is that they are performed on a *thing* or an *object*. Furthermore, in order to perform these actions, a certain set of tools or equipment might be required. It is also reasonable to extend the understanding of a process by assuming that the actions within the process will have to follow a certain discipline. It is also necessary to have *someone* performing this set of actions. The output or the end result of these activities is one or more deliverables.

1.4.2   A Sample Cooking Process

This explanation of a process is better understood by using a cooking example [Younessi and Henderson-Sellers 1997]. Consider the process of preparing a meal. It starts with the raw materials with which you want to cook the meal, and the tools that are necessary to carry out the tasks. In the case of baking a cake, the materials include the flour, butter, eggs, and additional raw materials; the tools include the pots and pans, oven, and other associated tools. These are the *technological* aspects of the process of cooking a meal.

However, the cake will not properly bake unless the raw materials are mixed in a certain proportion, and in a specific sequence. This information may be available in a book or a video that describes the mix and the sequence in baking the cake. This detailed recipe or baking method to be followed is the *methodological* aspect of the process of baking a cake.

Finally, the cook may be influenced by motivational factors (for example, the cook may be a professional who is paid for his work or a mother who bakes for her family). The general condition of the kitchen—including whether it has enough ventilation and light, whether it is air conditioned, and whether it is ergonomically designed—also plays a significant role in the final output. Thus, the skills of the cook and the environmental conditions in which the process is taking place constitute the *sociological* dimension of the process of baking a cake.

Each of these dimensions of the process needs to be considered carefully in order to produce a quality product. The study of this process can lead the cook to change the process when the cake is baked next time around, or it may allow a process expert to modify the process *while* the cake is being baked. This can be easily done only if the process is well defined and is divided into suitable components that lend themselves to change—they are the malleable part of the process.

1.4.3 The Orthogonal Process Relationship

The three dimensions of the process are not sequential to each other. That is to say, when the cook is mixing the dough, all three dimensions mentioned in the earlier section are in play. There is the "what" or technological aspect of dough, butter, and oven; the "how" or methodological aspect of the cookbook; and the "who" or sociological aspect of the cook. A number of activities are performed within each of these dimensions in order to achieve the overall objective. Furthermore, each of these three dimensions is made up of a subset of the overall set of activities within a process. A collection of a subset of such cohesive activities can form a component of a process, or simply, process-component.[8]

The activities from one dimension of a process relate to the activities of the other dimensions. Most of the time, activities from the three dimensions happen simultaneously. Taking the cooking example further, we may start with a cookbook, peruse it, and decide what we want to cook. Or we might know what we want, and refer to the correct recipe as we cook. Another example is that the cleaning and setting up of the kitchen (sociological dimension of the process) may go on, along with the study of the recipe (methodological dimension of the process).

In all practical cooking situations, the three dimensions of the process are executed depending on the management of the overall process discipline. We can say that the dimensions of a process are *orthogonal* to each other—each influencing the other aspects of the dimension. Figure 1.3 shows the dimensions of a process and their orthogonal relationship.

Based on this detailed example, we make the following observations about the process:

- A process is essentially made up of three dimensions.
- Each dimension of the process can be a process in itself.
- Processes comprise a set of activities.
- A collection of a subset of cohesive activities may be called a process-component.
- Activities within the processes have a flow.

---

[8] Readers comfortable with the basics of a process may find it helpful to take a quick look at the process-component for baking a cake, as shown in Figure 3.3. Other readers should wait till they reach Chapter 3 for further elaboration on and creation of a process-component.

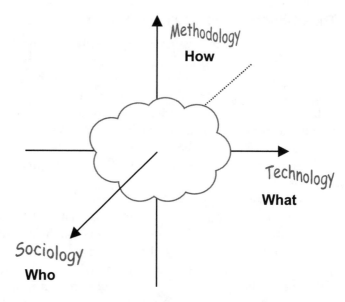

Figure 1.3 *The orthogonal relationship of process dimensions*

- Activities from all three dimensions may be conducted at the same time.
- The relationship between the three dimensions of a process is orthogonal.

The above discussion intends to create an understanding of what a process constitutes, and what its various dimensions are (namely, the what, how, and who of a process). This understanding is crucial in our understanding of software and quality processes that are discussed in subsequent chapters of this book. This results in a quality process for software development, with specific process components that are focused on quality assurance and quality control.

1.4.4 Process in Software Context

Is following a standard software development process sufficient to produce quality? In my opinion, the answer is no. A separate and sustained effort at quality is required that is distinct from the standard software development process.

There is a distinction between the software process (commonly referred to as software development process or software engineering process) and

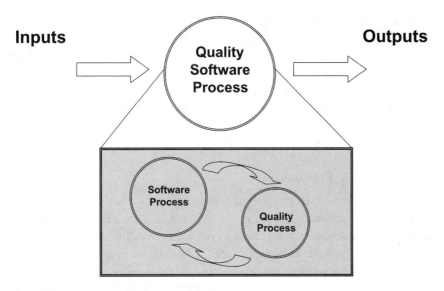

Figure 1.4   *Quality Software Process*

the quality process. Together, the software process and the quality process make what I call the "Quality Software Process," as shown in Figure 1.4. This is discussed in further detail below.

1.4.5   Software Process

I am using "software process" as a generic term to describe software development processes. While many software development organizations have processes of their own, others prefer to "buy" these development processes, which are available off the shelf. Software processes are also available in CASE tools. Examples of some of the off-the-shelf software processes include RUP, OPEN, MeNtOR, Catalysis, ICONIX Crystal, FDD, and XP. See Process Tools Using UML for a list of available processing tools.

In the context of UML-based projects, a process has to suggest how a particular diagram is produced. Then it has to provide detailed guidelines on how the various diagrams are put together to create complete models. It has to suggest the level at which the diagrams have to be used. A process further suggests the dependencies of the diagrams on each other. These are necessary aspects of a process which influence the quality of the model, which in turn influences the quality of the code that plays its part with the data quality to provide overall system quality.

While a process can provide details of all the necessary activities, tasks, roles, and deliverables, merely describing these details is not enough for a good process. It is important for a process to provide details on how these elements of a process are put together and enacted in an *iterative* and *incremental* fashion. Chapter 3 discusses these iterative and incremental aspects of a quality process in greater detail.

1.4.6 Quality Process

Quality process, as part of the Quality Software Process (shown in Figure 1.4), is almost an independent entity. Although it heavily influences the software process, and is in turn influenced by the enactment of the software process, it still has its own activities and tasks and process-components (see Chapter 3), and together they make up a suite of process-components of their own. The purpose of this quality process is to ensure that the software process produces quality models and quality products. Additionally, the quality process also ensures feedback to itself—that is, a quality process has to ensure its own quality by applying the same principles, concepts, and techniques that it applies in ensuring the quality of the standard software development process.

A quality process deals with four things:

1. Quality of the software process being employed for software work. This is discussed in greater detail in Chapters 2, 3, and 4, where the process aspect of quality is the key topic. The management aspect of quality is discussed in Chapter 2 and its estimation aspect is discussed in Chapter 5.

2. Quality of the software models being produced through the software process. This is a separate discussion outside the scope of this book, but discussed in a separate book on model quality in UML-based projects [Unhelkar 2003].

3. Quality of the software product being produced at the end of the software process. This deals with quality control, more traditionally called testing, as discussed in Chapter 6. There are also some measures of quality, as discussed in Chapter 5 on estimation metrics.

4. The activities, roles, and deliverables associated with its own self (that is, the value of the *quality process* itself). The quality of the

quality process itself is derived from this discussion (see Chapters 3 and 4).

A quality process not only helps to produce software that satisfies the needs of the end user, it also helps to improve productivity by reducing costly errors. As shown in Figure 1.5, by a rough estimate, if it costs only $1.00 to fix an error in the early part of a software development lifecycle, it can cost anywhere between $20 and $200 to fix the same error when it is discovered later in the lifecycle. A quality process ensures that we don't hurry through the software development process and don't cut corners to meet the target dates. Brooks [1995] aptly describes the truth of the matter when he quotes: ". . . Focus on *quality*, and productivity will follow." Brooks argues, based on Jones, that costly and late projects invest most of the extra work and time in finding and repairing errors in specification, design, and implementation. Brooks offers data that show a strong correlation between lack of systematic quality controls and schedule disasters.

We have established the importance of quality process; now we summarize the difference between the normal development process and a quality process. The process that deals with software development is what I call the software process. This has been discussed earlier, and it varies depending on the type of projects we have. For example, development

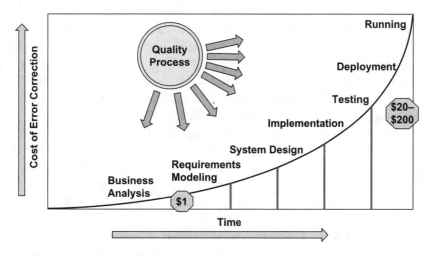

Figure 1.5 *Quality processes reduce costs of error correction, thereby increasing productivity*

and integration projects need to use a process that enables design and development of large numbers of new classes, components, and database tables.

However, a package implementation project must use the process in a way that enables detailed capture and documentation of the business requirements and functionalities. And, again, a data warehousing project will need to use the process differently from the way it is used in the previous examples.

A quality process deals with each of these software development processes and their variations. The quality process ensures that the software process has the correct checkpoints and has the right amount of quality techniques applied at those checkpoints to ensure that the project is on track. Typically the quality process comes in between the various iterations and increments related to the software process.

Together, the quality process and the software process become the "Quality Software Process," as shown earlier in Figure 1.4.

1.4.7   Quality Assurance and Testing: Let's Not Confuse Them

Quality assurance usually gets confused with testing. This has been aptly highlighted in the UML arena by McGregor and Sykes [2001]. Many times we hear: "The product is in QA." That is not the correct interpretation of quality assurance. What is meant by QA in this context is actually quality control or testing. This error is not limited to day-to-day users or developers but even to people dealing with popular processes. For example, Jacobson, Booch, and Rumbaugh [1999] in the *Unified Software Development Process* talk about quality assurance as a set of tools that are used to test applications and components. Once again what is implied are tools that would help to automate product testing.

That, of course, is only one function of QA. Perry correctly differentiates the two: "The role of quality control (QC) is to measure products against a standard or attribute." Thus, according to Perry, the purpose of QC is to identify defects and correct them so that a defect-free product is produced. QA is separate from QC and deals with the overall management of quality.

In this book we apply the overall quality assurance function to the projects that use UML. We do not restrict ourselves to mere QC or testing, although this testing aspect of QA does happen to be an important part of our QA strategy and is discussed separately in Chapter 6.

Furthermore, we extend our discussion of QA to include not just the management of the quality process but also the management of the overall quality function. This requires attention to obtaining resources and forming quality teams (their management, quality planning, budgeting, and so on), as discussed earlier. It is only when the product is produced or the database is loaded or the integration is complete that the final aspect of QC or testing comes into play. So to correctly restate the common phrase that "the product is in QA": The product is in testing or QC.

1.5   Modeling and Quality

1.5.1   Purpose of Modeling

Modeling enhances quality. To understand this better, let us consider why we model. As shown in Figure 1.6, modeling serves two clear purposes [Unhelkar 1999]:

- To understand the complex reality
- To be a creative cause for a new reality

A model is necessarily incomplete as it cannot, need not, and perhaps should not incorporate every possible detail of the real-life situation. By creating an abstraction of the otherwise complex reality, modeling assists in understanding that reality. This is important to note because it emphasizes modeling in all types of projects—including a modeling effort in a legacy environment where, say, a COBOL application has been running for the past 20 years. Creating a model, however brief, is imperative in understanding that "old" legacy application. In a new development,

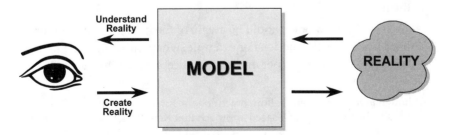

Figure 1.6   *Purpose of a model (based on Unhelkar 1999)*

modeling provides great help in understanding of the complex and fluid requirements.

In addition to this important aim, modeling also instigates the creation of new reality. We don't simply model what we know we want. Our modeling effort educates us so that we come to know what *else* we want. Many times a user who sees the prototype (a type of model) of a system *changes* her requirements and *adds* new requirements. As we will see later, this should be done as early in the lifecycle as possible.

Modeling provides the end user with a means of giving input long before the final product is ready. A model is a means of involving the end user or the sponsor of the product in its creation at an early stage of its lifecycle. It provides for a new paradigm, a paradigm that Kent Beck in his keynote address at TOOLS 2000 called "conversations."[9] Modeling facilitates conversation between the one who owns the problem (in defining it) and the one who has to provide the solution for it (in casting the solution iteratively).

1.5.2   Modeling Caveats

Despite its advantages, use of a model in both understanding the reality and creating new reality has its own limitations. It is essential to be aware of these limitations to enable us to make quality use of modeling as a technique. Some of the specific limitations of modeling are:

- A model is an abstraction of the reality. Therefore, it does not provide the complete picture of the real situation. A model, therefore, is subject to the interpretation of the observer.

- Unless a model is dynamic, it does not provide the feel for timing. Since the reality itself is changing with time, if the model does not change accordingly, it will not be able to convey the right meaning to the user.

- The user of the model should be aware of the notations and language used to express the model. For example, when the design of a house is expressed using a paper model, it is necessary for the user to know

---

[9] Although along with many fellow practitioners, I share my doubts on the scalability of XP, the programming-based approach that Kent Beck has initially put forward. In XP you don't just base your "conversations" with users on a model, but actually show them the final output—a piece of executable code—albeit in minuscule parts at a time.

what each of the symbols means. Nonstandardized notations and processes can render a model useless.

- A model may be created for a specific situation, or to handle a particular problem. Needless to say, once the situation has changed, the model may no longer be relevant.

1.5.3   Understanding Modeling Spaces in Software

Appreciation of the value and the limitations of modeling provide us with the necessary background to start applying the modeling approach to practical software development. But before we can do that, we need to take a step back and consider the areas in software that we need to model. More importantly, though, we also need to consider the areas in which we need to model. These areas are what I call "modeling spaces," as shown in Figure 1.7.

Out there, the reality is a cohesive whole. Whether it is a real software system, or a real baby, it has to be treated holistically. However, when we

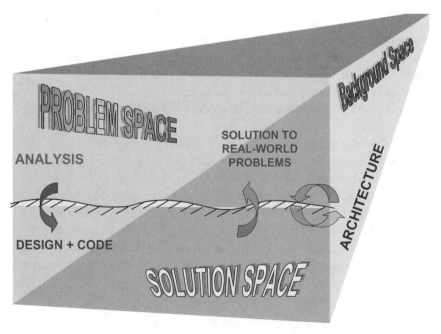

Figure 1.7 *The three major modeling spaces*

create a model for the same, we have the opportunity of slicing and dicing it so that it becomes more comprehensible. At the very least, this provides us with various "views" of the model, depending on our interest. A more robust approach to quality models is not only creation of various views of the same model, but separate models themselves, which are sufficiently cohesive to provide a complete and holistic view, whenever needed.

However, this creation of separate models provides the advantage of modeling (understanding and creation of reality) in an area of interest and in an area where the objectives of the project are directly served by the modeling effort. For example, a project that deals with implementing a third-party Customer Relationship Management System (CRMS) package has greater use of a modeling technique to specify the problem only. There is no point, in such a project, to model the solution as well—for the solution will be provided by the CRMS package.

In order to create an understanding of the spaces in which we should model, consider briefly the background of software development itself. Little more than 50 years ago we, the computing community, started off with an interesting approach—we simply provided solutions. Twenty years ago, when I took up my first job writing COBOL, the IT community was still eagerly and enthusiastically providing a wide array of solutions. Programming was "cool," and I programmed many complex algorithms for the "fun" of it. Sometimes, I gave such programs to my users, and let them figure out a problem to which they could fit my solution.

Medicine is considered a far more mature industry[10] not only because of the number of years it has been around, but also because it never provides a solution without first asking and understanding the problem. Even today, when I walk in to my family doctor's office, she is in no hurry to write a prescription without asking me first whether it is my head that hurts or my tummy. Until the relatively recent advent of well-researched methodologies, which are also supported by industrial-strength CASE tools, software developers had no qualms in "prescribing" solutions for a problem that had not been properly understood and documented.

The IT community is maturing as it learns from its mistakes. First and foremost, we recognize the need to understand the problem that exists. What is the purpose of the system that is being created? This is followed

---

[10] It is only fair to acknowledge that the medical profession has more experience than the IT community. Doctors have been handling viruses for millenniums whereas computer viruses are much newer.

by a model for the solution that is provided. This is the technical or design part of the model. And no modern-day software, especially Web application software, is built from scratch. There is always a background architecture that influences both the capabilities of the solution provided and the understanding of the problem.

Therefore, for the sake of creating an understanding of the modeling work, we divide all the software related work into three spaces:

1. The Problem Space
2. The Solution Space
3. The Background Space

1.5.4 Problem Space

The problem space obviously deals with the understanding of the problem. Primarily this is the problem that the user or the potential user of the system faces. Less often, it can also be a technical problem. In any case the problem space deals with all the work that goes on in understanding the software or system problem that is yet to be developed. In the case of projects dealing with existing legacy applications, this problem space handles the creation of a formal model of what exists, followed by a model of what is needed.

Major activities that take place in the problem space are documenting and understanding the requirements, analyzing the requirements, investigating the problem in detail, optionally creating a conceptual prototype, and understanding the flow of the process within the business. Thus, the problem space is entirely focused on what is happening with the business or the user.

Advanced readers will appreciate that as a nontechnical description of what is happening with the user or the business, the problem space needs those UML diagrams that explain the problem without going into the specifics of the technology used to provide the solution. These UML diagrams are primarily the use case diagram and the activity diagrams, followed by high-level class and sequence diagrams, and optionally state chart diagrams.

1.5.5 Solution Space

The solution space is primarily involved in the description of the solution. Models in this space take the information made available in the problem space in order to create and provide a solution that satisfies the needs of the user understood in the problem space. Therefore, this is a technical space and deals primarily with the technology used to provide the solution to whatever the problem might be.

Activities in this space need detailed understanding of the programming languages, programming environments, databases, middleware, Web application solutions, and a number of other related technical details. Good understanding of technology is therefore imperative to work well in the solution space coupled with a good understanding of how models in this space relate to the underlying technologies.

For advanced UML readers, the primary diagram used in the solution space is the class diagram. These design-level class diagrams contain the lowermost details including attributes, types of attributes, their initial values, operations, their signatures, and so on. This is followed by sequence diagrams, together with their messages and protocols. State chart diagrams and object diagrams can be used sparingly here. Finally, in order to complete the solution we will also need component diagrams, which may be initiated in the background space (discussed next). The component diagrams represent the executable chunks of code or libraries (in a Windows environment, these will be the .exe and the .dll files), which are finally incorporated in the software solution.

1.5.6 Background Space

The background space deals with two major aspects of software development that are not covered by either the problem space or solution space: architecture and management.

Management deals primarily with the planning of the entire project and does not necessarily form part of the problem or the solution space. To rephrase, management *includes* both the problem and the solution space. There are a number of activities within management that are handled in the background by the person playing the role of the project manager. They include planning the project; resourcing the project hardware, software, and people; budgeting and performing cost-benefit analysis; tracking the project as it progresses so that the various iterations are performed per the requirements of the process; and providing the checkpoints that yield quality results for the roles in the problem and solution space.

Planning activities fall under the general category of management, or to be precise, project management. While authors like Cantor [1998] have written about project management *with* UML, I personally don't think

UML provides any direct assistance in project management. Yes, we have the job of managing such projects, but whether or not the UML within the projects is helping in the activities of project management is a moot point.

Architectural work, on the other hand, deals with a large amount of technical background work that must consider major issues of architecture of the solution, existing architecture of the environment in the organization, and the operational requirements of the system (requirements of the system in operation—for example, the stress and the volume and the bandwidth that the system needs).

Further background issues include the important strategic aspects of reusability of programs, designs, and even architecture. These activities will most certainly require the local knowledge of the way in which the environment works, and the industrial knowledge of the availability of reusable architectures and designs. In all modern-day software systems, making software in-house is almost sacrilegious, unless the avenues of buying it, or at least some sizeable component of it, have been exhausted. This all-important "make versus buy" decision is heavily influenced by the fact that work in this space is abstract yet precise. Explicit models of software or components greatly influence the decision to buy (or not to buy) them.

The background space will need help and support from UML in modeling the deployment environment as well as in reusing both architecture and design. Advanced readers will notice that the diagrams that the background space uses as provided by the UML are primarily deployment diagrams and component diagrams. More importantly, though, the background space will end up using material in the UML domain that deals with analysis patterns, such as the work by Martin Fowler [1997], *Design Patterns* by the Gang of Four [Gamma et al. 1995], *Cognitive Patterns* [Gardner et al. 1998], *Anti Patterns* [Brown et al. 1998], and so on.

We have thus divided our work in modeling software in three domains or spaces. It is important to remember that these three spaces are not watertight compartments; these spaces—especially the background space—are in three dimensions, as shown in Figure 1.7, and are dependent on each other. Ideally, it should be possible to pick a point anywhere within the three dimensions of the three spaces and apply the criteria of quality to that point. Each such point that is subjected to quality assurance will have a component in it that belongs to the problem space, another component that belongs to the solution space, and another element that belongs to the background space.

1.6   UML and Quality

UML facilitates communication. It provides a mechanism to create and share models in an industrially accepted standard of the Object Management Group (OMG). The OMG officially adopted the UML 1.1 specifications in November 1997. After a number of revisions and iterations, the current accepted standard is UML 1.4. The current work going on at the OMG is to create the UML 2.0 standard. The focus of the work in UML 2.0 is the UML infrastructure, the UML superstructure, the OCL, and the Diagram Interchange capabilities.[11]

The UML enhances communication by improving the dialogue between business and technology and among businesses and technologists. Thus, it plays a major role in reducing the chances of project failure due to bad communication (which, as you will recall from Section 1.3.5, contributes to 20 percent of project failures). Needless to say, this has a direct bearing in improving and enhancing the quality within the project.

But before we start dealing with UML, it is important to clarify two common yet crucial *misunderstandings* about UML:

- That UML is a language (as in a programming language)
- That UML is a methodology (as in a full process or methodological approach)

In order to arrive at a satisfactory clarification, let us deal briefly with the history of UML.

1.6.1   A Brief History of UML

Fowler [1996], in his tutorial at OOPSLA 96, lamented:

> With a plethora of notational differences, many of which are entirely arbitrary, the simple modeler such as myself feels like banging the gurus' heads together until they pick a common cardinality symbol.

This plea was true of almost all practitioners utilizing methodologies. So overcrowded was the field that the OMG's special interest group on analysis and design described 27 different object-oriented methods, with some of the followers of these methodologies at war with each other—spurring

---

[11] For more details, see www.omg.org/technology/UML.

Jacobson [1993] to write, "Cease the methodology war." Hutt [1994] in his two books has surveyed between 16 and 21 methods.[12]

Apart from this large number of *recognized* methodologies, there were a number of second-generation methodologies [Henderson-Sellers and Edwards 1994], and probably many others that were never published or that were homemade concoctions derived from one or more of these recognized object-oriented methodologies. The effect of this is confusion in the software development community, followed by debates between programmers and designers [Dodani 1994] with most end users preferring to sit on the sidelines rather than betting on the wrong horse.

Who could be bothered about quality in this scenario? Luckily for the practicing modelers, and for the benefit of quality, the first results of such efforts could be seen as early as a year before Fowler's plea—with the announcement of the Unified Method (a version less than UML 1.0), at OOPSLA 95 in Austin, Texas. This was the UML in its inception phase,[13] and it was brought about by the unification of three popular approaches to object-oriented design [Booch, Rumbaugh and Jacobson 1996]: Booch, Object Modeling Technique, and Object-Oriented Software Engineering (whose commercial version is Objectory).

After a few iterations and a lot of input from various individual and organizational members, this unified approach was announced as the Unified Modeling Language. Presumably, one of the reasons why it was not stamped as a "method" was that it was a unification of notation and other modeling elements; the actual approach to, or the process of, development derived from these three popular methodologies and a number of other popular methodologies, still remained separate—even as this book is published.[14]

Thus, one of the things to note is that the UML is not a methodology, but a common and standard set of notations and diagrams that can be used by different processes, as shown in Figure 1.8.

Furthermore, the OMG has accepted the UML as a standard *modeling* language—to be used primarily for specifying, constructing, visualizing,

---

[12] These include Booch, Coad et al., Demeter, Fresco, Fusion, SOMA, Objectory, Rumbaugh, Shlaer/Mellor, SSADM, and Wirfs-Brock et al., to name but a few.

[13] For RUP users, a subtle pun intended.

[14] As I understand, the unification of process is under way at the OMG and can be called the "Unified Process."

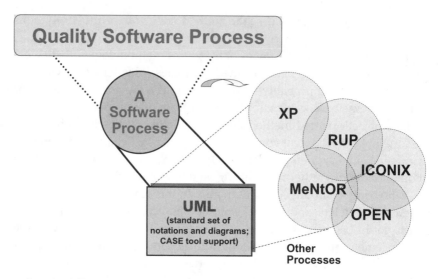

Figure 1.8   *UML, processes, and quality*

and documenting the artifacts of an object-oriented software system. Thus, it is *not* a programming language, although together with a programming language for implementation, it provides an excellent mechanism to develop software systems.

1.6.2   Quality of UML versus Quality by UML

There is a difference between "Quality *of* UML" and "Quality *by* UML."

When we discuss the quality assurance of UML-based projects, our main interest is in the latter—the value, in terms of quality, added *by* the UML to our project. As practitioners, and especially as users of UML, we are not too deeply involved in the quality *of* UML itself. However, as researchers or process consultants, we would like to have some idea about the emergence of the UML as a standard, and the reasons for its robustness.

The attempt to unify methodologies, as discussed earlier, was not just a concoction of various approaches put together. In fact, it was not even a unification of notations to start with—but the creation of a metamodel (model of a model) that would provide the ground rules for creation of models and, optionally, corresponding notations. Creation of the metamodel for UML has attracted far more attention and effort than the notations themselves.

1.6.3 Metamodels and Quality

OMG has provided for four levels of modeling, as shown in Figure 1.9. They are:

- Level 0: The Level 0 model is an instance-level model. It is a representation of a unique instance of an object. A diagram that only depicts instances, such as this account or that customer, falls within this level. Creating models at this level helps when we are dealing with a single instance of an entity. For example, if there is a need to differentiate a particular checking account in a bank from another checking account, the two need to be modeled as instances, and would be done so at this level of the metamodel.

- Level 1: The Level 1 model is a representation of a collection or group of instances resulting in a class-level representation. Numerous diagrams can be used to represent not only a collection of objects, but also a collection of behaviors, relationships, and so on. Models at this level provide the mold from which many items (objects) can be produced—making this Level 1 modeling work more abstractly than the Level 0 modeling.

- Level 2: The Level 2 model is not a simple model, but a model that relates all the representations of Level 1. This model shows how the classes, relationships, and behavior shown at Level 1 relate to each

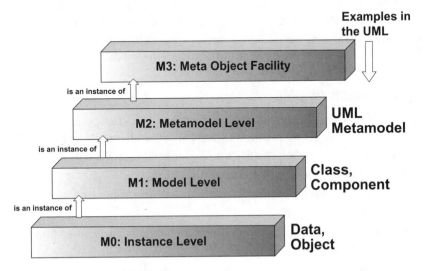

Figure 1.9 *OMG's four-level architecture*

other. Thus, this metamodel provides the ground rules for enabling the creation and linking of diagrams drawn in Level 1 and plays a crucial role in enhancing the quality of UML. The metamodel at this level lays down the ground rules for UML usage—leaving the users free to create their own variations to satisfy their own particular modeling needs (provided they do not transgress the rules laid down by the metamodel).

- Level 3 (the MOF, or Meta Object Facility): This is the overall repository from various modeling domains such as process models (as would be required once unification of process takes place) and UML-based models—and provides the source for new modeling domains including the process modeling work.

For UML, in Level 2, there is a comprehensive metamodel. Those responsible for the UML have spent most of their time in this model. Metamodels play a vital role in enhancing the quality of UML, for they provide the basic rules that both the developers and extenders of UML and the CASE tool vendors have followed. Metamodels are more like barriers on a freeway—their impact is in *preventing* fundamental modeling errors rather than merely correcting them.

Also, most well-known CASE tools comply with the UML metamodel, enabling a certain standard across the industry. Needless to say, this has a major impact in improving communication and, thereby, quality. Finally, multiple levels of modeling can also be combined in complex modeling exercises, resulting in better comprehensibility of diagrams. This multilevel modeling is a part of UML 2.0 initiative.

1.6.4   Quality by UML

UML is a modeling language that is used to visualize, specify, construct, and document software artifacts [Booch, Rumbaugh, and Jacobson 1999]. Therefore, in considering quality for UML-based projects we have to consider the effect of using UML on:

- Quality of visual representation of the artifacts, diagrams, and models

- Quality of the specification that provides detailed attributes for the UML artifacts and diagrams

- Quality of the construction of relevant software resulting from the visual UML diagrams

- Quality of the documentation of the artifacts and diagrams to provide additional description that would suffice for the quality requirements in creating corresponding models

Each of these quality aspects of UML needs further discussion to ensure that we understand the impact of UML on them, and how their quality can be enhanced.

1.6.5   Quality of Visualization

While "a picture is worth a thousand words," the challenge in software modeling is to represent pictorially that which is inherently nonvisual. However, that challenge in itself would not be insurmountable, but for the fact that we also need to model the nascent thought processes of a user. The UML's ability to show both processes and software elements visually, spanning the entire lifecycle of software development, is the key to improving the quality of overall visualization in software development.

The UML, through its "class" representations, can bring the reality (real passengers, flights, and seats in a typical airline reservation system) close to the people working in solution space by modeling Class::Passenger, Class::Flight, and Class::Seat as shown in Figure 1.10. The small semantic gap between models and reality, as provided by the use of object-oriented technology, improves the quality of visualization. However, in

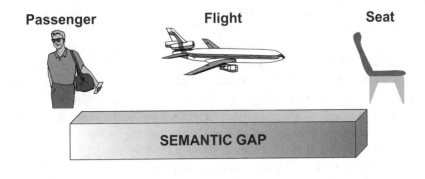

Figure 1.10 *Small semantic gap in object-oriented technology (based on Unhelkar 1999)*

this quality exercise, we also attempt to improve the quality of visualization by improving the quality of the artifacts produced by the UML itself.

As a visual modeling language, the UML has a direct bearing on the creation of, and the quality of, visual artifacts produced in a project. Decades ago one of the common and popular visual artifacts was the humble flowchart. A flowchart used to be constructed by using a commonly understood set of notations and some associated conventions. In my early attempts—almost twenty years ago—at visual modeling with a flowchart, the only *tools* I could use were paper and pencil, and at the most a stencil.

The flowchart technique was followed by the advent of Software Engineering [Somerville 1989], which used Data Flow Diagrams (DFDs) and Entity Relationship Diagrams (ERDs). While DFDs and ERDs were popular, they still were derived from technology; data was the main theme of these diagrams, and ERDs primarily helped model relational structures. Thus, in the absence of something like the UML, there was very little in terms of visual modeling that could be used to describe comprehensively the behavior or the business process for which the software was to be written.

The UML provides an excellent means to produce visual models—and in the three different modeling spaces. While the UML is not entirely diagrams (and there are associated specifications and documentations), still a substantial amount of UML (at least half) is made up of a number of notational elements and their corresponding diagrams. This provides an extensive amount of diagramming techniques (far more than flowcharts, DFDs, and ERDs did) to satisfy modeling needs in all three work spaces.

Furthermore, the quality of visualization is not only enhanced by the use of the UML as a standard, but also because of the large number of CASE tools that support these visual diagramming techniques. In verifying and validating these diagrams, we will consider a "quality approach" to producing them. We will then subject the diagrams to detailed checks for their syntactical and semantic correctness and completeness. Finally, we consider the detailed quality control and testing exercise on the resultant software. A quality software process encompasses all these aspects of quality development, crosschecking, and testing.

1.6.6   Quality of Specification

While the core contribution of UML is to provide detailed visual artifacts, they still need to be supported by specifications. Specifications go along with UML artifacts and the diagrams. For example, a use case, visually represented by a UML standard notation, would still have a lot of accompanying specification that may not be visual. Specifications start with simple things like the name of the use case, its stereotype, or the various relationships that a use case has with other use cases and actors. Everything that is outside of the visual diagram falls under the specification. And certainly the UML goes a long way in improving the quality of specification by:

- Attaching the specifications to the visual models

- Enabling the projects to decide, in addition to the standard recommendations, which areas of a particular element, or diagram, they want to specify

- Allowing (through CASE tools) these specifications to be available in various formats such as a company intranet, Web page, or a set of documentation

One of the ways these specifications and their quality can be further improved is by not producing all specifications at one time. Providing steps and guidelines to produce specifications in an iterative and incremental fashion, together with the visual artifacts, is the responsibility of the process. This is discussed in greater detail in Part III—which deals with quality processes.

1.6.7   Quality of Construction

If UML were to remain at an abstract level, it would not serve the valuable purpose of controlling what the programmer does. In a way, the purpose of the UML is to visualize and specify in the problem space that which will be actually developed, implemented, or constructed in the solution space. Certainly UML through its "visual and specification" characteristics directly contributes to improved quality of construction. A code that is constructed based on proper UML-based modeling would fare much better in both its validation and its verification. Classes and class diagrams, together with their specifications (for example, accessibility options, relationships, multiplicities), ensure that the code produced is inherently superior to code produced without the benefit of UML-based modeling.

Some tools (for example, TogetherSoft) provide what they call "live source." This facility shows the programmer a piece of code while at the same time showing the designer the corresponding class. Such a direct relationship between a model and its construction vastly enhances the quality of construction.

1.6.8   Quality of Documentation

While quality of construction is important, organizations have realized that code is not the only asset they have in IT. Accompanying documentation during all stages of a software lifecycle is an equally important asset, if not more so. This became evident during one of the largest time-bound projects that the IT community undertook—the Y2K project.

One of the first steps in approaching the Y2K cleanup, in any organization, was taking stock of the IT assets [Unhelkar, 1999]. This inventory exercise usually only revealed code or databases. People realized that to make sense of these pure programming-based assets was taking a lot of time and effort. Documentation has thus become paramount—not only the one that accompanies the code, but also the documentation that goes with models, prototypes, and other such artifacts. The UML suggests documentation accompanying all of its diagrams. Each diagram has a corresponding documentation, which may or may not reside with its specifications.

Furthermore, creation and quality of documentation is expedited when they are based on document templates (I occasionally call them documentation patterns). It is worth noting that we are not merely talking about the quality of documentation that accompanies the UML diagrams. Overall quality of *any* documentation produced in a UML-based project improves because relevant UML diagrams can be embedded in those documents (external to UML), thereby improving their readability and the overall communication in the project.

Documents in a quality-driven project are usually based on predetermined templates, as opposed to creating them from scratch. Such templates are provided as part of commercial processes, and are well worth the money spent to buy them. Decisions on documentation templates that accompany the UML diagrams can be made by project team members before the start of the project. Thus, overall, we see how the quality of documentation in a project is enhanced by the UML.

1.6.9   Summary of UML Diagrams and Their Importance in Modeling Spaces

As mentioned earlier, the UML follows the rigors of a metamodel. This results in a set of diagrams that have a set of underlying rules specifying how to create them. The metamodel also helps to provide rules for cross-

Table 1.1 *UML diagrams in practice*

UML diagrams	Model representing the . . .
Use case diagrams	functionality from user's viewpoint
Activity diagrams	the flow within a use case or the system
Class diagrams	classes, entities, business domain, database
Sequence diagrams	the interactions between objects
Collaboration diagrams	the interactions between objects
Object diagrams	objects and their links
State chart diagrams	the lifecycle of an object in real time
Component diagrams	the executables, linkable libraries, etc.
Deployment diagrams	the hardware nodes, processors, and optionally, corresponding components
Package diagrams*	subsystems, organizational units
Robustness diagrams*	architecture by ensuring separation of interface from business models

* indicates two additional diagrams to the original list appearing in Booch et al.'s *The UML User Guide*

diagram dependencies. The following table summarizes the UML diagrams and the modeling aspect of a software solution represented by them. CASE tools dealing with these modeling techniques are summarized in UML CASE Tools.

Further to this description of the focus of the UML diagrams, Table 1.2 summarizes the relative importance of each of the UML diagrams in each of the modeling spaces and to each of the major modeling roles within the project. While project team members can work in any of these modeling spaces using any of the UML diagrams, good quality models will result by understanding the importance of the diagrams with respect to each of the modeling spaces. This is shown in Table 1.2.

As is obvious from this table, modelers are not precluded from using any of the UML diagrams, but Table 1.2 provides the *focus*—in terms of which UML diagrams to use—for a particular role within a project. This information can be invaluable in organizing the quality team, as well as in following the quality process that will create and check these diagrams.

Table 1.2 *Importance of UML diagrams to respective models*

UML diagrams	MOPS (Business Analyst)	MOSS (Designer)	MOBS (Architect)
Use case diagrams	*****	**	*
Activity diagrams	*****	**	*
Class diagrams	***	*****	**
Sequence diagrams	***	*****	*
Collaboration diagrams	**	*	
Object diagrams	*	*****	***
State chart diagrams	***	****	**
Component diagrams	*	***	*****
Deployment diagrams	**	**	*****
Package diagrams	***	**	****
Robustness diagrams	*	***	*****

* = least important, ***** = most important

1.7   Quality Assurance Techniques of Syntax, Semantics, and Aesthetics

Having discussed the various quality aspects of modeling that are enhanced by the UML, we now discuss the manner in which these qualities, exhibited by the UML-based models, can be verified and validated. Some of this verification and validation deals with the visual aspects of the model, others with the specification, construction, and documentation aspects of the model. Note, though, that the prescriptive aspect of such verification is a part of model quality rather than process quality and, therefore, outside the scope of this work. In order to produce quality models, we have to ensure that:

- All quality models should be syntactically correct.
- All quality models should represent their intended semantic meanings and should be consistent in representing that meaning.
- All quality models should have some semblance of aesthetics in them—which exhibit the creativity and long-sightedness of their modelers. This also means they are symmetric and complete in what they represent.

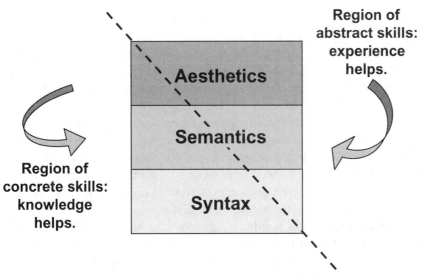

Figure 1.11   *Quality of models: syntax, semantics, and aesthetics*

As summarized in Figure 1.11, the words *syntax, semantics,* and *aesthetics* are chosen to reflect our techniques to verify and validate the models. One of the reasons why these words correctly represent our quality-assurance effort is that most of the UML-based models are stationary. While the UML models do represent structural and behavioral aspects, they are all stored in a CASE tool. Because of their relatively static nature, quality of the UML-based modeling deliverables can be greatly enhanced by applying the syntax, semantics, and aesthetic checks to them. Here we have a look at each of these types of checks.

1.7.1   Quality Models—Syntax

All languages have their syntax. Latin and Sanskrit have their own syntax, and so have Java, XML, and UML. However, two major characteristics of the UML differentiate it from the other "languages":

1. It's a visual language, which means it has heaps of notations and diagrams.
2. It's a modeling language, which means it may not compile!

Needless to say, incorrect syntax affects the quality of visualization and specification. And, although a diagram itself cannot be compiled, incorrect syntax at the diagram level percolates down to the construction level, causing errors in creating the software code.

CASE tools help enormously to ensure that syntax errors are kept to a minimum. Rules of association and creation of default visibilities (for example, "private" for attributes) are some examples of how CASE tools help to reduce syntax errors.

In the case of UML-based models, when we apply syntax checks, we ensure that each of the diagrams that make up the model has been created in conformance with the standards and guidelines as specified by the OMG. We also ensure that the notations used, the diagram extensions annotated, and the corresponding explanations on the diagrams all follow the syntax standard of the modeling language.

Figure 1.12 shows a simple example of a rectangle representing a dog. The major focus of the syntax check is that it is, indeed, a rectangle that is meant to represent animals (or other such things) in this modeling mechanism. The rectangle is checked for its correctness, and we ensure that it is not an ellipse, or for that matter an arrowhead, representing an animal.

In terms of UML models, a syntax check is a checklist of all things we want to check off that must comply with the syntax for the diagrams and associated artifacts of the UML as laid out by the OMG. Permissible vari-

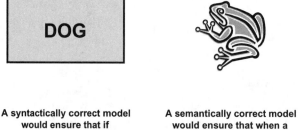
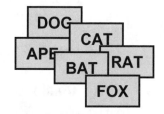

A syntactically correct model would ensure that if a rectangle has to represent an artifact, then literally "no corners have been cut."

A semantically correct model would ensure that when a DOG has to be represented, it is a DOG and not a FROG that gets represented.

An aesthetically sound model will strive for balance. The representation of the DOG will not be too big or too small; it will be readable and changeable. Also, it will not represent too many elements.

Figure 1.12 *Application of syntax, semantics, and aesthetics*

ations to these diagrams complying with the metamodel can become a project-specific part of the syntax checks.

1.7.2 Quality Models—Semantics

While one of the qualities enhanced by rigorous syntax checks is the quality of construction (read "compilation"), one cannot be satisfied merely by a program that compiles and executes correctly, but does not give due credence to the manner in which it is interpreted.

In Figure 1.12, we want to see a dog represented by a rectangle with the word "dog" written in it. Writing the word "dog" within a rectangle might be syntactically correct, but would be semantically wrong. This is because, as shown in Figure 1.12, the class dog is actually representing an object frog. If a class dog is specified for an object frog, that class dog will have to "learn" to croak (that is, a method "croak" will have to be added to the class dog). In the absence of such a method, the class dog will not know how to croak—but the software system will!

The semantics aspect of model quality not only ensures that the diagrams produced are correct but also makes sure that they faithfully represent the underlying reality. In UML, for example, business objectives as stated by the users should be correctly reflected in the use case diagrams, business rules, constraints, and pre- and post-conditions documented in the corresponding use case documentation.

Once again, the models are not the executables, and therefore it is not possible to verify and validate the purpose of the model by simply "executing" them, as one would with the final software product (the executable). This is when we apply, more rigorously than in the syntax checking, the traditional and well-known quality techniques of walkthroughs and inspections. These techniques are described in greater detail in Chapter 2, when their use is suggested to ensure that the semantics of the models produced are correct.

We can play act each of the use cases and we can play act an entire diagram. We can have people going through the use cases and verifying the purpose of each of the actors and those of the use cases, and whether they present what the business really wants. This is the semantic aspect of verifying the quality of a UML model.

While the syntax can be verified by anyone who has sufficient knowledge about the UML, the semantics of each of the UML diagrams and the models in which these diagrams sit needs a little more experience. As shown in Figure 1.11, semantics verification and validation requires more abstract knowledge than mere syntax checking, and *that* requires more experience in using UML and corresponding business rules in real projects. The connotations of this statement are that it is important to include the users and to entice them to participate in all quality walkthroughs, inspections, and play acting in verifying the semantics of each of the models.

1.7.3 Quality Models—Aesthetics

Once we have the syntax and the semantics right we need to worry about the aesthetics of the model. How many use cases are there on a diagram? Is it possible that a system with ten use case diagrams, each with five to six use cases, may be accurately representing a use case model? Despite the accuracy of this overall model, it is also possible that some of the use case diagrams are overloaded compared with other diagrams. For example, one use case diagram may have 20 use cases (not wrong from UML viewpoint, but ugly) and another use case diagram may have only one (albeit an important one).

The aesthetics aspect of the model's quality requires a combination of knowledge and experience. In ensuring the aesthetics of the UML models created, we need to have not only the knowledge of UML and the knowledge of business, but also very good knowledge of the CASE tools and the environment in which they have been used. We need experience in more than one project before we can successfully apply the aesthetics aspect of model quality to the UML model.

A good metrics program within an organization will also be very helpful in improving the aesthetics of the model.

Finally, these three aspects of quality checks—the syntax, semantics, and aesthetics—should not be treated totally independent of each other. A change in the syntax can change the meaning or semantics behind a sentence or a diagram. While syntax gets checked at the ground level, minutely and for each artifact, an error in syntax may not be limited to the error in the language of expression. Here is my favorite example. Consider this example of a plain English sentence that has apparently nothing wrong with it as far as grammar is concerned:

I saw a broomstick walking across the ground.

This sentence doesn't appear to make too much sense unless you, like me, have just finished reading one of J. K. Rowling's[15] *Harry Potter* books. A syntactic change to the above sentence can be effectuated as follows:

> I saw a broomstick, walking across the ground.

The comma inside the sentence has made the meaning of the sentence acceptable—especially to ordinary folks.[16] This happens in the UML as well, wherein the syntax and semantics may depend on each other. For example, the direction of an arrow showing the relationship between two use cases will certainly affect the way in which that use case diagram is interpreted. Similarly, aesthetics or symmetry of diagrams facilitates easier understanding, making the semantics clearer and comprehensible to their readers. We leave the model aspect of quality to a separate discussion but with the suggestion here that in assuring the quality of UML-based diagrams, readers will have to consider in detail these three aspects of syntax, semantics, and aesthetic quality of the models.

1.8   Quality Assurance of Software Process: Necessity, Sufficiency, and Malleability

There is a basic difference between a process and the models that reside within it. The models are static. The models are produced at *a* point in time. They have syntax and a semantic meaning to which we can apply quality-control criteria. Even the models that are supposed to represent the dynamic behavior of the system[17] are not dynamic.

The process that produces these steps, however, has specifications for the model, as well as a detailed set of activities and tasks enabling us to

---

[15] Starting with *Harry Potter and the Philosopher's Stone,* my teenage daughter and I read with avid interest all four works of fiction by J. K. Rowling. When I finished reading *Harry Potter and the Goblet of Fire,* I almost changed this example. I now believe, together with a million other readers, that not only can broomsticks walk, but they fly comfortably with people on them!

[16] Potter fans may read this as "Muggles"—see J. K. Rowling's other works.

[17] In UML, there are hardly any genuine dynamic models—a dynamic model would be something like a prototype of a steam engine, giving out a real whistle and steam! The state chart diagram comes closest.

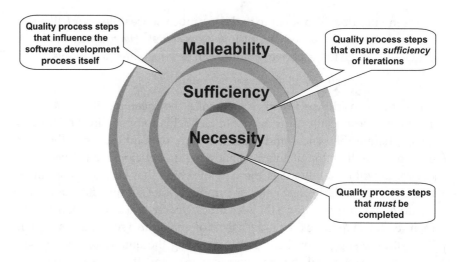

Figure 1.13   *Quality process levels: necessity, sufficiency, and malleability*

produce the model. Furthermore, as discussed in Section 1.4.1 (defining the process), a process not only describes what to produce (the deliverables) and how to produce them (the activities and tasks) but also who produces them (the people, or more appropriately the roles they play).

Because of the fluidity that exists in a process, it is better (than putting together a syntax and semantic checklist) to ensure its quality by:

- Making some aspects of the process mandatory
- Describing process artifacts that satisfy more than just the basic necessity
- Allowing the ability of the process itself to change

These are the necessary, sufficiency, and malleability aspects of quality in software processes as shown in Figure 1.13 and described in further detail below. Chapter 3 describes in greater detail the application of these concepts in practical UML-based projects.

1.8.1   Quality of Process—Necessity

Necessity of a process describes the steps that are a must before any deliverable of value comes out of the process.

For example, in baking a cake, the process description should ensure that the role of a cook; the flour and butter; and the very basic steps of mixing the flour, putting it in the oven, and removing the cake at the right time are mandatory. These are the *basic necessities* of baking a cake, without which there would be no cake.

Necessities of a process may not have much elegance about them. They can be a simple set of tasks cobbled together in a project task list or plan. Their execution is also likely to be linear, following the waterfall life-cycle of software development.

1.8.2   Quality of Process—Sufficiency

A process can be said to be sufficiently described and followed when it outlines all the process artifacts that provide for more than just the basic necessities.

In the example of baking the cake, sufficiency of the process can be judged by the aspects of the process that describe additional roles such as helper and taster, additional materials such as a decorative cherry placed on the cake, or a bookstand to hold the cookbook, and steps to make the process further satisfactory such as using a timer and cutting the cake into the right size to enable easier serving.

Sufficiency brings in the concept of elegance in process. When applied to UML-based projects, this means the application of the principles of Iterative, Incremental, and Parallel (IIP) development.

1.8.3   Quality of Process—Malleability

In discussing what the process should produce, and how it should produce deliverables, it is likely that the quality of the process that is producing the deliverables gets missed.

An ordinary process has its description—as in the steps and the roles executing those steps—preset. These steps are not easily changeable, especially when their execution has already started.

The ability of a process to lend itself to change by accepting feedback from the users of such a process, before and even during its execution, is what I call the malleability of the process.

The malleability aspect of the process comes from the architecture of the process itself: some aspects of a process that make it malleable include how the process is put together from its building blocks (provided of course the process has building blocks), how easy it is to configure such a process, if the process is a process-CASE tool itself, or if it can be easily input inside a CASE tool enabling the changing and creating of new processes suiting differing project requirements.

The malleability aspect of a process makes it a quality process, because it helps the process engineer provide additional emphasis on activities and tasks that are important to the project, while it eliminates tasks that might not be relevant to the given situation.

If not deployed and managed properly, processes tend to be cumbersome and bureaucratic. Malleability of a process ensures that the project, and the quality of the product, doesn't suffer from these drawbacks. However, we cannot apply a checklist to the malleability aspect of a process. This quality aspect of the process must be built in or architected by the producers of the process.

1.9   Reuse, Patterns, and Quality

The first aspect of object-orientation that fascinated the IT community was reuse. This led to the pattern movement that has permeated every aspect of development, especially designs. Figure 1.14 tries to depict why patterns are even more fascinating to the designers and programmers. Patterns provide the essence of a design and the designer fills up the rest. However, patterns are not restricted to designs. For example, Eriksson and Penker provide an excellent description of how the concept of patterns can be applied, together with the UML, to model business processes [Eriksson and Penkar 2000] (as against technical designs). We discuss here these important concepts of reuse and patterns with respect of quality.

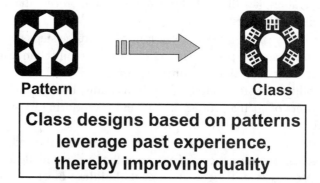

Pattern   **Class**

Class designs based on patterns leverage past experience, thereby improving quality

Figure 1.14   *Reuse and patterns*

1.9.1   Increasing Productivity through Reuse

One of the initial pushes of object-orientation was reuse. It was assumed that because object-orientation provided the ability of a class to inherit from another class, it would lead to large-scale reuse, thereby increasing productivity. Earlier, before the OO wave, reuse did exist in terms of cutting and pasting of software, followed by well-organized subroutines. However, the ability of object-oriented programming languages to inherit both the characteristics and the operations of existing classes led to a major push for software reuse.

Reuse faced a number of challenges, though. It appeared that writing software that could be potentially reused was relatively easy—searching for and finding such software and then eventually incorporating it in the end solution was fraught with technological and sociological challenges. It was realized, though, that if a class is modeled and developed correctly, and tested thoroughly, then reusing it will not merely increase productivity, but will also improve the resultant quality of the new inherited classes. Furthermore, it was realized that if classes are modeled following the principles of encapsulation, it results in localization of errors and thereby improved maintenance and quality.

1.9.2   Reusing Expert Knowledge and Experience

Reuse was too good a concept to be restricted to code-level reuse. Designers started thinking in terms of capturing the "conceptual thinking" of experts and reusing that for their own designs. This was thought not only to reduce time in design, but also to improve the quality of the resultant design. The pattern movement resulting from the works of the Gang of Four [Gamma et al. 1995] has received rapturous response precisely for this reason—their "Design Patterns" is a set of models that encapsulates the past experience of the industry and smoothly integrates with the new designs (models) being produced. Reusing these "models of thought processes" reduces the chances of errors that exist if a modeler starts a design from scratch. This pattern line of thinking has been applied to analysis patterns, cognitive patterns, and so on.

1.9.3   Applying Standards

Reuse of code and design implicitly results in project-level standards. For example, if a class is based on a class template created for the project, it is likely to have similar naming standards for attributes and function, and may have all the "getters and setters" already created in a skeleton form. These standards can then be scaled up to the organizational level, paving the way for uniform and quality-conscious mechanisms, to creating designs and writing code. This results not only in ease of creation of artifacts, but also in ease of quality checks during inspections and reviews, as some of the basic checks of naming standards for use cases, classes, and even documents within the projects are likely to pass. Thus, reuse and standards are closely linked with each other, and with quality. Furthermore, not only does reuse result in local standardization, such standardization, in turn, facilitates reuse. This is because reusable code and design needs a standards application that will enable easier location and incorporation of these reusable entities.

1.10   Quality and Usability

Usability is the ability of the software to help the users achieve their goals [Constantine and Lockwood 1997]. This is an important issue to be considered in any discussion on software usability. For example, usable software may be very easy to use and may have all the "bells and whistles" features, but if that software is not able to satisfy a particular user requirement then the usability of the software does not add value to the software quality.

Hudson, in listing the top ten user-centered techniques (and correlating them to the ISO13407 human-centered design standard), has put the actual creation of GUI design as the last—the other nine include user analysis, low-fidelity prototyping, navigation design, and scenarios of use. These techniques enable creation of usable software that helps the user achieve her goals in the easiest and simplest possible way. However, since the goals of the user can change, it is essential for usable software to "grow" along with the growing requirements of the user and her growing knowledge and expertise of the software.

1.10.1   Principles of Usability

Constantine and Lockwood [1997] and Constantine [1993] describe the laws of usability followed by the seven principles. The great law of usability states, "The system should be usable by a user with knowledge and experience in the application domain but no experience with the system—

Usability includes

- **Syntactical Correctness**
- **Semantic Consistency and Completeness**
- **Aesthetic Symmetry**

AND

All the above changing with changing needs and experience of the users

Figure 1.15 *Quality and usability*

without help or instruction." This law indicates that it is important for the software system to be "instinctively" usable. However, this law does not tell us about the training needs of the users in *their application domain.* It is up to a good user to know his application domain, and the usability of the software should not be blamed for any lack of application knowledge.

The lesser law of usability states "the system should not interfere with or impede efficient use by a skilled user having substantial experience with the system." This law recognizes the need for the system to "grow" with the user. For example, I need all the help and tool tips when I use the system for the first time. Later on, as I grow in expertise, this additional help may become more of a hindrance. Usable software recognizes this and enables expert users to use the system without providing unnecessary help.

The principles of usability stated by Constantine and Lockwood include support, structure, simplicity, visibility, reusability, feedback, and tolerance. Each of these principles provides a comprehensive quality angle to the software being designed and produced.

1.10.2 Navigability of Interfaces

In most graphical environments, it is essential for the screens and forms to be organized in a logical and cohesive manner, depending on the needs of the users. For example, a senior insurance broker logging on to a system will usually look for control totals on the insurance risks and premiums accrued, rather than calculate the amount for a particular claim. Similarly, an employee going to an employee portal within the organization and looking for her outstanding annual leave may then want to navigate to her salary and tax screens, rather than the outstanding policy applications. These are some fine nuances in designing the navigation of screens and related interfaces. This navigation becomes all the more important in an Internet-based application, where the logical grouping, dependency, and performance of Web pages are vital for the usability of the application.

1.10.3 GUI Design and Quality

While the user interface is considered separately in any discussion on the software usability, it still remains an important factor in improving the software usability. An interesting discussion on the user interface aspect of usability occurs in *Object Modeling and User Interface Design: Designing Interactive Systems,* by Mark Van Harmelen [2001].

1.11   UML-Based Projects—Types

In "Best of Booch," edited by Ed Eykholt [1996], Booch says, "While it is unfair to apply stereotypes to any specific projects we make some broad generalizations." Booch then proceeds to highlight the differences between sizes of projects based on factors such as the language of implementation. For example, C++ projects tend to have large numbers of developers (in the hundreds), compared to Smalltalk development projects that have less than a couple of dozen developers. Further highlighting the "language debates" between projects, Booch says, "Such religious attacks are plain silly, but for some projects they do sometimes reflect a deeper truth." We see here an attempt to classify projects in various groups such as early adopters of object technology, size, success, failure, and so on. This helps us understand the nature of the projects, and thereby helps us to plan and execute them.

In this discussion, we attempt to create a rough classification that enables us to apply the rigors of quality to these projects, keeping their objectives in mind. At the beginning of this chapter, we discussed how quality is dependent on the purpose and the objectives of the user of the product. That is the reason we want to classify projects depending on the objective with which UML will be used in these projects. In outlining each

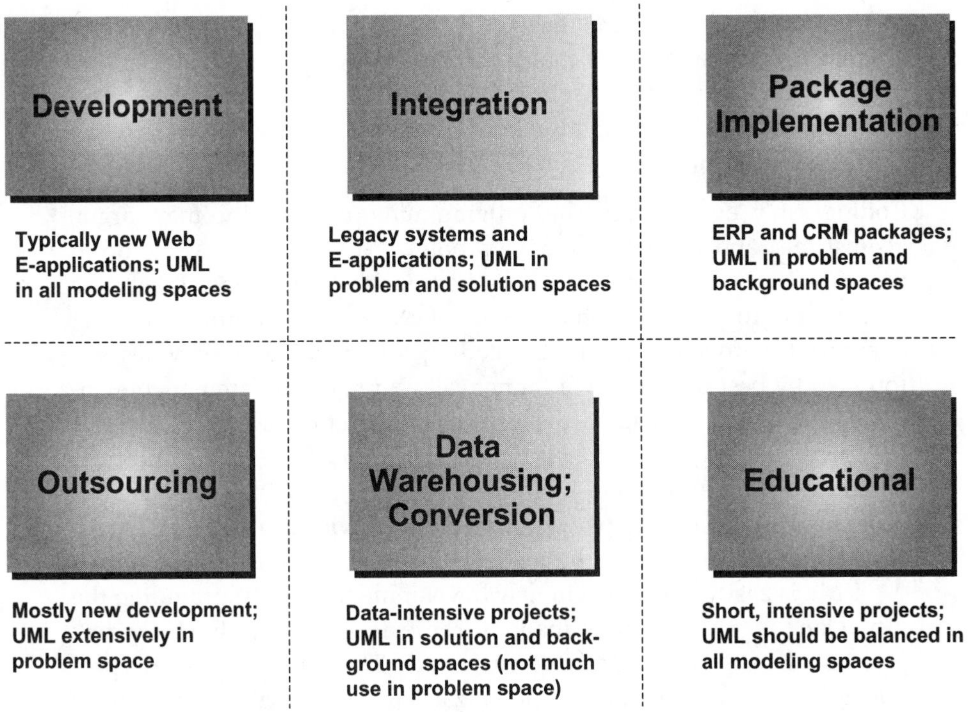

Development	Integration	Package Implementation
Typically new Web E-applications; UML in all modeling spaces	Legacy systems and E-applications; UML in problem and solution spaces	ERP and CRM packages; UML in problem and background spaces
Outsourcing	Data Warehousing; Conversion	Educational
Mostly new development; UML extensively in problem space	Data-intensive projects; UML in solution and background spaces (not much use in problem space)	Short, intensive projects; UML should be balanced in all modeling spaces

Figure 1.16   *Some UML-based project types*

of these project types, I am building the background for how the UML can be used to its best advantage, resulting in corresponding quality. Needless to say, these are not watertight compartments and you will find that in each of these project types there is some influence and effect of other project types as well. Following are the six project types that have used the UML and are likely to derive quality benefits by its application:

- Development Projects
- Integration Projects
- Package Implementation Projects
- Outsourcing Projects
- Data Warehousing and Conversion Projects
- Educational Projects

The expressiveness of the UML expands further, as it gets applied in these varied project types. This also demands significant quality effort, as the manner in which the UML gets used changes with the project types. Therefore, understanding the UML in the context of the projects is very helpful in quality improvement.

1.11.1 Development

Coding isn't everything. The programming community may argue against this, and indeed they have a point. All the work that we do in modeling software has to eventually be translated into code. Taking the argument to the extreme is the concept of eXtreme Programming. In that approach to software development, coding is at the center of activities surrounded by best practices. We cannot call eXtreme programmers pretentious—for they have named their approach extreme, indeed! I do agree that programming becomes the final activity, and therefore purpose, of whatever we do in terms of UML-based modeling. We model so we can program. However, UML plays a vital role in providing a standard means of communication between the customer (or user) and the programmer.

UML is easily applicable in new development projects, providing the visual language for business analysts. These are, of course, the lucky few projects where everything starts from scratch. The era of the dotcoms producing new software, and the organizations writing large e-commerce applications from scratch, fall into this project category. The advantage of these types of projects is that the paraphernalia of existing code databases and architecture does not hamper them. You can pretty much create what you want to create. Modeling does have to interact with architecture and requirements, but all of these are new. The code-generation facilities of UML CASE tools can be used here more than in other types of projects.

Development projects have the highest amount of freedom and at the same time the highest amount of risk. Therefore, not only is modeling using UML vital for these projects but it is also the iterative and incremental aspect of a process vital for these projects. Quality in these projects has no benchmark. Quality is perceived by users as they start using the product, and the earlier products in a particular domain set the "rough guidelines" on the acceptable levels of quality.

1.11.2 Integration (with Legacy)

While considerable new development was happening in start-up organizations, established, large companies did not have the freedom to develop brand-new, stand-alone applications. I classify projects as "integration projects" if their new development must interface with, send messages to, or retrieve information from a large, existing, legacy database or a COBOL application. Businesses that have invested millions of dollars and that have successful legacy procedural code written in COBOL and Pascal cannot totally dump these (usually mainframe-based) applications for the sake of new Web applications. However, they still have to cater to the high demand for their information and data to be shared with their Internet-savvy customers.

Especially after the Y2K fix, the investment or the capitalization in legacy software systems is so high that any medium- to large-scale project invariably has to contend with integration issues. While presenting the legacy data to the Internet-enabled user, the new development has a job of retrieving data, massaging it, and presenting it to the Web user, at all times ensuring that the integrity and the security of the data is not violated. Integration projects have far less freedom than new development projects, in terms of creating models and choosing languages and databases for implementation.

In terms of quality, though, there is a benchmark—a level of expectation—that the developers have to deal with when they are writing code and designing systems that have to integrate with existing systems. Existing applications, although not sophisticated in their interfaces, have lasted mainly because of their robust algorithms that the business has come to depend on. This puts extra demand on the developers, as it is not sufficient to simply provide an application with a good interface. More work is needed to ensure that the current level of software support is not disturbed by the integration effort.

UML remains important in these projects not only for its ability to "forward model" what is eventually the new part of the system, but also due to a need to create models of systems that exist. The concepts of refactoring, discussed by Fowler et al. [1999], can be applied in these projects, wherein we recast the existing applications to improve their performance. In an integration project, refactoring may happen but is not mandatory. New aspects of modeling will need to know the interface to the existing system requiring extensive amount of modeling work in all three modeling spaces.

The UML work in the problem space will be based on the modeling of additional functionalities the user wants from the system. For example, integration applications might need use case diagrams to pictorially show what the existing legacy application is doing. However, modeling in these projects might also be a simple representation of information that already exists—now perhaps accessible through the Internet. In the solution space, Class diagrams may be used to represent the current legacy system and its potential interface. The background space, with its need for architecture, will be complex in integration projects because there is not as much freedom in integrating with existing applications as with new development. Issues like the current platform, languages that can run on the current platform, the need for executing on or integrating with the new platform, speed, bandwidth, and security level are some of the things that have to be considered in the background space in these integration projects.

1.11.3 Package Implementation (ERP, CRMS)

The Enterprise Resource Planning and the more recent Customer Relationship Management System waves have created an era of the hugely popular third-party packages that organizations find beneficial in implementing directly—as against major in-house software development projects. Examples of these packages include SAP, PeopleSoft, and Siebel.

One of the major challenges of these package-implementation projects is, how much business should be reengineered and reorganized, so that maximum benefits can be derived by implementing the package? The reverse is also true, where there is a need to customize the package to fit the needs of the business. The need to understand the business before customizing the package seems to be less understood, leading to the costly budget overflows and failures of projects implementing these packages.

The UML, through some of its diagrams that are used in creating a model of the problem space, can greatly assist in specifying and customizing these third-party packages. Specifications, through a suite of UML diagrams, make it relatively easy to implement and—more importantly—test the implementation of these packages.

Quality assurance has a different meaning in these package-implementation projects. This is because quality activities are not focused on the development of new software modules but on how to ensure that the needs of the business are properly understood and documented within the capabilities of the package being implemented. In these projects, the amount and extent of software development is limited to customizing the software modules by changing and extending them.

Therefore, package implementation projects have less work for the programmers, but a relatively large amount of modeling work in the problem space for the business analysts. However, if the software package being implemented in the organization was itself developed using the UML, then it is essential that the programmers involved in the package implementation project are conversant with the UML. This is because the UML makes it easier for the implementers of the packages to understand the capabilities of what can and can't be done through the software package's customization.

1.11.4 Outsourcing

Despite a growing number of organizations using outsourcing, not only as a means to keep the costs down, but also to free up their resources to pursue core business, the ground is fertile for miscommunication and misunderstandings. UML seems to be the right technique to minimize these misunderstandings and improve communication between parties involved in an outsourcing project. In such projects, UML is used not only for its modeling capabilities, but also for its ability to scope and control the deliverables. For example, some large projects have used the UML in their terms of contracts, where payments were tied in with delivery of software modules that would satisfy a complete use case or a suite of use cases within a diagram. This is an important spin-off of using the UML for outsourced projects.

The basic purpose of using the UML, though, is specifying requirements and creating the design. In typical outsourced projects, two parties are involved—the one that specifies what has to be produced (developed) and the one that satisfies the needs of the specifications by actually doing the development. The party that does the specifications uses the UML in the problem space. The party that does the development starts the project by "reading" the UML-based specifications, followed by actual design work in the solution space.

It is much easier to produce a set of Use Case and Activity diagrams with its common and relatively well-understood set of notations and pass those files across to the outsourced organization, for their developers to understand what is required. The quality issue, of course, assumes that mere diagrams are not sufficient to specify the entire requirement. However, it is a much faster and efficient way of dealing with a separate development entity that might usually be located in a separate city or country, than trying to describe the requirements in a few hundred pages of descriptive language.

Because of the ease of putting functionalities within each of the use cases, it is also possible to track UML-based development across geographical and time borders. With UML literacy on the rise, the major issues in outsourcing projects—scope, control, communication, and reporting structure across different boundaries—are handled much better in such outsourced projects.

1.11.5 Data Warehousing/Conversion

Kimball et al. [1998], in their well-known work *The Data Warehouse Life-cycle Toolkit,* talk about dimensional modeling for a data warehouse. They argue for dimensional modeling as the next step in modeling a data warehouse, stating that the ER modeling approach may not be sufficient for major data warehousing needs. However, use of the UML is likely to benefit any effort to create an extensive model of what is stored in the database. The UML provides a wide spectrum of modeling techniques, and the ones that benefit data warehousing and data conversion projects center around the Class diagrams. The Class diagrams provide a means of documenting relational data storage. This ability of classes to represent tables can be used to create and refine schemas, as well as to provide the ability to manipulate the data through the class behavior.

If the data warehousing project is considered a complete project on its own (that is, it is not just related to data, but is responsible for the business functions as well), then UML, through its Use Case and Activity diagrams, can provide an excellent modeling mechanism in the problem space.

Conversion of data obviously benefits by its representation through Class diagrams as well as Package diagrams, as these diagrams ideally represent the relational tables.

1.11.6 Educational

While the UML is little more than five years old, it is robust enough to be used in teaching object-orientation. With its generic appeal, the UML can be, and is, used to teach good software engineering. Therefore, the UML plays a major role in educational projects. Higher-level degree students and participants of industrial courses benefit when the concepts of software engineering and good modeling are explained by using the UML in teaching assignments.

The application of UML in these academic exercises requires some premeditation. For example, it is essential to consider which diagrams to start with in teaching UML, and the basic process of moving from one diagram to another. Encouraging the students and participants to "think with the

UML," and applying that thinking to the three modeling spaces, is important in good teaching and industrial training. Some of these concepts of the application of the UML in education can be applied in large-scale deployment of the UML, where project teams transitioning to this software engineering approach may have a need for formal training and mentoring.

In typical academic environments, educational projects using the UML tend to last between one and two semesters, with the total typical workload between 14 and 24 weeks (assuming three hours of lecture time per week). It is essential to teach UML as team projects rather than individual projects. By the time the students have reached their senior year in undergraduate courses, they have usually formed allegiance to some programming languages. In learning the UML, however, students should be encouraged to keep programming languages aside till the last moment, when construction of software is attempted from the models.

Students should also be encouraged to discuss and make formal presentations of their work, as this not only facilitates learning, but is the practical scene that students will face as they enter industry. Presentations can follow the inspections and reviews, using the workshop techniques discussed in Chapter 2. This will certainly enhance the quality of the project work and enable faster understanding of the concepts. A common error, though, is that the UML diagrams themselves are treated as the end deliverables of the course assignments. Students should be encouraged to place these models within the context of the overall deliverables of requirements and design. This may require the CASE tool-based UML diagrams to be linked to, or inserted in, other deliverables. If this is not possible, students should certainly be encouraged to consider what additional documentation and specifications they need to explain the UML diagrams in more detail.

In making these educational projects as real as possible, students and course participants must be encouraged specifically to play the roles of business analysts, system designers, and architects as the modeling work progresses.

1.12 UML-Based Projects—Size and Scalability

Using a sledgehammer to drive a nail to hang a small photo frame is a "misfit" scenario. Sometimes, we have to admit, that is what happens when projects adopt the UML. For example, a relatively small project comprising three programmers and a three-month time frame may end up undertaking extensive UML-based modeling just because it seemed a good idea at the time.

The reverse is true more often, with teams of 50+ developers coding away to glory, with no modeling whatsoever to facilitate communication and quality. Lack of sufficient and appropriate modeling leads to considerable frustrations among project team members, and a large overhead is usually discovered later in the project. Projects that do not balance their modeling needs proportionately to their time and budget end up going around in circles, and team members finally place the blame on the UML.

Here, we are giving thought to the size of a project in order to minimize the waste that happens due to "misfit" scenarios and, better still, to enable application of the UML at the right level of project requirements. It is hoped that this will have a positive impact on the overall quality of models and deliverables produced, on the process that is followed to produce them, and eventually on the final product.

In classifying projects based on their size, I have applied a rough guideline of time, cost, and people, shown in Figure 1.17. Needless to say, these divisions are not set in concrete, and many practical projects will fall on the fringes of these divisions. The idea is to understand the relevance of the UML in the context of these project sizes. Furthermore, this classification is not in lieu of the previous classification of project types. The project types and the project sizes are orthogonal to each other, and projects will exhibit both characteristics.

Unlike project types, though, project sizes tend to scale up, putting additional demands on the quality requirements as well. While the hope is that a project that is planned, organized, and modeled correctly will have fewer "creep factor" problems, there will be formal needs for projects to be scaled up depending on the business opportunities, changing focus or, although unlikely, availability of more resources.

1.12.1 Small Projects

A small project is one with five to fifteen people and a project length of from three to six months. For a project with fewer than five people and shorter than three months, it may not be worthwhile to consider using the UML for modeling. Likely types of projects in this category include small, new development projects. Projects conducted for "experimental purposes," where an organization is trying a pilot project to produce software using a new Web application server or merely to "check out UML," are also considered small projects. Typical educational projects, where stu-

Small

Rough Guidelines:
5 to 15 people;
3 to 6 months;
<$1M

Examples:
Pilot—where organization
is trying out UML;
Educational—usually to
be completed within a
semester

UML documentation tool;
Minimal process;
QA effort depends on
context

Medium

Rough Guidelines:
15 to 50 people;
6 to 12 months;
$1M to $10M

Examples:
Medium-sized package
implementations;
Extensions to and
integration with legacy
applications

Two iterations of a
process are a must;
Social issues in projects
start appearing

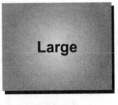

Large

Rough Guidelines:
50+ people;
More than 1 year;
>$10M

Examples:
Large ERP and CRMS
implementations;
Part of work outsourced;
Data warehouse
implementations

UML, together with
very formal process,
usually with a process tool;
High-ceremony process;
Social factors crucial

Figure 1.17 *Some UML-based project sizes*

dents are involved in UML-based modeling for a period of around 14 weeks, can also be categorized as small projects. The purpose of these educational projects is different from industrial projects; therefore, despite being a small project, an educational project may end up considering the entire gamut of UML modeling techniques.

An interesting observation on small projects in the industrial setting is that UML might be used across all its breadth, but the depth of its usage may not be high. This means that the UML diagrams might be used in the problem and solution space, and perhaps only some diagrams might be used, or experimented with. Work in the modeling spaces may also be limited to problem and solution space. Given the time, and perhaps the objectives of such projects, there is less opportunity to conduct extensive architectural modeling work in the background space.

The experimental or pilot projects are likely to have high visibility mainly because the results from the projects might be used to make further decisions related to, say, deploying the UML throughout the organization. It is important for these projects to be completed on time.

Furthermore, these projects will have less opportunity to apply the full iterative and incremental process to support UML-based modeling.

This also means there is very little opportunity to outsource projects or to consider package-implementation projects as small projects. Despite being low-ceremony projects, as far as processes are concerned, it is still important for the project team members to follow some guidelines to ensure that the modeling technique of UML is given a fair try. Therefore, we recommend at least one formal process iteration.

The focus of small projects is specific and the team will necessarily need an experienced mentor. This is because in these small projects, there is a fair bit of learning expected of the team members and the organization.

Occasionally, some data-conversion projects fall into the small-project category if the conversion has to be completed within a short time and is treated separately from the main functionality-based project. Thus small projects will most likely have one iteration, create a full breadth of UML-based models, may not need intensive process to accompany the model, and will have to produce results in a short period, usually three months.

Technically, these projects will use programming languages and data-bases to implement the project, but the organization may not always depend on the results from such projects to conduct its business. Since small projects are likely to be pilot in nature, their output and the experience gained in producing such output might be used to help the decision makers make choices in modeling, process, languages, and databases.

One other aspect of small projects is the use of CASE tools. These projects may not necessarily need a high-end CASE tool because of the low number of people involved and the short duration of the project. Documentation of the UML artifacts, however, should be done within an acceptable form of CASE tool because without such a tool, the project may not fully benefit from the application of the UML and may end up misleading the decision makers within the organization. This is especially true of organizations that are transitioning *any* modeling, let alone the UML.

1.12.2 Medium Projects

A medium project is one that is neither small nor large. This may not be a sufficient definition, though. A relatively formal description of a medium project is one having between 15 and 50 people and which lasts for around a year or more. Budgets for such medium-sized projects range from $1 million to $10 million. Once again, this is not to say that project budgets, time, or personnel outside of these ranges do not exhibit the characteristics of medium projects, just that they will benefit more by keeping the goals, benefits, and quality considerations arising out of the small or the large projects.

Such a project can also be a pilot project, but conducted with an angle to benefit the business more productively than just the small experimental project. It will have a smaller budget than a large project, but one that lets the organization procure necessary CASE tools; set up the necessary development environment, usage, and customization of off-the-shelf packages; and try out the use of methodologies.

While medium projects can follow more ceremony in the application of the "software process," they can still get away with two serious iterations (a draft iteration and a final iteration).

1.12.3 Large Projects

A project with more than 100 person-years worth of effort and with a budget of more than $10 million (but closer, perhaps, to $50 million) can be categorized as a large project, needing the application of UML in a different way than the other two project types. A large project using the UML extensively can belong to most of the five project types described earlier—the exception being the educational project type, where we don't envision application of all concepts of the UML at the same level of depth and breadth as in an industrial project.

To start with, no large project should be attempted without sufficient knowledge and some experience of both the UML techniques and iterative and incremental software development processes. Therefore, a large project should not start as a large project itself. A large project can verge on the definition of a program that can be made up of multiple projects. The difference, though, between such multiple projects and a very large project is the relatively cohesive nature of the large project. Large projects use the UML in both its depth and breadth. This means large projects get to use all diagramming and documentation techniques of the UML within all three modeling spaces.

From a quality angle it is important to note that large projects have a certain amount of integration and also possible package implementation that requires what I call "reverse modeling." While reverse engineering is a much broader term to indicate attempts to create models from code, "reverse models" can be called creation of models from any of the existing artifacts including code, ER models, data flow diagrams, flowcharts, plain English documentation, talks with the users, architectural descriptions, or any such things that exist in the knowledge pool of the existing environment.

Large projects typically need to create complex models from the existing models as well as existing systems, in order to understand what these existing legacy systems are currently doing. Modeling the existing legacy applications, however briefly, is a precursor to an extensive exercise in modeling what is expected of the new systems. Models of problem space, solution space, and, most importantly, architectural models in the background space will be produced following a high-ceremony quality process and will be subject to elaborate quality-assurance techniques and rigorous quality control.

The UML itself is scalable; however, that scalability has to be supported by the judicious use of CASE tools. This tool support is almost mandatory in any large project, because without such CASE tools to support modeling exercises between multiple teams, the UML can end up producing more confusion and frustration. Large projects must have sufficient budgets set aside to procure tools and to create a formal development environment. Also, because of the large number of people involved over a longer time frame, coordination among people and teams can only be made possible by extensive use of UML CASE tools that enable documentation, reporting, configuration management, and consistency among various modeling spaces. CASE tools produce a wide variety of reports and in various ways from the same model, making it easier for users to participate in large-scale modeling exercises by looking only at parts of models and diagrams, and only at their relevant level. For example, the ability of almost all UML CASE tools to hide the attributes and operations from the descriptions of classes is a boon in large projects, where simplified business object models (class diagrams) are usually read even by the users and domain experts involved in requirements modeling. CASE tools also enable intranet Web-based publication of the models, making is easy for far-flung teams and global users to participate in the software modeling exercise. Quality assurance in large projects requires extra effort in terms of traceability of requirements, and this is obviously facilitated further by the use of CASE tools.

These large projects also need a comprehensive and robust software process. There is a further need for configuration of such a process before the start of the project, followed by the malleability of the process to change as the development proceeds. Web application architectures and servers, various middlewares, and patterns and frameworks play a crucial role in such large projects. Therefore, these projects cannot do simply with a mentor for a short time. They are not mere investigative projects, but are directly linked to the performance of the organization as a whole. They need people on board who are comfortable with both UML and the process being followed during these software developments.

1.13   Putting it All Together (Key Points)

- Discussed the elusive nature of quality, especially in the context of software.

- Attempted to define quality and highlighted the fact that quality is an attribute "of something" and therefore cannot be defined on its own, without a context.

- Defined what is quality assurance and how it differs from testing or quality control.

- Defined the four different priorities vying against each other in a project: budget, time, functionality, and quality. Of these four, quality is the least measurable and most elusive. Therefore, it tends to get thrown out when pressure is applied by budget, time, functionality, or their combination.

- Defined the six different levels of quality within a software project: data quality, code quality, model quality, process quality, management quality, and the overall creation and management of the quality environment. Of these, model quality, its associated process quality, and the overall quality environment are of direct interest to us in this book.

- A process has three dimensions: the what, the how, and the who. All three dimensions exist within a process at the same time. They form part of a software process as well as a quality process.

- Modeling and quality are interrelated. Modeling helps us not only to understand the reality but also to create new reality. Within software development environments, modeling occurs in three different spaces or regions of work. The problem space creates models to understand the business and functional issues of the system, the solution space creates models of the solution as well as traces the solutions to the problems, and the background space creates models of the architecture as well as provides for project management and quality management.

- The UML enhances quality because it provides an industry-standard mechanism to communicate within and among projects.

- The UML enhances the quality of visualization, specifications, construction, and documentation work going on within a project.

- Not all UML diagrams apply to all modeling spaces—Table 1.2 presents the focus of each of the UML diagrams to respective modeling spaces.

- There are three levels of quality-control checks: checking the syntax of the models, making sure that they semantically represent what they are meant to represent, and seeing that the models have some aesthetic sense around them.

- Quality assurance of software process deals with the necessary aspect of the process, followed by the sufficient aspect of the process, and finally the malleability of the process or its ability to change.

- Reuse and patterns have a direct beneficial effect not only on the productivity of the project, but also on its quality. Quality and usability of the software produced are interrelated because usable software is perceived by users as having higher quality.

- There are six different types of popular UML-based projects: new development, integration, package implementation, outsourcing, data warehousing/conversion, and educational projects.

- These projects could be further categorized as small, medium, and large.

1.14 Bibliographic Notes

A summarized description of the three modeling spaces and the UML diagrams that appear in these modeling spaces appears in an article I wrote based on this book. See the Australian Computer Society's official publication, *InformationAge*, October–November 2001, "Demystifying the UML," pp. 56–61 [Unhelkar 2001].

In my earlier process work, and many times in practice, I have compared the three dimensions of a process with white clouds. This is a phenomenon I have observed during my many flights home to Sydney from the West Coast (San Francisco or Los Angeles). The journey is entirely over the Pacific Ocean and there is hardly any land in sight. Formed by the unhindered marriage of the sunrays with the Pacific Ocean, these white clouds stretch in abundance for thousands of miles—as far as the eye can see, or the plane can fly. They represent a process whose growth is relaxed yet certain—providing an ideal model for my process-based work. Osho

[1978], quoted below, provides one of the best philosophical descriptions of white clouds that has benefited my own process thinking:

> A white cloud is a mystery—the coming, the going, the very being of it. A white cloud exists without any roots . . . but still it exists, and exists abundantly. . . . All dimensions belong to it, all directions belong to it. Nothing is rejected. Everything is, exists, in a total acceptability.

The other interesting aspect of the above-mentioned journey is that you pass over the International Date Line. It is a funny experience to grow a day younger or a day older (depending on the direction of your flight), literally within seconds.

For a list of some popular CASE tools that help create UML-based models, see UML CASE Tools.

1.15 Frequently Asked Questions (FAQs)

Q1: Do I need to understand both process and modeling before I can apply quality to them?

A1: Yes, your understanding of process should be developed independent of your understanding of models. Once a good understanding of both process and models is developed, quality can be applied to them.

Q2: If my project is running late, which of the three checks (syntax, semantics, or aesthetics) should I drop?

A2: Syntax checks will be relatively easy to execute. This is because most CASE tools help you draw syntactically correct UML diagrams. Therefore, you should not skip the semantic checks of all models.

Q3: Is the separation of the three modeling spaces important?

A3: Yes, it is important to understand modeling in problem, solution, and background spaces. What is more important is to keep in mind that eventually these models will be intertwined with one another and that there is no need to specifically work towards keeping these models separate. The division of modeling work in these three spaces ensures that the roles working in these modeling spaces have a clear understanding of what they should be focusing on.

Q4: Is UML a process or a methodology?

A4: No, UML is an industry-standard set of modeling techniques, which need a process around them. A process (also commonly known as a methodology) may differ in its approach, but can still use UML as a common set of communication mechanisms.

Q5: How do I handle a project that is extremely large, and beyond the description of large projects discussed here?

A5: Large projects are discussed here to show how their usage of the UML differs from medium and small projects. Extremely large projects will need the application of the concepts discussed here, many times over. The actual concepts of how the UML should be applied do not change.

Q6: How does quality management relate to project management?

A6: Quality management is, in a way, managing a "subproject" within a full software development project that is specifically focused on the quality aspect of the project. Thus, quality management uses almost all concepts of project management in terms of people, planning, and execution, but is focused on quality assurance and quality control of the processes and deliverables in the project. These issues are further discussed in greater detail in Chapter 2.

Q7: You discuss the three dimensions of a process as "what," "how," and "who." What about "when?"

A7: The three dimensions provide the core of a process. Additional dimensions will arise and will be relevant to practical projects. However, incorporating them in a process becomes easy if the basic three dimensions are defined.

Q8: We have an old legacy system. We have to replace it. How can modeling help?

A8: Modeling can help by enabling you to create a good understanding of the existing system. This will involve limited modeling of what exists. This will be followed by models related to conversion of data and reengineering of business processes. Modeling will of course play a major role in creating new business processes.

Q9: I am a process consultant. Do I need to understand UML meta-models?

A9: Yes, any process person who customizes and implements processes needs to understand metamodels. However, project managers who are merely "users" of a process may not want to spend too much time understanding the metamodels of the UML.[18]

Q10: Despite working hard on the usability aspect of our software, it is not getting recognized as such.

A10: Consider including the users more than you have been in modeling requirements and conducting usability studies. Consider cross-cultural issues, particularly if the software is developed in a different country from its users. Ask the users to prioritize their usability concerns and address the most important ones first. Create prototypes (even if they are nonexecutable prototypes or create storyboards or mind maps).

1.16 Exercises

E1.1: What are the pressures on quality?

E1.2: How would you define quality? And what are the issues in defining quality?

E1.3: What are specific quality issues in software development?

E1.4: What are the levels of quality of interest to us in UML?

E1.5: What are the three dimensions of a process, and how do they apply to a software process?

E1.6: How is a quality process different from a software process?

E1.7: Describe the aspect of quality assurance that ensures that the correct end result is produced.

E1.8: How does modeling help in projects where there is a large amount of existing legacy code?

E1.9: Describe the three suggested modeling spaces within software.

E1.10: What are the different types of quality aspects enhanced by UML?

E1.11: How is the aesthetic of quality models different in nature from their syntax and semantic aspects?

---

[18] Comparison between what is within the realms of a process and what is modeling is derived from *www.MethodScience.com*.

E1.12: In addition to the knowledge of UML, what else is needed in assuring the semantic quality of UML?

E1.13: Describe the difference between malleability of a software process and its necessity and sufficiency aspects.

E1.14: Malleability of software has to deal with the software process feedback loop. Explain.

1.17 References

Booch, G., J. Rumbaugh, and I. Jacobson, "The Unified Modeling Language Tutorial," *The OOPSLA 96 Conference,* San Jose, Calif.: October 1996.

———, *The Unified Modeling Language User Guide,* Reading, Mass.: Addison-Wesley, 1999.

Brooks, F., *The Mythical Man-Month,* Reading, Mass.: Addison-Wesley, 1995.

Brown, W., Malveau, R. "Skip," McCormick III, H., and Mowbray, T., *Anti Patterns: Refactoring Software, Architectures, and Projects in Crisis,* John Wiley & Sons, Inc., 1998.

Cantor, M., *Object-Oriented Project Management with UML,* Wiley, 1998.

Card D. and Comer E., "Why Do So Many Reuse Programs Fail?" *IEEE Software,* 11(5), September 1994: 114–115.

Cheng, M.J., "My words are very easy to understand," *Lectures on the Tao The Ching* (translated from the Chinese by T.C. Gibbs), Richmond, CA: North Atlantic Books, 1981.

Constantine, L., "Getting the user interface right: Basic principles," *Proceedings of Software Development Conference,* San Francisco: Miller Freeman, 1993.

———, *Constantine on Peopleware,* Yourdon Press Computing Series, Upper Saddle River, N.J.: Prentice Hall, 1995.

———, and L. Lockwood, *Software for Use: A Practical Guide to the Models and Methods of Usage-Centered Design,* Reading, Mass.: Addison-Wesley, 1997.

Coplien, J., "The Column without a Name: Setting the Stage," *C++ Report,* 6(8), (October 1994): 8–16.

DeMarco, T., and Lister, T., *Peopleware: Productive Projects and Teams,* Dorset House Publishing Company, 1987.

Dodani, M., "Archaeological designers," *Journal of Object Oriented Programming,* May 1994.

Eriksson, H., and M. Penkar, *Business Modeling with UML; Business Patterns at Work,* OMG Press, 2000.

Eykholt, E., (ed.), *Best of Booch,* New York: SIGS Books & Multimedia, 1996.

Fowler, M., "A Survey of Object-oriented Analysis and Design Methods," *OOPSLA 96* Tutorial No. 45, San Jose, Calif.: October 1996.

Fowler, M., *Analysis Patterns: Reusable Object Models,* Reading, Mass.: Addison-Wesley, 1997.

————, et al., *Refactoring: Improving the Design of Existing Code,* Reading, Mass.: Addison-Wesley, 1999.

————, with Scott, K., *UML Distilled* 2d ed., Boston: Addison-Wesley, 2000.

Frakes, W.B., and Isoda, S., "Success Factors of Systematic Reuse," *IEEE Software,* 11(5), (September 1994): 15–19.

Beizer, Boris, *System Testing and Quality Assurance,* New York: Van Nostrand Reinhold, 1984.

Gabriel, R., "The Quality without a Name," *Journal of Object-Oriented Programming,* 6(5), (September 1993): 86–89.

Gamma, E., et al., *Design Patterns: Elements of Reusable Object-Oriented Software,* Reading, Mass.: Addison-Wesley, 1995.

Gardner, K., Rush A., Crist, M., Konitzer, R., and Teegarden, B., *Cognitive Patterns: Problem-solving Frameworks for Object Technology,* Cambridge University Press, 1998.

Gates, B., *Business @ The Speed of Thought,* Viking, 1999.

Glass, R., *Software Runaways: Monumental Software Disasters,* Upper Saddle River, N.J.: Prentice Hall, 1997.

Greatrex, C., (KPMG Director), "Achieving Excellence through Effective Management of your IT project," *Proceedings of ITProject Management by AIC Conferences* (April 1996).

Henderson-Sellers, B., and J. M. Edwards, "A second generation OO methodology: MOSES," *Object Magazine*, 1994.

Hutt, A., *Object Analysis and Design, Comparison of Methods*, OMG/Wiley, 1994.

Jacobson, I., "Time for a cease-fire in the Methods War," *Journal of Object Oriented Programming*, July/August 1993.

Jacobson, I., Booch, G., Rumbaugh, J., *The Unified Software Development Process*, Reading, Mass.: Addison-Wesley, 1999.

Kimball, R., et al., *The Data Warehouse Lifecycle Toolkit*, Wiley, 1998.

Lanier, J., "The Frontier between Us," *Communications of the ACM*, 40(2), (February 1997), 55–56, Special Anniversary issue on 50 years of computing.

McGregor, J. and Sykes, D., *A Practical Guide to Testing Object-Oriented Software*, Boston: Addison-Wesley, 2001.

Osho, *My Way: The Way of the White Clouds*, Dorset, Mass., and Queensland: Element, 1978.

Perry, William, *Quality Assurance for Information Systems*, QED Information Sciences, MA: 1991.

Somerville, I., *Software Engineering*, Reading, Mass.: Addison-Wesley, 1989.

Unhelkar, B., 1999, *After the Y2K Fireworks: Business and Technology Strategies*, CRC Press, 1999.

———, "Demystifying the UML," Australian Computer Society's official publication, *InformationAge*, October–November 2001, pp. 56–61, St. Leonards, NSW, Australia: IDG Communications.

Van Harmelen, M., (ed.), *Object Modeling and User Interface Design: Designing Interactive Systems*, Boston: Addison-Wesley, 2001.

Younessi, H., and B. Henderson-Sellers, *Object Magazine*, 7(8), 1997: 38–42.

Yourdon, E., The Rise and Resurrection of the American Programmer, Yourdon Press Computing Series, Upper Saddle River, N.J.: Prentice-Hall, 1998.

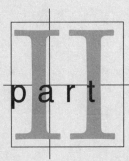

part II

Organizing and
Enacting the Process
for Quality

Part I covered the theory behind the elusive nature of quality. When we discuss the process related to software development, we are not simply talking about verifying and validating what has been produced, we are also discussing a sustained effort to organize and follow the discipline of producing models and software. Part II considers the comprehensive organization and execution of the quality function with a detailed emphasis on the *process* of developing UML-based software. In other words, in Part II, we discuss "how" the quality function is organized and carried out in UML-based projects. The people issues ("who"), so elementary in producing good quality, are also discussed. A brief outline of Part II follows:

- Chapter 2 discusses the quality management function with special emphasis on the people and organizational aspects of quality management.

- Chapter 3 discusses the Quality Software Process, which encompasses both the software development process and the accompanying quality process.

- Chapter 4 focuses on the practical enactment of the Quality Software Process.

- Chapter 5 discusses the crucial issues of estimates and metrics in a UML-based project, topics that will interest managers directly.

2 chapter

Quality Environment: Managing the Quality Function

Good software does not come from CASE tools, visual programming, rapid prototyping, or object technology. Good software comes from people. So does bad software.
—Larry Constantine [1995]

Putting This Chapter in Perspective

People produce good quality. Therefore, organizing and managing people and the roles they play is essential to producing good quality in software projects. This organizational aspect of quality is described as a "quality environment." Creating and managing a quality environment falls under the realm of quality management, which, in turn affects—and gets affected by—all aspects of general management. The primary areas of management with respect to quality discussed in this chapter are planning and organizing people, processes, and the physical environment. This chapter also focuses on the sociological ("who") aspect of the quality function—the people who form the project and quality teams, their relationships to each other and to the external members of the project (the users), and the processes they follow in order to carry out their quality-conscious tasks.

The Prime Reader: Quality Manager, Project Manager, Director/VP

2.1   Quality Management

2.1.1   Quality Environment

This chapter discusses organization of the quality function, or quality management. It is effectively the tip of the quality context triangle (see Figure 1.2)—the quality environment. An effective quality environment includes the people who perform the quality checks, their organizational structure, and how those responsible for quality checks should interact with the rest of the project members. Quality management is a part of project management and, therefore, utilizes all aspects of management itself. This involves understanding the project in the context of the overall business, identifying and organizing teams, putting together a detailed process, setting standards, facilitating modeling, managing external relationships, and so forth.

A well-organized project team is also able to monitor and track projects—a fundamental aspect of quality. When we organize quality-conscious project teams, we organize teams that can hit a "moving target." These quality teams bring together various players who will influence the actual quality of the software and, equally importantly, will influence the *perception of quality* within the project. Therefore, quality teams bring people together who will understand the problem, produce the models, produce the product, test it, deploy it, and use it. Good project teams also consider the roles that handle training, help desks, and so forth.

Based on the above, we move forward by setting the scene for the nontechnical aspects of management as well as quality management. Organizing and documenting the *necessary* and *sufficient* aspects of a quality process is essential to being able to shoot at the moving quality target. These are issues that go beyond software modeling, and they are discussed here with the aim of positively influencing the outcome of a UML-based project.

2.1.2   Nontechnical Management

Meyer [1995] has discussed in great detail the *non*technical role of a project manager who deals mainly with team formation and management. This nontechnical project manager role includes the sociological or human aspect of management that is applied to project teams and quality teams within the project. This application of sociology by managers to project teams is crucial to producing quality, because in the final analysis people produce quality—albeit supported by good tools and processes.

Goldberg and Rubin [1995] also discuss the importance of team formation, especially with regard to its structure and operation. A crucial aspect of their discussion is organizing teams in such a way as to carry out a successful reuse program in an object-oriented environment. This is because the sociological aspect of a development project is critical for both reuse and project quality. For example, it is a common experience that ownership of the reusable component is an emotional issue for the person who owns that component—requiring careful support from the project manager when the component has to be modified—especially if errors are found.

Quality-related work also generates emotions among project teams. For example, people entrusted with quality assurance and people whose work products (deliverables) are subjected to quality checks are often at opposite ends of the emotional spectrum. This happens because those entrusted with quality function must enforce the process and seek out errors in the deliverables or work products; the producers of the models may not always appreciate it.

While these sociological challenges in an object-oriented environment are well known, they are simply the extension of sociological challenges confronted by all teams—particularly the global teams that we come across in an outsourced project [O'Hara-Devereaux and Johansen 1994]. Team formation, operation, and motivation are not simple tasks, mainly because they do not seem to follow a given formula. Constantine, during the panel discussion on these soft issues at OOPSLA 96 in San Jose, stated:

> It is easier to communicate with machines and solve the problems; but with people, it is difficult. This is mainly so because people are very difficult to generalize.

However, handling this difficulty is precisely at the heart of the success or failure of a particular project. Today's Information and Communication Technology (ICT) industry is such that most equipment, development environments, architectures, and commercial off-the-shelf software and components are easily purchased—perhaps at a fraction of the cost spent to develop them. The differentiating edge, however, as Kriendler [1993] points out, is created by a "company's work force and the quality of their development processes." The skills and ability of the work force come to fruition depending on the way the teams are organized and managed, and the quality is improved through the quality process applied in development. Work forces and processes are discussed at length in subsequent sections.

2.1.3   Process and Quality

A significant aid to creating and managing quality teams is a good software process (shown in Figure 1.4). A process provides the necessary infrastructure of activities to carry out a successful project. Thus, a project and the process used within a project are interdependent. A process on its own cannot achieve much unless it is supported by good management skills. However, management itself also needs a well-thought-out process.

The responsibility of a quality-conscious process is not limited to simply producing software—although that is a significant deliverable in any software project. We want to produce a software product that evolves, scales, and changes according to the needs of its users. However, these needs continue to change almost daily, and so does the perception of quality. Therefore, we need a process that also handles the changing quality needs.

A quality-conscious process has some necessary steps and other sufficient steps. Furthermore, such a process includes a mechanism to improve the software process itself. Thus, the process has a component that enables the improvement of the overall process. This is the malleable aspect of a process and interests us from both software development and quality viewpoints. These necessary, sufficient, and malleable aspects of a quality process provide the additional focus of a quality process—the separate and sustained effort to produce a good quality product, good quality software models (such as our UML-based models), and a quality environment.

It is interesting to note how, at times, this necessarily separate and sustained effort toward quality gets treated as a part of normal software development. The reasoning behind this is: If everyone involved in a project accomplishes what he or she has to do in the best possible way, the eventual product is a quality product.

One can immediately challenge this thinking by asking, "Who decides what everyone should do?" While no one can deny that quality is everyone's responsibility, it is a greater responsibility for some than for others! It is this focused responsibility on quality that is derived from a separate quality function within the overall process. It is important for a process to be well thought out, put together, instantiated, and deployed. This is a part of the quality function, which is followed by enactment and monitoring of the process.

In order to achieve the process discipline (or discipline in following a method[1]), it is necessary to plan and organize the quality function in the same way that normal project management functions are organized. Thus, we use all the concepts of project management in quality management, but still maintain quality management as a distinct function with its own set of activities, tasks, roles, and deliverables.

An example of the confusion that can otherwise result is seen when we ask the basic question, "Who creates and maintains a quality plan?" Theoretically, either the project manager or the process consultant performs this work. However, it is more appropriate to assign this to the role of quality manager. If quality is everyone's responsibility, then, despite all good intentions, it will end up being no one's responsibility.

This is not to say that people are not sincere in their desire to bring quality in their work. In fact, information technology—despite being only half a century old—is full of people who take utmost pride in their work. Many IT professionals eat, breathe, and live code—and eventually, the work they produce is of very good quality. What we intend in this discussion is to create a quality environment and inculcate a quality discipline that results in quality by individuals and teams. If management facilitates a separate and sustained quality effort, by enabling verification and validation of models and products, organizing and motivating people, and providing a planned approach to quality assurance activities, then the work of those innumerable sincere IT professionals will be that much more effective.

2.2   Team Organization

Since quality is "by the people," it is essential that project managers recruit, organize, and manage software teams in the best possible way. This is true of all types of software projects, but much truer of object-oriented projects

---

[1] The discipline of methods is a science in itself. Creation and configuration of methods needs a scientific approach that eventually translates into their practical deployment, enactment, and monitoring. For more details, see *www.Method-Science.com*.

that use the UML. In discussing the importance of success in an object-oriented project, Goldberg and Rubin [1995] correctly point out the role of the organizational aspect of the project:

> Objects are not new. They were tested, were found to work, and are still around. But they continue to be used successfully only where appropriate organizational and management contexts are created.

This section describes how to create that context by organizing the quality function around people. Distinct emphasis is placed on the people who are developing software and the people who are responsible for the quality-assurance aspect of that software. Creation of this context starts by discussing the team organization in terms of the model (or ideal) roles performed by people within project teams.

Do note, however, that the models presented here are to be treated as reference models. It is *not* mandatory that teams are organized around these models precisely. Therefore, these team models should be used only as a basis to create teams needed for various types and sizes of projects. For example, a large data warehousing project will need more than one database manager, and certainly multiple administrators, whereas an outsourced project will have many business analysts but very few programmers.

While most roles will make at least some contribution in all three modeling spaces, in practice, it is found that roles tend to cluster around the primary model space in which they operate. For example, the business analysts tend to work more closely with the users than the programmers do. Therefore, the suggestion here is to create a team that is made up of roles that cluster together. Because we have grouped all our work in software development into the problem space, the solution space, and the background space, groups or clusters of roles are organized accordingly.

2.2.1 Organizing the Roles in the Problem Space

Having given sufficient importance to modeling in the problem space, it is now important to consider the roles that work in this modeling space. Figure 2.1 shows the problem-space roles played by project-team members. As mentioned earlier, the way these roles operate within the problem space, the way they relate with each other, and the way they relate with roles from the other modeling spaces can change depending on the project. The following sections discuss the most primary roles that work to create the Model Of the Problem Space (MOPS), their brief skill requirements, and how they impact the overall quality of the system.

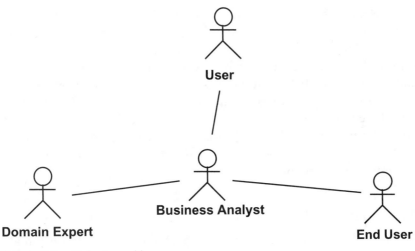

Figure 2.1   *Roles in problem space*

2.2.2 Business Analyst

This role is at the heart of modeling in the problem space. The business analyst (BA) is responsible for understanding the requirements of the business, documenting them in UML standard, and analyzing the specification and documentation to create additional diagrams that will be useful to the system designers. It is important for the business analyst to be able to communicate with all levels of users and management, because a business analyst continually interacts with the users, their managers, and the project managers. This results in appropriate management of the user expectations by the BA—a key part of the business analyst's role. Some of the valuable attributes of a business analyst include the ability to organize workshops, run them smoothly, direct the discussions during the workshops, extract the maximum requirements through good interview techniques, and encourage the users to voice their priorities and concerns as early in the project as possible.

However, a business analyst cannot stop at that. In UML-based projects, the business analyst should also be able to document the results of the discussions during workshops and interviews using the use case diagrams, use case documentations, and activity diagrams. With increasing experience, the BA can also use additional UML-based diagrams such as sequence diagrams and state chart diagrams.

Furthermore, it is commonplace for good BAs to use the basic class diagram to indicate the core entities in the problem space. This representation of the core entities as classes showing simple class-to-class relationships between them provides a robust starting point for further analysis and design. Note that when the BAs create the models of software systems, they are referred to as requirements modelers (RMs). In small projects, these two roles tend to merge. However, medium to large projects, especially the ones dealing with package implementation and outsourcing, will have two separate roles (BA and RM), and two or more individuals performing these roles.

2.2.3   User

The user (also called the user representative) is the person who eventually uses the software within a business environment. Typical examples of users are the account executives, the tellers, and the branch managers in a banking or insurance domain. Examples of users in a manufacturing domain include operators on the shop floor using the software to monitor their inventory or calculate the capacity of a car's engine, for instance. (This book does not delve into engineering software, but concentrates on information systems and information processing applications in all industrial sectors.)

Users play an invaluable role in providing quality—by providing the right interpretations to high-level objectives requirements. User representatives in software projects should be drawn from the field—employees and contractors who have hands-on experience in using the existing software, or people who are well versed with the existing business processes. Users are responsible for describing the existing business processes, followed by what would be ideal in new business processes that can be supported by the new software. It is important for the people playing the role of users to be able to distinguish the core requirements from the "nice-to-have" things. Many users, especially in the Web applications area, find the user interface aspect of the software interesting (and at times fascinating). These users should be encouraged to concentrate initially on the expected functionality of the system.

It is also worth noting that many users have moved into business from IT. These users are ideally suited to play the role of a user representative on the project. While communication is crucial to the success of this role, users may not run the requirements modeling workshops and may not document the requirements themselves. In UML-based projects, even if the users don't create them, they must be able to read the use case and activity diagrams, and should be able to pass comments on their appropriateness. Thus, users provide the front line of quality function in terms of reviewing the business processes documented (using the UML diagrams) by the business analyst.

It is also important to note that users may not be interested in the detailed syntax check of the UML-based diagrams—their interests lie in the semantic meanings behind each of the diagrams and the elements on the diagrams. Users should be allowed to be as subjective as they can in their description of the current problems and future expectations—leaving the interpretations and documentation in the UML to the BA. If users are not UML-literate, they can receive a brief summary of use case and activity diagram notations. In my experience, if presented properly, explaining the basic notations of use case and activity diagrams to the user community does not take more than a couple of hours. Once the user group becomes capable of reading the UML diagrams, and starts to participate in the workshops and discussion sessions, model quality improves immensely.

Finally, users can also vary their role and become acceptance testers. Users are in the best position to conduct acceptance testing, as they know the problem domain and are the ones who have helped specify and prioritize the problem. In conducting an acceptance test, the user focuses on whether or not the functionality specified in the MOPS through the use cases and activity diagrams has been satisfied.

2.2.4   End User

This role is different from that of the user in that the user is part of the organization and is most likely an employee or contractor representing the business. Examples of end users, on the other hand, are the customers standing on line in front of a bank counter or a post office. Before the advance of the e-commerce era, the end user had hardly any direct interaction with the business systems. Today, though, because the end user is the initiator and the beneficiary of the interaction with the business system, it appears as an important role in the MOPS.

In modeling good quality systems, it was not uncommon to get an end user on board on a short-term basis to provide input to the software model being created. Consider, for example, a hospital system. Doctors and nurses in a hospital can spare some time (typically ranging from one to two hours per week) to pass comments on the needs of the end user and how the requirements should be shaped to include current and future needs.

Needless to say, the end user is neither interested, nor skilled, in UML diagrams, software processes, and so on. A plumber or an accountant using a tax-calculation package may not mind explaining (for an hour or two) what the package should do, but beyond that it is stretching the role of the end user. Despite this rather peripheral association of an end user in a software project, it is important to get good potential end users onboard in order to extract appropriate requirements from them—particularly in Web-based applications where the end user will be signing on to the actual system and using it.

Thus, examples of such users include the bank customer who logs on to the Internet to access her account information, and who wants additional features such as account transfers, relevant legal advice on the transfers, interest calculations, and so forth, on the Web site or portal. With the $24 \times 7 \times 360$ degrees (around the globe) access, end users should be analyzed for their language needs, cultural sensitivities, color choices, and legal requirements. An end user trying to access information from China, for instance, faces different legal restrictions from another end user in Australia. A good MOPS has to build on the needs of the end users by talking to, interviewing, and encouraging them to participate in workshops where their needs can be analyzed, documented, and prioritized.

2.2.5   Domain Expert

More often than not the domain expert (DE) is a consulting role. This might be true even if the DE is a full-time employee. A person who has at least five years of extensive and current experience in the business domain is suitable to play this role. A MOPS for an insurance system, for example, would benefit from the advice of a person who has extensive experience in the insurance business, and who is not merely familiar with but is fully knowledgeable about the current rules and regulations, recent legal changes regarding the obligations of the insurance providers, the current relationship of the business with its underwriters, and so on.

The fact that the information about the business domain is the foundation of any problem specification cannot be overemphasized. This vital element of the requirements is brought to the project by the DE. Furthermore, input and advice from the DE not only helps to shape the correct and current requirements of the project, it also enables future thinking, thereby providing the opportunity for the BA to create requirements models that encompass potential requirements once the system is deployed. Refactoring of requirements is made possible by input from the DE.

2.2.6 Prototyper in Problem Space

A prototyper in the problem space has the job of creating a look-alike of the thought processes that describe the problem and the functionality required to handle the problem. Note that this is different from creating the prototype in the solution space (discussed in Section 2.2.13). Because the focus is on the functionality rather than on the solution, the person responsible for this role doesn't need to be a programmer. The prototype at this level can be a manual set of screens or classes, and the walkthrough of this prototype can also be a manual process of stepping through the screen spaces. There is no requirement for this prototype to be an executable; hence the prototyper should not be concerned with a lack of technical ability.

A prototype in the problem space is meant to jog the thinking of the users, end users, and domain experts to enable them to understand what to expect and, additionally, what is possible. This eventually has a positive impact on the usability of the system, because the users of the system will have thought of the most optimum way in which the system can be used to satisfy their function. Constantine and Lockwood [1999] have correctly identified the importance of treating user interfaces as systems in their own right, and paying attention to their design from the outset. DEs can provide great assistance in designing a usable system.

2.2.7 Organizing the Roles in the Solution Space

The roles in the solution space, shown in Figure 2.2, are far more technical in nature as they strive to produce a Model Of the Solution Space (MOSS). The importance of these roles is in their technical knowledge and experience. However, people with business skills can also make valuable contributions

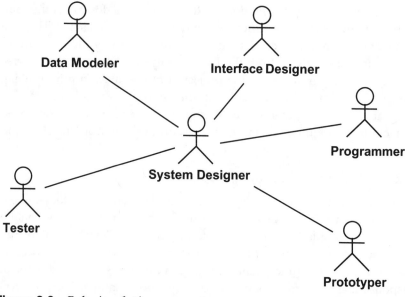

Figure 2.2 *Roles in solution space*

in modeling the solution space by participating in high-level technical reviews, understanding the capabilities of the technology, and modifying the business requirements and expectations based on these technological capabilities.

2.2.8 System Designer

The system designer (SD) works in the solution space, creating a solution-level model that can be implemented by the programmer. Thus, an SD has a need to interact with the business analyst in order to understand the requirements model that she has created. The SD also interacts with the programmer, explaining the designs, modifying them depending on the changing requirements or constraining technologies, and ensuring that the designs are conveniently and correctly implemented. Thus, the SD plays the crucial role of identifying solution-level classes from the business domain model created by the business analyst.

Ideally, a system designer should have at least five years of IT experience, enabling the person to understand the capabilities of implementation technology. Because of the rapid changes to the technologies, such as programming languages (for example, Java and C#) and environments (for example, WebSphere and .NET) and associated databases, it is essential for the person in this role to understand these technologies sufficiently to create good quality designs. This also means that for medium to large projects, it is essential that the person has at least two years of design experience using the UML. Large projects will need more than one person playing the role of a designer.

2.2.9   Data Modeler

The data modeler (DM) primarily creates database schemas with the help of class diagrams of the UML. The data modeler plays a more crucial role in integration projects (than in normal development projects), wherein there is a need to create not only a new database, but also interfaces to older legacy or transaction-based databases. In e-commerce developments, designing the content management system (CMS) is vital to this role.

DMs, especially in a relational environment, concentrate heavily on table design, index design, normalizations, and efficiency issues, which are all mapped to the class designs in the solution space. Furthermore, in association with the SDs, this role also makes use of patterns in creating interfaces to databases, ensuring the robustness of the DB interfaces, as well as their flexibility. Finally, the data modeler may be called in during creation of the test database—especially in populating the database with selective records.

2.2.10   Interface Designer

An interface designer (ID) deals with the layout, design, and navigation of the interfaces. There can be variations to this role focusing specifically on the user interfaces. This is because the primary interfaces of the system are the graphical user interfaces (GUIs)—where most of the effort of this role is directed. However, an interface can also be to another system, database, or a device such as a key card reader. If it is within the skill set of the person fulfilling this role, these interfaces will also be designed by the interface designer. Alternatively, SDs can treat this as a variation of their role—thereby creating the designs for interfaces other than the GUIs.

Finally, reports also provide a vital interface to the system. Reports (design, layout, and printing) can be considered a part of this role. In large systems, report creation and layout is vital enough to be dedicated to not just one role, but to a team of people fulfilling the role of report designer.

2.2.11 Programmer

Known also as a coder and implementer, the programmer represents the first set of software skills known to the IT community, ever since we took the giant leap of programming computers by doing more than just changing the physical wires going from one socket to another. The programmer is the *all-important* foot soldier who converts the designs produced by the system designer into workable code. This requires that the programmer is fully knowledgeable and as experienced as possible in the technology of implementation.

However, with the advent of components, and especially comprehensive middleware and application servers, programmers find themselves slowly fading from the intense line-by-line programming scene. For example, in a package implementation project that deals with a CRMS package, almost 75 percent of the code will already be available, and will not be written inside of the project. This leads us to think of the projects where such code is getting produced, and certainly the programmer in all its variations plays a crucial role in producing the reusable packages and components.

Nevertheless, the difference between component-based development and in-house line-by-line coding is that in the case of the former, programming activity is viewed from the industrial viewpoint, rather than specifically from the organization. Overall, in the industry, the role of the programmer is changing to a person who brings together various components, does a quick unit test, and releases them.

Furthermore, in the PC industry, a programmer is required to be skilled in multiple languages. These days a Web programmer is certainly expected to know VB script, JavaScript, HTML, and XML—in addition to having a good command of at least one of the VB, Java, or C++ programming languages. Present-day programmers cannot remain productive learning one programming language, as programmers once did.

Despite the changing role and its moving away from writing to assembling code, this role remains important in any software project. The skills, knowledge, experience, attitude, and motivation of a programmer have a direct bearing on the productivity and quality of code, and the overall software. These attributes are also important in sociological areas related to the reuse programs and parallel team development.

2.2.12 Tester

The tester is responsible for the quality control of whatever has been produced by the programmer. He is another foot soldier who continually aims to find defects in the programmer's work, and ensures that once the defects are fixed, they are retested. This role can become technical if the tester is writing test harnesses that run through the code being tested with a large amount of carefully selected or created test data. However, as an acceptance tester doing only black-box testing, it is the business knowledge that takes precedence over the technical knowledge. The focus of the technical tester is not just the satisfaction of the functionality, but the manner in which the code works, and more importantly, integrates. This role is discussed in greater detail in Chapter 6.

2.2.13 Prototyper in Solution Space

The prototyper in the solution space is usually a technical person, responsible for the creation of the technical prototype. A technical prototype tries out the system designs created in the MOSS, with respect to the language and database of implementation. This requires that the prototyper is comfortable with the technology of choice, just as much as the programmer and tester operating in this role are.

The prototyper in the solution space can work together with the programmer (in small projects the programmer herself can play this role) to decide whether the prototype will be thrown away, or whether it will evolve in the actual system. Both approaches have their own advantages and limitations, but I prefer to create a throwaway prototype, as it serves the purpose of extracting good requirements without confining the final solution to the restrictions of the prototype.

2.2.14 Organizing the Roles in the Background Space

Concomitant with its name, the background space encompasses roles that stay in the background and influence both the problem and the solution spaces. These roles produce the MOBS (Model Of Background Space). Roles common to all modeling spaces are also considered as working in the background space. Some of these roles are shown in Figure 2.3. Most of these roles require people with considerable prescience in their respective technical and business domain.

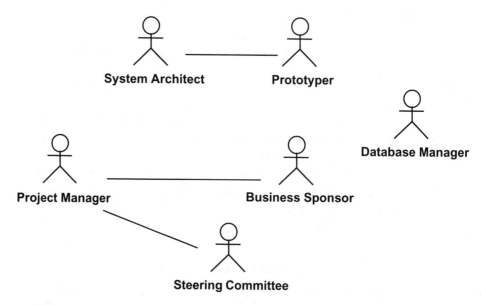

Figure 2.3   *Roles in background space and some common roles*

2.2.15 System Architect

The system architect is a technical visionary who views the solution in its entirety. This role ensures that the designs created by the system designer are implementable in the given technological environment. The system architect is a careful reader of the operational requirements, and may even participate in the creation of the operational requirements by providing, in the early stages of the software lifecycle, input and insight regarding the capabilities of the languages and databases from an operational viewpoint.

A system architect produces the architecture of the system by bringing in the best of reuse, patterns, frameworks, component libraries, and security architectures. The system architect, together with the prototyper in this space, plays a crucial role in evaluating packages before they are purchased. The system architect also influences the reuse occurring within the project—at design level through patterns, and at coding level through components. Routine functionalities such as charting and printing should not be written from scratch, but should be incorporated in the system architecture. However, support from creation of reusable components (production of reusable artifacts as against consumption of it) is the responsibility of the enterprise architect—or an architect functioning at the enterprise level, rather than simply at the project level.

2.2.16 Prototyper in Background Space

The only reason this role is mentioned separately from the role of a prototyper in the solution space is the level at which it operates here. A prototyper in the background space is not concerned with the functionality and navigation or the design of the solution. Instead, he focuses on the overall fit of the packages and components that the system architect is dealing with in the existing environment. Therefore, this prototyper plays a role in the evaluation of application servers and packages much before the project team sees them.

2.2.17 Database Manager

This role continues to interact heavily with the role of data modeler. However, I have kept it separate here in the background space because a database manager has the prime responsibility of managing the database that has been created in the solution space. This work continues on an ongoing basis in the background, requiring a careful understanding of not only the database schema but also the nature and contents of the actual data sitting in the database. More often than not, and especially in small projects, one person may play both roles of the database manager and the data modeler.

2.2.18 Common Roles

As mentioned at the start of this discussion on roles, each role has the capability of influencing work going on in all three modeling spaces. The roles mentioned here, though, have a direct bearing on everything that is happening in the project. Therefore, they are considered under a separate heading here but shown in Figure 2.3.

2.2.19 Project Manager

The role of a project manager (PM) encompasses a wide spectrum of responsibilities including planning and organizing the project, procuring the resources, launching and tracking the project, and reporting on the progress to the steering committee or its equivalent. However, the most important aspect of the role of a project manager is risk management. All management boils down to risk management, even more so in a software project. The deliverable is a software product that is subject to wide interpretations by the user and the business community within the organization.

A project manager in a UML-based project should also be comfortable with the iterative and incremental aspect of the process. This is a paradigm shift in terms of project management techniques. Delivery of the solution is not a singular affair, but is iterative, requiring the project manager to move away from the traditional sign-off culture at each phase of the deliverables. Despite the iterative approach to development, though, it is the responsibility of a project manager to plan the project and set the expectations of all parties involved in the development. Creation of iterations, their durations, and their enactment are important parts of the planning process that a project manager has to undertake.

The PM ensures that the possibly wide interpretations of the requirements are narrowed down to manageable options, although they may never be fully eliminated. This role demands a fine balancing act to keep the technology, methodology, and sociology together in order to crisply define the product and thereby manage the risks.

A variation of the role of a project manager, especially in a large project, is the program director, who oversees multiple projects and an ongoing program transitioning to the new dimensions.

2.2.20 Steering Committee

The steering committee brings together skills from the senior management disciplines within the organization. Joint decisions, while taking longer to arrive at, are almost invariably better than individual decisions. Therefore, forming a committee and empowering it to make the final decisions on all major issues related to the project ensures that the business objectives are kept above the interests of a single person. In addition to being a part of the committee, the project manager reports to the committee.

The committee can be made up of the business sponsor, the domain expert related to the project, and the senior management from business and information systems. Additionally, for projects that impact the external image and the external relationships of the company, it is advantageous to have marketing, legal, accounting, and related disciplines represented on the steering committee. The viewing of the prototypes and the interim deliverables by the committee will have a positive impact on the quality and timeliness of the project.

2.2.21 Business Sponsor

The business sponsor is the initiator of the project. This is the person whose business activities need the necessary software support, and this is the person who has gone to great lengths to justify the need for and managed the funding for the project to provide such software support. This person is also ultimately responsible for the way in which the budget is spent.

While leaving the operation of the project to the project manager, the business sponsor is continually involved in tracking the progress of the project—the functionalities provided and the budget and time spent. Therefore, ideally, this is the person who the project manager communicates with, in order to monitor and realign the risks within the project. The business sponsor is primarily interested in realizing the business benefits the project was set out to deliver. In the final analysis, the business sponsor determines the success of the project in its ability to address the problem space.

2.2.22 Organizing the Quality Team

Similar to the common roles discussed above, the quality roles cut across all modeling spaces and provide direct input into the activities, tasks, and deliverables happening in the three modeling spaces. Thus, in a way, they are common roles that are played out in all modeling space. They are discussed here separately because of their importance in all aspects of a project and are shown in Figure 2.4.

2.2.23 Quality Manager

Quality management derives from project management, but focuses on the quality aspect of the project. This requires the quality manager to have independent access to the steering committee that will enable him to provide feedback to the steering committee on the quality aspect of the project. In small projects, the organizational aspect of the quality manager's role—such as procuring the quality resources, organizing the test teams, or buying a process CASE tool—may be carried out by the project manager. However, independence of the quality function is maintained only by assigning that role to a person external to the project. For medium and large projects, quality manager has to be a separate full-time role, with a separate schedule and budget, and a sustained effort on the overall process discipline, project management, and, finally, quality control.

The quality manager organizes the inspections, reviews, and audits of the UML-based diagrams, the deliverables that contain these diagrams,

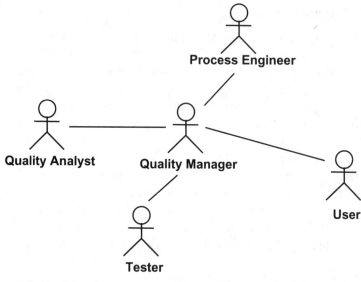

Figure 2.4 *Quality roles*

and the overall modeling, process, and programming efforts. The quality manager also focuses on the soft factors like the quality of the work environment (environment factor), the communication through the project, and the motivational aspect of the project. These factors make it necessary for the quality manager to function closely with the project manager.

2.2.24 Quality Analyst

The quality analyst executes all the elementary quality functions within the project. A quality analyst is a common name used to refer to anyone within the project who is made responsible for overseeing the quality of a particular deliverable. This requires the quality analyst to be capable of understanding the UML-based models, the process activities and tasks, as well as being able to appreciate the technologies used within the project. Ideally, the quality analyst is someone who has already done some modeling and process-related work in other projects. Previous experience creating the models and deploying a process can provide significant insights that the quality analyst can use during the inspections, reviews, and audits performed throughout the project.

This role, however, is not involved with the organizational aspect of quality, which is left up to the management of the project. Instead, the quality analyst works to ensure that the UML deliverables have been subjected to the syntax, semantics, and aesthetic aspects of the quality checks (see the accompanying CD for a suggested list of checks) and that the necessary and sufficient aspects of the Quality Software Process have been enacted. In the problem space, the quality analyst works closely with the business analyst to identify, capture, document, and analyze the requirements. In the solution space, the quality analyst works with the system designer in terms of the quality of her advanced class diagrams and database schemas. The background space requires the quality analyst to apply the quality techniques to, say, the deployment diagrams, to the operational requirements, and to the use of patterns in creating component diagrams.

Thus, the quality analyst provides an independent and robust check on the process as well as the product within a project. Depending on the size and type of the project, many people can fill this role. For example, a new development project needs quality analysts at all three modeling levels, but a data warehousing project needs this role to perform more intensely in the solution space—dealing not only with the development process, but also with the data-conversion process and the integrity assurance of the new data.

2.2.25 Process Engineer

A process engineer, also referred to as a process consultant because of the relatively temporary nature of the job, is a person responsible for the creation of a software engineering process for the project, its deployment, and the support of its enactment. It is worth noting that a process engineer herself does not enact the process—that is the responsibility of the project manager. But a process engineer is around the project long enough to provide support in fine-tuning the process, modifying the templates, and providing process-related feedback to the project and quality managers.

Furthermore, if the process is deployed using a process CASE tool, then the process engineer must ensure that the tool is configured correctly to reflect the process needs of the project, that the process elements, such as templates for the deliverables, are readily available to all project members, and that the feedback loop of the process is established within the process tool. This is handling the malleable aspect of the process quality.

2.2.26 User

While the prime responsibility of the role of the user, as mentioned earlier in the roles in the problem space, is to work closely with the business analyst, the user is also an important quality person. This importance stems from the fact that the user is ideally placed to perform acceptance testing. Working along with the quality analyst and the tester, the user can create good acceptance test plans that will test the functionality specified in the first place.

Since the user is involved in the creation of use cases, activity diagrams, and sequence diagrams in the problem space, he can also help to create comprehensive test cases from the model of the problem space. Successful testing also provides the user with hands-on experience in using the system, paving the way for subsequent user training sessions that will be needed toward the end of a project. However, it is worth noting that while users are good at ensuring that the system is functioning correctly, they are not as effective at performing specific destructive and/or technical testing such as testing the boundary conditions, abnormal screen displays, and system crashes due to technical (and also other nontechnical) reasons. These tests are left up to the technical tester.

2.2.27 Tester

A tester is responsible for quality control of the product. This includes, but is not limited to, testing of the software product. For example, a tester creates test designs and test cases and, after conducting tests, records the results. Unfortunately, while the quality of test scripts and test programs is of utmost importance, and while the programmer who has written the code is in an ideal position to write the test programs as well, mainstream programmers tend to neglect this task. This leads to interesting situations like discovering a bug in a test harness or test program written by a tester who is not qualified to be a programmer. Therefore, it is important to consider the variations to the tester role, occurring in all three modeling spaces as the functionality, technology, and architecture get tested separately. Automated testing tools also require the tester to be comfortable with the use of the tools in running tests—especially regression tests. Testers can be involved in writing test programs and test harnesses, and keeping these test programs updated as the system design and coding of the main system progresses.

2.3   The Quality Environment

The quality environment encompasses the roles that make up the project, and the quality team within the project, as discussed in the previous section. However, a quality environment is more than just a collection and structure of roles. There are many underlying factors that make up a quality environment. Some of these are discussed here with the aim of having an additional positive impact on the people developing the product and encouraging the quality management to identify similar factors in their projects.

2.3.1   E-factor and Quality

The physical environment in which the team operates is a subtle yet important factor in producing good quality. The effect of the environment on quality has been discussed very well by DeMarco and Lister [1987] and it has been defined as the "e-factor." Some examples of these e-factors are:

- Physical disturbances caused in a team environment. These can be simple day-to-day events such as telephone calls, paging, or even playing music through the PC speakers, and may not have been given much thought by the managers. Because a software programming environment is quite different from a manufacturing environment, the effect of any raucous noise on quality should not be ignored. It's important that the quality manager considers the frequency and types of these kinds of disturbances.

- Sitting arrangements of the teams, their proximity to each other and to the user groups, can be correlated to productivity and quality. The influence of these factors cannot be discounted in producing quality models and quality code. I have been personally involved in multimillion-dollar projects where due to earlier lack of planning, the architect and designers have had to sit in the corridor leading to the rest rooms. It is highly advisable to provide modelers, programmers, and other roles in the project with sufficient space of their own, as well as common meeting areas, which do not disturb individual workers.

- Provision of office tools. Whiteboards, flipcharts, data projectors, recording equipment, and so forth, are considered routine in today's development environment, but may not be well organized. We have all struggled with dried-up whiteboard markers, and we have all propped up data projectors on books and other supports. Often, whiteboards that are meant to print on paper don't do so. On their own, none of these individual factors make or break a project—but collectively, they create an environment where mental modeling suffers.

- Frequency of changes to the physical organization of the teams. It takes time for people to settle down in their work environment, and changing the physical work environment should be done with due consideration for the possible loss of productivity and quality. A case in point is the writing of this book. The quality of thought processes and the speed of writing them down would both suffer if the physical place where I sit and write were changed too frequently.

These are some examples of e-factors that affect software development. Each project has its own variation of these factors, and many more. Prudent quality management ensures that these factors are sought out, discussed, and resolved. The best time to start handling these factors is early on in the project, when there is time, opportunity, and a budget to address them.

2.3.2   Soft Issues Specific to UML-Based Projects

While e-factors affect software development, they apply to any software project. The nature of software development, as discussed in Chapter 1, is nonlinear. This means it is difficult to identify a one-to-one relationship between productivity and the number of hours spent in designing and coding a system. This nonlinearity is exacerbated when we deal with modern-day object-oriented systems that depend heavily on good modeling (using the UML, of course), component-level reuse, and integration issues with existing legacy applications. In these projects, sometimes the productivity may be very high, and the resultant deliverables appear to fulfill all quality criteria. At other times the productivity chart may slope down, dragging quality along with it. The reason for this, in addition to the physical environmental factors discussed in the previous section, is what we call soft factors.

The soft factors specific to UML-based projects (that are implemented using object-oriented technologies) are summarized as follows:

- Parallel team organization: When subsystems are internally cohesive but externally loosely coupled with each other, it is possible to have them designed and developed in parallel. This is possible provided the interface between various modules and packages is kept firm, and not allowed to vary. However, dependency of one team on the interfaces provided by another team introduces elements of social conflict. If a team does not implement interfaces that another team depends on, nothing in the overall system will work. Also, if and when interfaces change, the social impact of those changes should be carefully managed.

- Reusability: Those who produce reusable designs and code have to put in that extra effort in order to generalize their output to make it easily reusable. The credit of using such reusable code, however, goes to the consumer rather than the producer of the code. This is more of a sociological situation, rather than a technical one, and requires a sociological solution. Creating a linchpin role [Henderson-Sellers and Pant 1993], or making someone responsible for reuse in all projects, is the kind of solution this soft issue demands.

- Length of employment: While specialists are needed on every project, they may come in for a short time, provide their consulting expertise, and walk away. It is important that roles such as the project manager, quality manager, and enterprise architect are not contracted out for short periods. Experience suggests that long-term employment—or a contract that sees the project through to the end—tends to encourage reuse and improve quality.

- Senior-management support: Use of UML along with a robust process, and its deployment in relatively older environments, is a big challenge. This is the challenge of transitioning to a new paradigm as discussed by Henderson-Sellers and Serour [2000, 2001]. Any paradigm shift needs support from senior management, but more so in using object-oriented techniques because it is not just the modeling and programming paradigm that changes—the iterative and incremental process of managing a project is a challenge in itself. Support from senior management (for example, the steering committee) is considered crucial to this soft issue of transition to a new development and process environment.

- Legal issues (copyrights, royalties, and downloads): Software products, unlike physical products like cars and bicycles, are easily borrowed and not returned. Legal issues spring up from the need to protect the intellectual property of the pattern producer, or a reusable component, or even a book like this one. Cox [1992] has discussed the problems of copyright and royalty payments associated with a set of reusable components, suggesting that instead of selling copies of software packages, royalties should be paid on a usage basis. This soft issue is already taking a position of importance in the world of e-services (Web services), where it is not just a component being sold, but an entire service such as employee payroll or insurance claims.

2.3.3   Communication in a Quality Environment

A major aspect of a quality environment is the flow of information within the organization. Here, I am talking about social communication as against merely the information system model and architecture communication. In discussing soft factors relating to project management, it is essential to discuss the manner in which the leadership communicates with the team, as well as with other players in the project. Communication includes keeping team members informed about issues such as changing delivery schedules, realigning risks, procuring additional hardware or CASE tools, and changing the seating arrangement of the team members. Some of these may appear frivolous to project managers who are more concerned about time and budgets, but the impact of the way in which sociological changes are handled is crucial to the well-being of the team and the eventual quality of the product produced. Regular communication is also important. While an occasional email from a CEO addressing 15,000 employees might be acceptable, a weekly email from the project manager to a team of 15 people can and does have a far more gelling effect on the team. Some suggested (and tried) communication mechanisms include:

- The company's intranet (or internal Web site) can provide information on issues such as team status, achievements of major milestones, and changes to standards being used.

- Emails provide one of the easiest and cheapest mechanisms to communicate. It is not uncommon for effective project managers to spend an hour of their prime morning time replying to all emails they have received. Keeping the project team updated on the progress of the project, and providing administrative information (such as messages) can and should be done through this medium.

- Phones provide the medium to communicate—especially when teams are spread out geographically. However, the phone is not just a routine communication medium. For example, phone interviews with domain experts and with users in different locations should be conducted by business analysts with thorough preparation.

- Newsletters are also effective. No matter how good the electronic medium of communication, it should be supplemented with traditional newsletters within the organization. Launching the project, achieving significant milestones, and sharing technical experiences can all be promoted in a regular newsletter.

- Project goals and objectives should be visibly promoted. This can be achieved by the simple yet effective means of making the crucial aspects of the project available for everyone to read; for example, framing high-level objectives and the context diagram, and hanging them on a wall in the project area, is my favorite mechanism to let everyone know about these important matters. The context diagram that shows all external entities and the context of the current system is an invaluable source of communication and discussion within a project. It also helps to explain the project objectives. Since these objectives and the project context are not expected to (and should not) change much during the project, framing these two pages and putting them on a wall serves as a key communication mechanism.

- Use videos and CDs to create a summary of the project background and goals, or create a video or CD of the documentation within the project. This is invaluable in practical projects—resulting in an increased understanding of the project goals, improved reuse, and subsequent improvement in quality. Creation of user manuals, support manuals, and initial training manuals have all been a part of this communication medium in many successful projects I have been associated with.

2.3.4 Telecommuting

Telecommuting is becoming popular because it saves time and effort in commuting to work. It is especially effective during the development work that does not require all members of the team to be present at the same time. For example, after all the design decisions are made, individual class coding does not need the entire team to be present. These are the situations where telecommuting is extremely beneficial to both the individual and the company. Erudite project management should expect, and in fact facilitate, at least one or more days per week (20–50 percent) of the work through telecommuting.

While more readily acceptable in coding types of work, one may also expect contributions by domain experts, and certain users who are geographically spread out, but who have the business knowledge to contribute to the project through telecommuting. However, it is more likely that this soft concept will play a significant role in the solution space. The discussion on telecommuting, though, continues to raise the important question of work ethics while working from home. Telecommuting has the advantage of enabling people to work in a relaxed way, without the pressure of a dress code or forced social interaction. However, people will have to be more responsible in describing the tasks and estimating the amount of time they think the tasks will take.

2.4   Project Sociology

2.4.1   Four Models for Project Teams

Real project teams are made up of real people. Therefore, like people, teams are difficult to generalize. However, having an understanding of the purpose for which a team is formed, its background structure, and its dynamics can be very helpful in creating a successful team, and keeping it motivated right through the project. Understanding team models is an appropriate precursor to creating and understanding software models with the UML. To achieve that understanding, it is worth considering how Thomsett [1994] has further developed Constantine's [1989] excellent description of the various ways in which teams can be organized in a software development project, as shown in Figure 2.5. The four possible team structures include:

- Closed: These teams follow the traditional hierarchical structure and are good for traditional development and maintenance of legacy applications such as payroll and accounting systems.

- Open: These teams perform as collaborators. There is very little hierarchy and no tradition. The lack of hierarchy is particularly appealing to new programmers.

- Random: These teams are innovative. They are comprised of very few people (three or four) and they are put together to achieve a short-term breakthrough goal. Obviously, due to the lack of structure, they cannot be expected to perform in a cohesive manner for an extended period of time.

- Synchronous: Constantine calls these Utopian (out of the world) teams. They perform on total understanding and harmonious

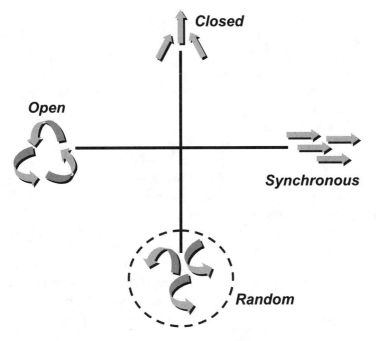

Figure 2.5   *Possible team structures (based on constantine 1989)*

alignment. This is the team structure that every project manager
hopes to achieve.

Our aim is to create a team based on the utopian model that is able to function coherently and with minimum control. In terms of Transactional
Analysis (TA, discussed later in Section 2.5), we strive for a team where all
members function with an "I am OK—You are OK" life position. The team
members will suspend their Child tendencies until it is appropriate to let
them out and instead will work using the Adult part of their personality.

2.4.2   The Best-Fit Approach to Creating a
Homogeneous Team

The crux of project formation is identification, recruitment, and organization of team members. Description of job roles, rewards structures, and
personal growth all follow from the most fundamental part of team building—recruitment. While a quality team has its objectives and roles well
defined, it is also a team that is put together by a careful process of getting
the right people. This process starts with the appointment of a project

manager. As seen later in the discussion of the process-component of business evaluation,[2] the steering committee or a similar body responsible for the project performs the important task of nominating a person with the right skills and experience to run the project or the program. This person is either put in charge of a preassembled team (not a favorable situation), or allowed the freedom to organize her own team.

In assembling a team, it is vital to keep in mind that those people who are effective individually may not necessarily be able to perform well in team environments. Barring the utopian team discussed in the previous section, all teams have to face the challenge of gelling the people together. Team-building exercises can only improve on the people you have—getting the right people is a more basic challenge.

The suggestion is the best-fit approach, as shown in Figure 2.6. The aim is to create a team that is likely to function as smoothly as possible. It is possible that such a team is *not necessarily* made up of the best technical people. The project manager and the quality manager who are responsible for assembling the team should be prepared to let go of a technically superior person if, based on interviews and reference checks, it is apparent that the

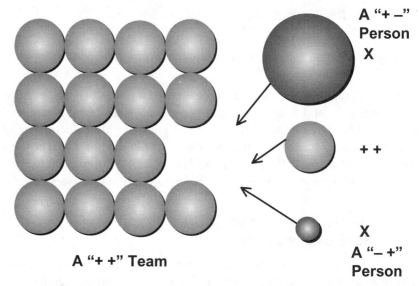

Figure 2.6   *Creating a homogeneous, smoothly functioning team—the best fit approach*

---

[2] Process-components are described in detail in Chapter 3.

person does not fit in very well with the existing team members. The end result of this selection process is a team where most members fit well with each other, and the team itself fits well with the rest of the organization. Lack of cohesiveness has caused an untold amount of misery in some of my practical projects. Although the individuals were technically brilliant, no amount of good UML-based modeling helped me.

Homogeneity of the team, as suggested by the best-fit recruitment approach, is vital for quality. A highly technical, competent programmer who does not fit well, or who introduces or leads some of the games (discussed in Section 2.5.4), would eventually influence quality negatively. Negative attitude results in decreased productivity far more than the ability of a single programmer to produce complex code.

It is therefore imperative to focus the recruitment procedure within the organization toward considering people who have a strong Adult personality and who operate from the OK position (these TA terms are also discussed in Section 2.5). Using formal questionnaires to ascertain personality types and subjective interview techniques are common ways to ensure team homogeneity. In cases where technical competence is the overriding factor in a project, special short-term roles should be created with specific objectives in mind. Once those objects (for example, creation of a distributed architecture) are achieved, that role should be disbanded. This will obviate the possible mediocrity that may result from overzealous application of the principle of homogeneity of the team, as discussed here.

2.4.3 Flattening the Pyramid

Organizing the team structure follows assembling the right people. While the four possible team structures discussed earlier can be very helpful in achieving this goal, and while the utopian team remains the goal of every project manager, it is also essential to create a team organization that is not hierarchical. This is essential not only for the project team members onboard for the long term, but also for the specialist staff that might be added to the project from time to time, and who may not be interested in succumbing to a direct reporting structure.

Hammer and Champy [1994] have discussed "flattening the pyramid of the organizational structure" in their reengineering approach to business. The same idea can be applied to software project teams, as well. A utopian team is not organized in a hierarchical pyramidal fashion, but is rather much flatter, as shown in Figure 2.7.

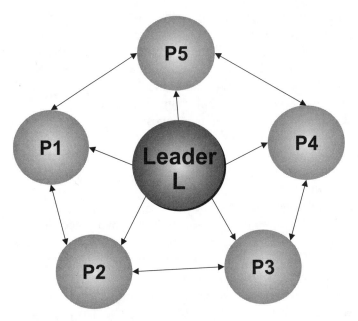

Figure 2.7   *Flattening the pyramid (top view of a "++" team)* [Unhelkar 1996]

In order to understand this flatter structure, you have to view it from the top. Figure 2.7 is the top view of a flatter, nonhierarchical team. A flatter team structure means that the team does not have a rigorous reporting structure that goes up to the project manager. Instead, the project manager plays more of a facilitator role, organizing and coordinating activities and creating and managing the environment rather than being didactic. He also facilitates the processes and tools that ensure quality within the project.

A typical team with a project manager and five role members, when viewed from above, looks like that in Figure 2.7. Development can benefit by viewing the team organization from the top (the vertical view), because it does not carry the hierarchical notion of traditional team structures. This is a flat *circular* arrangement with many advantages in terms of organization and communication. For example, communication is now facilitated not only between the leader and members (L-P1, L-P2, and so on) but also among members (P1-P2, P2-P3, P4-P5, and so on). The position of the leader is not viewed as superior (as it would be in a front view), but is seen at the same level as the other members of the team. The leader is the facilitator in this case. Thus, this model of team structure caters to the static and the dynamic aspect of its functioning.

2.4.4 People in Reusability

Reusability is correlated to quality as it alleviates the need to remodel and retest a large amount of software. However, successful reusability is an equally important people issue that was mentioned in the list of soft factors earlier. Reusability influences people. For example, people who have experience with reuse find it smoother and easier to create reusable designs and code than people who have never seen the benefit of using someone else's code. Lim [1994], while discussing the effect of reuse on quality, productivity, and economics, says:

> Finally, we have found that reuse allows an organization to use personnel more effectively because it leverages expertise. Experienced software specialists can concentrate on creating work products that less-experienced personnel can then reuse.

For reuse and subsequent quality to succeed, it is important to weave the reusability aspects into the process itself. Product-based reuse achieves results, provided software processes that are themselves based on reusability support them.

Furthermore, the team organization should reflect these reuse-based processes. One required element of this reuse-based process is the development of an appropriate reward system. In functional development, rewards are given at the completion of major milestones. However, in OO development (especially due to reusability) there is a need to think ahead beyond the immediate problem and to separate current needs from general ones. While the UML provides the necessary fillip to achieve technical reuse, the need to *produce* reusable classes requires management to compensate those developing reusable classes either by providing lump-sum payments for contributions accepted into the organization's reuse library or by providing royalty payments based on actual class reuse [Kriendler 1993].

Another approach to team organizations, which just provides rewards to teams producing reusable code, is discussed by Henderson-Sellers and Pant [1993]. It is the creation of a common role with the responsibility for both the teams producing reusable software code (the producers of Meyer

[1995]) and the teams reusing the code produced. This is similar to Thomsett's recommendation of a linchpin role [Thomsett 1990], except that instead of vesting the responsibility with a particular role (person), the same is achieved in an organizational fashion.

While a detailed monetary reward structure is very helpful in promoting reuse, it is important to administer it in such a way that both producers and consumers of reusable components are rewarded. More importantly, though, the peer recognition for large-scale reuse, and recognition from the rest of the organization when the product is produced on time, is considered to be a precious reward for reuse. Positive reinforcement encourages members of a utopian team to undertake projects both "for" and "with" reuse, and programming teams will not mind reusing designs and code written by other members of the team. This results in the socially responsible work of teams generalizing their own code to enable subsequent teams to reuse it.

2.4.5   Parallel Development Teams

Object-oriented systems are usually built by putting together different subsystems. Meyer [1992] considers the division of the project into subsystems that can then be assigned to individual project teams for development as one of the two major responsibilities[3] of a project manager. While creation of packages is the technical aspect of dividing the development of software, creating corresponding teams and assigning the packages to them is an important sociological exercise.

A phenomenon that is as interesting as putting together subsystems and assigning them to teams is that of parallel teams. Because of the ability of object-oriented software to be encapsulated, it is possible to conduct development in parallel. This means that once the interfaces between two components or two packages are bedded down, the actual design of functions and code underneath these interfaces need not be dependent on each other. Thus, as long as the interfaces are not changed, the development of two packages can go on in parallel.

This concept of encapsulation also leads to some more interesting discussions. For example, Graham [1994], in his discussion on migrating to object technology, makes a rather bold declaration:

> This tested time-box philosophy means that it is quite permissible and safe to write the code before the design is done . . .

---

[3] The other one is to be in charge of the latest demo.

This bottom-up approach to object-oriented development comes in handy when we attempt to redesign existing systems, or attempt to integrate with legacy applications. For example, once a component has been identified and its interfaces bedded down, there is no harm in writing the code for this component before other components that use it have been designed. Alternatively, the components that use this component can have their code cut, while this particular component, which is being reused, may still be in design. It is essential to exercise caution in doing this, but proper encapsulation provides the possibility of doing this parallel development with potential advantages in terms of productivity and quality.

2.5   Transactional Analysis in Software Projects

Henderson-Sellers [1997], in his *Book of Object-Oriented Knowledge,* discusses the comparative growth of interest in objects: "Why all the enthusiasm for object orientation in the last five years or so when the object-oriented languages have been around for over 25 years?" Indeed, object technology finds resurgence in the new millennium due perhaps to plummeting hardware costs, supporting software such as operating systems being able to cope with objects, and of course the ability to model objects uniformly and effectively through the UML. We, the IT community, had no hesitation in embracing object technology despite its remaining dormant in the business arena for more than two decades. Even the UML, as is well known, came out of our attempts to discipline object-oriented development after it was well on its way to becoming a popular development approach.

Based on our discussions thus far in this chapter, it is obvious that objects and components bring with them as much sociological phenomena as technological. While psychological considerations in quality of software projects is not new (seen as early as Weinberg [1971]), on the sociological front, a resurgence similar to that in the object-technology field is happening in the fascinating field of Transactional Analysis. While being a part of standard management curriculum for decades, its practice in software projects is becoming more interesting in the last few years.

I have personally used this approach in practice [Unhelkar 1999] and found it deceptively easy and effective to learn and use, and most rewarding in managing multiple project teams. A practical software project manager has a limited time to learn psychology and sociology. That is where I found Transactional Analysis helpful and rewarding. This book is not the place to delve into the detailed theory of this sociological aspect of project management. However, I am outlining the approach here, together with its application in practical software team management, with a hope that it will help practicing project managers to create quality software teams, quality software team environments, and eventually quality software products.

2.5.1 A Brief History of TA

Just as object technology is not new, but has become popular after more than two decades due to the availability of cheaper hardware and the need for complex and quality software systems, transactional analysis, more than three decades old, is found to contain all the ideal elements to enable managers to handle soft factors appearing in technical development and project management in the area of object technology. TA has been popularized by well-known works [Berne 1964; Harris 1973; James and Jongeward 1971]; at the same time, its application to management was made popular through books like *The OK Boss* [James 1975] and *Practical Transactional Analysis in Management* [Morrison and O'Hearne 1977].

We consider the basics of TA in the following sections. This is followed by how these principles can be applied in forming and managing teams within the area of object-oriented software development using the UML. The basics of TA include the ego states and life positions[4] and games. Understanding these ego states, life positions, and games within a project environment makes a direct impact on the way the project teams are formed and managed.

2.5.2 The Parent, Adult, and Child Ego States

Individual project team members exhibit personalities. Ego states are what make up a personality. Each person has within themself three ego states. These are:

1. The Parent, which essentially comprises the *taught* concept of life. This is the information recorded from Parental sources, and is dated or archaic.

---

[4] A detailed discussion of these concepts is outside the scope of this book. Interested readers are referred to any of the TA in management books described earlier. For practical experience on its use in software projects visit *www.Method Science.com*.

2. The Adult, which is the *thought* concept of life. This is what is being figured out by the logical part of the mind, of what is happening out there.

3. The Child, which is the *felt* concept of life. This is the emotional part of a person.

Note that these ego states are within a person, and are different from real parents, adults, and children, and are therefore referred to in uppercase throughout. The structural aspect of our personality has a Parent, Adult, and Child (P-A-C) ego state. The difference in people is not of structure, but often lays in the dynamics of these ego states. These characteristics of the ego states can be summarized as follows:

- Ego states are phenomenological realities. They exist within a person and are not persons themselves.

- Everyone is structurally the same (everyone has a P-A-C).

- We differ functionally.

- Each ego state is important when expressed at the right time and place.

- It is the function of the Adult to decide the appropriateness of expression.

When a project manager is confronted with a decision-making process, data from all three parts of her ego states come into play.

The Parent data bring in her righteousness as well as prejudices and deal with such parental precepts as "work before play," "work hard," or "never leave a job undone." These data have organizational value for the team. However, all Parent data are archaic and do not deal with external reality that has changed since the Parent-data was recorded in the mind.

The Child brings in fun and joy, laughter and parties, and is concerned with plans for the weekend. It has motivational importance but does not care for objective reality. This aspect of a project manager's personality influences the team-building exercises, project launch parties, milestone achievement lunches, and so on.

The Adult is the *reality tester.* It is free from the prejudices and rigidity of the Parent, as well as from the emotional and carefree approach of the Child, in understanding what is real out there. However, a person doesn't need to ignore her Parent or Child—only to correctly identify it as such. In the decision-making process the Adult of an individual's personality functions like a computer. It takes into account the three sources of data (the Parent and Child within a person and the Adult reality) before arriving at a final decision.

2.5.3   The Life Positions

The emergence and display of the aforementioned ego states is based on life positions. Positions are the view formed by a person of the world and the people within the world [Berne 1972]. The possible views have been classified by Berne into four *life positions*.

1. *I am OK—You are not OK*: This is mostly didactic, and the person tends to respond from a position of superiority. The active ego state is Parent most of the time.

2. *I am not OK—You are OK*: This is a team member who always feels inferior. The active ego state is the adaptive Child.

3. *I am not OK—You are not OK*: This team member shuts himself out from the group, and in the extreme case withdraws completely.

4. *I am OK—You are OK*: This is the position of good leaders and motivators. These are the people who maintain universal respect for themselves and others even in utmost adversity. The active ego state is Adult most of the time, but Parent and Child are allowed uncontaminated display.

Creating software teams and assembling people within the teams is best accomplished if the life position of the people is "I am OK—You are OK." Not only do people exhibit life positions, but also teams, projects, organizations, and nations exhibit these positions. Needless to say, people cannot always be categorized into one or the other life position, but awareness of this view of the world that a person or team exhibits can play a crucial role in the success of the team.

This also enables us to map the software team models (based on Constantine) discussed earlier to corresponding life positions. As shown in Figure 2.8, the synchronous team is the most ideal team, and exhibits the most ideal life position of "I am OK—You are OK." The closed team would be ruled in a hierarchical manner, with the project manager telling everyone what to do and what not to do—thereby exhibiting the "I am OK—You are not OK" life position. The other two team models are still constructive team models and they fall somewhere in between. The other extreme of these life positions is the totally negative "I am not OK—You are not OK" position, which means there is no team at all and people are unable to work together in any sensible form, as is sometimes evident in kindergartens, parliaments, and the like. We will not discuss such situations here.

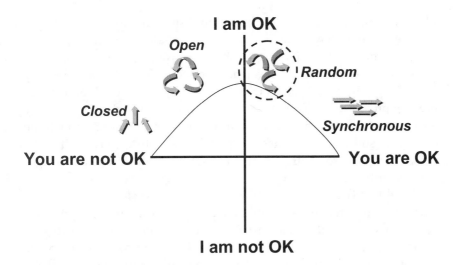

Figure 2.8   *TA life positions and corresponding team structures*

2.5.4   Games

The ego states and the life positions provide the backdrop against which people and teams function. Most of this functioning is psychologically a means to structure the time allotted. In software projects, this is the time given to complete the project or to achieve a particular milestone. In TA terms, people and teams tend to structure their times in one of the six possible ways: withdrawal, ritual, activity, pastime, intimacy, and games. Out of these possible ways to structure time, ritual, activity, pastime, and games have an important role in handling the soft issues of a software development work environment. The other two ways to structure time, withdrawal and intimacy, are usually outside the work environment—although individuals occasionally do tend to exhibit these time-structuring mechanisms, leading to very interesting challenges for the project manager.

Work can be a nine-to-five ritual—and some project team members quickly slide into the safety of this routine if put under pressure. Meetings, organizational charts, boring training sessions, and workshops can all be activities. And meeting in corridors or stepping out for a cup of coffee or a smoke at the stroke of every hour can be pastimes. Each of these time-structuring mechanisms of ritual, activity, and pastime can still be managed, and work can be accomplished in a formal, rigid way. However, games have the potential to annihilate software projects. Games, as referred to in TA, are not the same as the games of baseball or rugby. In fact, even those games tend to be so serious at times that they can no longer be called games in the true sense of the word. In terms of software project management, games are an ulterior and dishonest way to structure time, which eventually results in project failure through the underlying soft factors. Games can play havoc with quality, as it is the one factor that is so abstract that it cannot be easily measured, categorized, or corrected.

Berne [1964] defines a *game* as a series of complementary ulterior transactions progressing to a well-defined payoff. Games have concealed motivations and are almost always destructive in human relations (teams, in this case). However, since most of the working time is involved in some form of games, it is essential to develop a careful understanding of the nature of games. This reduces their negative impact on the functionality of the team.

Some of the examples of games have been succinctly described by Berne in *Games People Play.* Overtly, in their attempt to structure time they tend to encourage teams to make progress. *But then they keep on making progress without delivering value at all.* These types of team games have a relationship with the teams in IT that keep progressing without producing a single product. Organizations and projects seem to have a fair share of people playing these games, with some senior managers excelling in them. The key to producing quality products and delivering them on time is to *avoid* these destructive natures of games within software projects. This is accomplished by the use of Adult ego state, and a firm commitment to the "I am OK—You are OK" life position by the team members and leaders.

2.5.5   Games in an OO Project

Games are neither fun nor productive. They are a time-structuring mechanism that is almost always ulterior in nature. Since software development is a team event wherein all the nuances of social psychology (as discussed in the theory of TA) emerge, it is obvious that these games exist within development teams and that they are responsible for many software project and quality failures.

Examples of some games played in IT projects, and possible antidotes, are discussed here. Obviously more discussion and practical application of these concepts are needed and encouraged in IT projects, in order to successfully handle the sociological aspect of software development.[5]

2.5.6   Use It or Lose It

Constantine [1995] mentions the need of some programmers to use every available feature of the language. This results in a highly complex code with many of the functionalities present in the class or component only because that feature was cool to use, or was available in a particular language or tool. Brown et al. [1998], in *Anti Patterns*, discuss a software architecture "anti-pattern" of a Swiss Army knife, wherein a class or a component has literally hundreds of interfaces that are there to handle any and every imaginable (and unimaginable) situation. Many of these features might be provided just because the language of choice offers them, or just because a user has mentioned them likely to be needed "in the next ten years."

Project managers should discourage the use of technology features just for the sake of using them. Quality meetings, including quality workshops where UML-based designs are subject to quality checks, should ensure that every feature provided in a component or asked for in a use case has a corresponding genuine need in the problem space. Thus, the antidote of this game is justification. Generalization, needed for reuse and so on, can further complicate this game, but if those who are generalizing for reuse stick to their objective Adult ego state, they will have less need to generalize for the sake of generalization.

2.5.7   Cowboy Programming

This is a game played by people who disregard process disciplines. Dodani [1994] discusses examples of situations that reflect the cowboy programming game. This is a situation where the programmer aims to be the superhero of the project and, in the process, treats software development and quality processes with disdain.

---

[5] This *gamey* aspect of IT projects is discussed separately in my proposed book *Games IT People Play.*

Creation of a Quality Software Process that refers to a formal process discipline (as discussed in Chapter 3), insistence of the project manager on following the process, and the semantic and aesthetic checks provided by the process, are the best antidotes to this game. However, it is important for project managers to keep the practicality of process discipline in mind. If processes are didactic, and strangle the creativity of individual programmers [Unhelkar 1995], they can be used as an excuse for developers to continue to play cowboy programming. This balance between the need for creativity and obviating the need to play process games takes us in the realms of agile methodologies [Fowler 2002] such as eXtremeProgramming [Beck 2000] and needs further discussion, which is outside the scope of this book.

2.5.8   Flour Mix

The game of flour mix represents the creep factor so often discussed in IT project management. It is a game played by the developer (at times with help from the project manager) where she wants to add, with utmost sincerity, one more functionality before delivering the system. Then, to satisfy that functionality, she needs more time and resources. The development proceeds along the lines of an inexperienced cook trying to mix the flour with water in order to create the dough for baking bread. After an initial attempt to create the mix, the cook ends up with extra water. So, in order to compensate, the cook adds more flour. That leads to extra dry dough; hence she adds more water—ad infinitum.

As an antidote to this game, once a set of functionality is put together in a use case diagram, the approach should be to provide for that functionality in the first release. There is no restriction on changing the use cases or the class diagrams, but if that results in a change of scope, then that feature should be incorporated in a later release. The time-box approach to development, wherein a release is due every three months or so, can also be a possible antidote to this game. The Next Release Maybe (NRM) approach proposed by Meyer [1995], in which the requirement of the functionality is accepted, but only on the condition that it will be provided *not* in this release, but the next one, can also be utilized effectively to help break up this game.

2.5.9 Meetingitis

Meyer [1995] discusses a well-known problem in projects wherein the development team spends hours in meetings without deciding on anything or resolving any issues. UML-based projects are no exception. "Meetingitis" is a game that provides tools to structure time for workers who don't know what to do with their time or who are restless on their own. They just go to a meeting. This is indeed unproductive and self-defeating. One primary reason for meetingitis is a lack of clear objectives. Scott Adams's cartoon character Dilbert is popular not just because of well-presented jokes; there is a real Dilbert in every one of us, and we know it so well. The joke comes out of our personal experiences of knowing "what a waste that meeting was" and in the same breath we are setting up another meeting for next week.

Setting an agenda before the meeting, and reiterating that agenda in the first five minutes of the meeting, is an excellent antidote. Creation of a parking lot where all gamey issues can be parked is also very helpful in breaking up meetingitis. Other attempts to break up this game can include having an e-meeting instead of a physical meeting. If a physical meeting can't be avoided then try having a standing meeting—with no chairs. While these may appear to be drastic anti-social measures, the results they produce far outweigh the outcry that project managers may face initially. People should also be encouraged to come prepared for the meetings by reading through the agenda, and by contemplating solutions in their minds.

Meetings should be used for making decisions, not for investigating and research. In any case, being aware of the game is a definite first step toward breaking it up.

2.5.10 Deadline

Development teams play this game in many situations. When the team wants to look busy, it tries to approach the development with a *harried* approach (described by Berne [1964]). It appears to the onlooker that the team will die if it does not meet the deadline. There is a phenomenal amount of project activity—with people shouting and screaming, and compilations being fired every few minutes or seconds, and developers crowding around a lone hero who has just finished writing his 5,000th line of code in a killer class and has assembled it with the legacy wrapper.

"If the code doesn't build this time, we are all dead" is the common belief of the team. Then the deadline comes and goes, and the team still exists. So it brings in the next deadline. Deadline is a game played by people who feel they can only work under pressure. While that may be the case with some, creation of these false deadlines and the hullabaloo that surrounds them can be very unproductive.

The antidote to this game includes proper use of an interactive and incremental approach. The eXtreme Programming community provides the best antidote to this game by releasing their work on an almost-daily basis for the users to see. The chance of a project team suffering from deadline neurosis is thus considerably reduced. This approach is more effective in small to medium projects, as large projects will have to consider the issue of deadlines in the context of managing user expectations, business opportunity needs, and so on.

2.6   Popular Quality Techniques

We discussed at length the creation and management of teams, and the impact of sociological factors in these teams. This was important from a high-level view of organizing the quality function. We now delve into the lower-level techniques of actually carrying out quality functions. As was suggested in Chapter 1, ensuring model quality of UML diagrams includes a detailed checklist for each of the UML diagrams that ensures their correctness and completeness by checking their syntax, semantics, and aesthetics. The quality techniques that help us carry out these checks from elements (for example, a use case or a class) to complete models

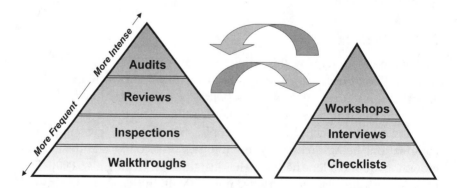

Figure 2.9 *Mapping among quality techniques*

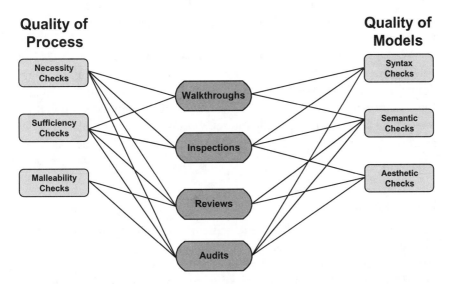

Figure 2.10 *Quality techniques applied to quality of process and models*

(MOPS, MOSS, and MOBS) include those of walkthrough, inspection, reviews, and audits. Each of these techniques can use the additional techniques of checklists, interviews, and workshops.

These same techniques can also be used to ensure that all the necessary activities and tasks of a process-component have been carried out in its enactment. Detailed audits of a process can also reveal its malleability. As shown in Figure 2.10, one or more of the quality techniques can be used, in combination, to accomplish the quality goals of the process and the models.

2.6.1 Walkthroughs

A walkthrough is the least formal of all quality techniques. It is simply a quick check of whatever has been produced. Walkthroughs are done to simply look through a UML diagram, a piece of code, or a database schema. The producer of the model or code himself can do a walkthrough. While it is a casual or relatively informal quality mechanism, it is important to treat this as a separate activity from the activity of developing a model or writing code. Walkthroughs are not necessarily done with the intention of finding errors (although if errors, incompleteness, or inconsistency is discovered it should be recorded, or corrections made immediately).

Walkthroughs may not check the artifact against a set of rules but rules can be kept in the back of our minds as we conduct a walkthrough. Sometimes, a checklist may be used to conduct a walkthrough, and still the intention is not to locate errors formally, but to simply ensure that no major gaps have been left in the model. A walkthrough can take up to an hour for a particular UML-based diagram—or deliverable such as a use case or a project plan.

2.6.2 Inspections

An inspection is done with the specific aim of finding errors. Thus an inspection is more formal and more robust in ensuring the quality of a particular artifact than a walkthrough. Although an inspection can also be done by the producer of the artifact (now with an aim of finding errors), it is highly advisable that the inspection of, say, a use case or a use case diagram is done by someone other than the one who has produced that artifact. If another person does the inspection, the chances of picking up errors are much higher than if it is done by the producer of the artifact.

A valid question at this point is, "If peers do inspections, what does a quality person do?" Quality analysts well versed in the techniques of producing the artifact can also conduct inspections. Alternatively, they can facilitate such inspections in a workshop environment. A checklist used at this stage provides the ground rules against which the inspection is carried out. These ground rules are also very helpful in keeping the personalities out of the inspection process.

Because more than one party is usually involved, preparation for inspections is very helpful. A time and place for inspections should be set aside and inspections on UML diagrams, and even quality and project plans, should be carried out on a regular basis. Results from the inspections should be formally documented, and fixes should be subject to reinspections. Inspections of UML-based diagrams may take between one and two hours. This is estimated on the fact that two people are usually involved in an inspection, and there is usually the need to ask questions and seek clarifications.

It is worth noting that formal inspections of usability, called usability inspections, still satisfy the requirements of inspection as discussed here.

In usability inspections the concept of inspection is combined with that of a workshop, leading to a more comprehensive inspection involving the producer of the artifact, the user, the quality person, and a peer who asks the maximum number of questions as she inspects the product. Such inspections will most certainly go beyond the two hours and may last up to a day.

2.6.3 Reviews

A review is a formal quality technique that ensures that a particular deliverable is meeting its syntax, semantics, and aesthetics criteria. In a UML-based project, a review can be carried out on an entire model—such as a MOPS or a MOSS. A review makes sense at the level of a model or a collection of diagrams, because we want to spend more formal time reviewing a model for the inconsistencies or incompleteness that are not apparent when only a single artifact is inspected.

A review is invariably done in a workshop environment. The ideal way to review UML-based models is to provide the models to be reviewed to the reviewers at least a day before the review—enabling them to familiarize themselves with the models created, and to allow them enough time to prepare their questions.

Reviews are ideally carried out by presenting the artifacts using formal presentation facilities such as the data projector, failing which the producer of the artifact would step through the model on the screen and the reviewers would stop him at any point to ask questions and seek clarification.

While the producer of the models has the responsibility of walking through the models, during this process he is not allowed to defend his model. All the criticisms that are heaped on the model are recorded. Although the reviewers can seek clarifications, these clarifications cannot be initiated by the producer of the model. For example, if a business analyst is presenting his use case diagram and sequence diagrams, he can continue to do so until he is stopped by a peer who wants to know the particular use case in which the message shown in the sequence diagram will appear. The business analyst must then explain the documentation of that use case, and show how an instance of that use case is explained by the sequence diagram.

Sometimes, in a quality review, it's necessary to allow the producer to refrain from providing an explanation immediately. For example, if a reviewer asks, "Why has this use case not been stereotyped?" the business analyst can provide the explanation during the review workshop. However, if a reviewer says, "You must stereotype this use case," and if the business analyst had a reason not to stereotype it, the explanation should be provided toward the end of the review workshop, and not during it. This is important in order to encourage the reviewers to ask as many questions as possible, and for the producer to sort out the issues before the system goes live. Detailed explanations of why a use case has not been stereotyped, although valid, prevent an average reviewer from asking the next question or passing the next comment—one that might be genuinely important for the quality of the artifact. Once again, the human aspect of keeping the personalities out of the review process is important to achieve the aims of an impartial review.

Reviews can be conducted against the detailed checklists for the UML diagrams (for suggested checklists, see the accompanying CD). They can also be conducted against the objectives of the system identified earlier on in the problem space. Prototypes can be used to review a particular deliverable—ensuring that the deliverable produced satisfies whatever was promised in the prototype.

Users should be involved in reviews whenever possible. Users will be able to make an important contribution during these quality techniques, as they bring with them the field knowledge. For example, a class diagram that satisfies all quality checks may still need improvement if the user mentions an operational requirement of higher hits per minute than originally specified. While such a requirement may not be directly related to a class diagram, eventually this requirement may end up modifying the class diagram in order to improve, say, the performance of the system. Overall, though, users are able to make more contributions to the MOPS reviews, as opposed to the MOSS or MOBS reviews.

Although reviews can be conducted at any point during the project, it is preferable to schedule them at the end of each iteration. While a review at the end of the first iteration is mandatory, the major iteration may have more than one review schedule. Furthermore, each of the packages or subsystems within the overall architecture may have its own formal reviews. Because of the more formal nature of the reviews, one envisages the participation of at least three roles in a review process:

- The person who has produced the artifacts

- The person who has sufficient knowledge to inspect the artifacts

- The quality person who is ensuring that the review process is correctly followed

Results from reviews should be formally documented in a review report. They are then circulated to all participating members and reported to the steering committee. Each review should end with a follow-up task list, including brief meetings to ensure that all errors and criticisms have been addressed by the producers of the artifact. A review may take up to one day, and a follow-up meeting around one hour.

2.6.4 Audits

An audit is the most formal of all quality techniques. It requires preparation, followed by a rigorous inspection and review of whatever has been produced. Thus, in a way, it encompasses the previous two techniques discussed. However, an audit has many more characteristics than an inspection or review. For example, the producer of an artifact being reviewed is usually a team, not a person. It is the responsibility of the entire project team to subject their deliverables—which could be an entire system—to a rigorous audit. Another interesting thing to note is that an audit can be done on a deliverable without the presence of the producer. Thus, an audit may use checklists and interviews more than a workshop.

Audits can be further divided into internal audits and external audits. Both audits have the capability to bring in not only the technological and sociological elements discussed so far, but also legal issues. For example, an internal auditor will be well within her rights to ask questions about the copyrights and license fees paid on a CASE tool being used to create UML diagrams. Thus, audits will look at finances, project plans, organizational plans, budgets, costs against budgets, and other such issues that may not be a part of a programmer's daily routine.

External audits are conducted when the organization lacks internal resources, when the project itself has been outsourced, or when there is need for an unbiased appraisal of the quality of what went on in the project. It is especially helpful in an outsourced project for the organization to commission a third party to perform an external audit on the state of the project. Depending on the legal contracts, such audits may or may not involve checking the financial aspects of the organization—in which case only project-level finances may be audited. Technical and project management issues are also subject to audits. An audit can last from a day to a week or more. However, keeping the scope of the audit itself in mind is important—in fact, auditors must be provided with written objectives of the audit, and should be made to stick to it. Furthermore, audits should result in a formal report on the status of the project, as well as possible suggestions for risk reduction and risk rescheduling.

2.6.5 Checklists

Checklists provide the most basic form of quality techniques. They can be used to conduct a walkthrough or an inspection. They can be used in a formal quality review or a detailed audit. Checklists provide the baseline against which the quality of a model or a product is verified.

For checklists to be successful, they should be carefully created by people who have sufficient experience in creating the artifacts themselves. For example, a quality checklist for a deployment diagram should be created only by someone who has previous UML-based knowledge and experience creating many deployment diagrams. Furthermore, checklists should be graded according to the urgency of the checks and their importance.

Other forms of grading and grouping are also acceptable—but throwing a checklist together with no consideration of the sequence can jeopardize the quality effort. For example, it is advisable to check the syntactical correctness of an attribute within a class before checking the correctness of an operation—because operations may depend on an attribute. The sequencing of checks can be further extended to the UML diagram level. An example is checking a state chart diagram for a class without having checked the class itself. A well-constructed checklist ensures that the class is checked first before the state chart is checked.

Checklists can appear in various mediums—paper-based checklists, electronic checklists that can do some basic calculations on the results of the checks (such as a checklist in an Excel spreadsheet that totals the results of "OK" and "not OK" responses), and checklists deployed on the Internet. Internet checklists are helpful in an outsourced project by providing feedback to the outsourcing partner on the status of a use case diagram or a state chart diagram.

Dynamicity of checklists is also important. If a part of the checklist is to be stepped through depending on the results of the previous check, then the "if then else" situation must be explained in the checklist itself. This is done by means of comments underneath the checks. For example, in checking the attribute of a class, a comment would be "go to the checks of initial values if this is a MOPS quality check." Dynamicity of checklists also means that the checklists should be continually updated to reflect the newer requirements of quality checks arising out of previous runs of the checklists.

The manner in which checklists are executed or used can also differ. For example, we can use the checklists provided in the accompanying CD to conduct detailed quality checks. But these checklists only provide the reference list—there is no mandate to fill out any results at the end of each check. However, other checklists may have a need for the quality personnel to fill out results or pass comments against each of the checks. Surveys of a social nature, such as checking the e-factor or quality environment within a project, may use such subjective checklists, where those who go through the checklist also write their answers, comments, and criticisms at the end of each check.

2.6.6 Interviews

Interviewing is a technique that not only validates and verifies whatever has been created, but also plays a decisive role in creating a good quality UML model and software in the first place. This is because many of the requirements in their early stages are best elicited and documented using interviews with users, end users, and project sponsors. Interviews are used by business analysts to deal with a large cross section of users, more than just the one or two users who might be onboard in a project.

Interviews require preparation. It is important for the business analysts or the quality analysts to prepare their questions in advance. This sets the agenda and tone for the interview, and also keeps the interviewer free from the responsibility of creating questions on the fly (running the risk of forgetting to ask an important question). However, provisions should be made within the preparatory lists to allow for extra questions based on the answers provided to previous questions.

Preparation for interviews also requires setting up time, and time-boxing the interview to stick to the prearranged schedule. Questionnaires for the interview may be passed on to the interviewee earlier—especially if it requires some research on the part of the interviewee to provide a satisfactory answer. For example, if a business analyst wants to interview an insurance specialist on the recent business regulations governing the claims process for a worker injured while away from the home city on business, then it is advisable to put that question in a list and send it to the insurance specialist well in advance of the interview.

Interviews are best conducted face to face. Telephone interviews, however well conducted, simply do not have the same effect as face-to-face interviews have. Even videophone interviews fail to draw the same response, in my opinion, as a physical interview. The reason for this is perhaps outside the current scope of our discussion but it can be certainly said with confidence that face-to-face interviews should be conducted wherever possible. A follow-up interview can be conducted over the phone, but it will still lack the descriptiveness resulting from an interviewer being physically present.

Recording of interviews can be a sticky point in some interviews. If interviewees are even slightly uncomfortable with a tape recorder, it should be avoided. If there is likely to be a lot of technical material resulting from the interview, someone should accompany the interviewer in order to document everything that is being said during the interviews. However, if the comfort level of the interviewee is not affected, then a tape recorder is the most helpful interview instrument—as we can replay the tape later to document the answers.

The manner in which interview questions are framed also affects the outcome. The choice is between objective questions that result in a plain "yes or no" answer, versus a subjective question that results in a detailed descriptive response. If the nature of your interview is a survey, wherein you have to receive, collate, and analyze responses from hundreds of participants, then an interview with "yes or no" or a grade of one through five or ten is helpful.

However, in most UML-based work in the problem space, subjective questions are more important than objective ones. For example, a good business analyst trying to interview an end user for an Internet-based query feature of an insurance claim will *not* ask a question like "Would you like to know the date you made your claim?" Instead, a better question is "What would you like to know about your claim?" If the response includes "date," a follow-up question would be "Why would you like to know about the date?" This approach results in a more comprehensive requirement model, as the end user in this case is likely to describe more features that she wants in the query than the business analyst herself can think of. Subjective interviewing is most beneficial in eliciting quality requirements. Long answers should also be tolerated, but the interviewer should try to bring the interviewee back on course by asking counter-questions that relate to the subject matter. Irrelevant answers can always be ignored, but the cost of not getting the answers at all is too high, especially in the problem space.

2.6.7 Workshops

Workshops, as a formal quality technique, provide immense benefits of group work. Workshops bring together project participants with varying expertise. Workshops can be organized for the purposes of inspections, reviews, and audits. They can also be conducted for requirements capturing and requirements modeling. Workshops provide the forum to express business requirements in the MOPS, but they are equally effective in reviewing a technical design, or getting a consensus on the use of a particular technology within the overall system architecture.

A workshop, however, is a rich source of gaming, as described earlier in the sociology of a project. Meetingitis, the game so popular with all project teams, and which results in a phenomenal amount of unproductive work, finds workshops an ideal playing field. Despite that risk, it is important to have well-organized workshops in a project; they bring together user groups, business analysts, and developers and enable them to sort out the objectives, the requirements, and the designs that would otherwise not be easy to sort on a one-to-one basis. It is therefore important to undertake some preworkshop planning to ensure that the administrative part of the workshop is addressed before the workshop proceeds.

A typical workshop administration may include a whiteboard, flipcharts, data projectors, and other audiovisual equipment. These are the basic things in a workshop, yet they have the tendency to disrupt the workshop. If functioning well, they tend to make the workshop more productive. For example, a whiteboard with a printing facility is a tool I can't praise enough. It is also recommended, especially during requirements workshops wherein a CASE tool is being used for UML diagrams, that the diagrams are projected on a whiteboard from the data projector. This technique provides the dual advantage of the good look and feel with color, provided by the CASE tool, and the ability to conduct discussions and corrections directly on the whiteboard using a marker, before the changes are incorporated in the tool itself.

All workshops must have a facilitator. In a review workshop, this can be the reviewer or it can be the quality person. A quality analyst is called upon to facilitate the workshop and to review the models. However, the skills to review a model and the skills to facilitate a workshop are not the same. A facilitator, for example, must be on her feet most of the time—cajoling and encouraging and at the same time keeping the objectives of the workshop in front of the participants all the time.

There are times in a workshop (typically after lunch) when discussions tend to die down and the room is left with a few seconds of awkward silence. Such situations can be best resolved by asking a leading question, or going through the parking lot of difficult issues thus far. The reverse of this situation is also true, wherein a workshop gets heated with about three different raucous conversations going on in the room at the same time. The facilitator in such situations should ensure that things don't become uncontrollable—the value of a coffee break, even if it is not scheduled, should never be underestimated in a workshop. In the absence of such special situations, the facilitator should stick to the time-boxes, especially the breaks. Workshop sessions should not last more than two hours at the most.

Play acting during workshops is an important aspect of quality techniques. Workshops, during quality reviews and audits, does not mean just sitting and looking at a UML diagram or deliverable from a quality angle. Play acting, by assigning elements on a diagram (actors) to people and stepping through the use cases, is very helpful for quality. While techniques like CRC cards are made up of such play acting, what is suggested here is extending the technique of play acting to verifying the quality of almost all UML-based artifacts.

For example, if you are doing a workshop to verify the quality of a state chart diagram, it is worthwhile to assign the states to the people present in the workshop, and make them responsible for the states as the workshop members step through the state chart diagram. People should be encouraged to voice their views during workshops, but the facilitator has the important job of keeping the workshops from degenerating into a game. Reviews of UML-based requirements can especially benefit by keeping a separate area on the whiteboard titled "parking lot"—wherein all issues related to, say, a use case that can't be resolved immediately are parked.

I tend to look at the emergence of difficult issues, or issues that are likely to hold up the progress of the workshop, with relief rather than concern. This is because the sooner we start having debates and the sooner the confusion surfaces in requirements and quality workshops, the better. If there is no discussion and no confusion early on, I view it with some trepidation—because there are no projects without confusion. It's valuable to allow those confusions to surface as early as possible in the project lifecycle.

Such issues, when surfacing during a workshop, should be welcome but should be parked in the parking lot. In addition to enabling the workshop to move forward, often you will notice that the issues that appeared insurmountable at the start of the workshop, and which were prominently placed in the parking lot, get resolved as the workshop progresses.

Finally, it is important to consolidate the workshop at the end, and to report on the progress. Summarize at the conclusion of the workshop what has been achieved, what should be done next (in terms of action items), and the strategy to handle parking-lot issues. A summary of the minutes of the workshop is circulated to all concerned parties, and the next workshop scheduled tentatively, if possible.

2.7   Standards and Quality

One of the important and significant contributions to quality is the judicious use of standards. This is because standards help alleviate gamey discussions, such as how to name a class or how to format a use case. Standards are not one single entity applied to the entire project. There are different standards and areas of their application. There are also different sources of standards. These are considered here with the view of improving the overall quality of the models and other deliverables in a UML-based project.

2.7.1   Areas of Application of Standards

Quality in UML-based projects depends on standards being applied to a wide variety of areas. Some of the areas of standards, as shown in Figure 2.11, are:

- Modeling standards. These standards dictate the notations, diagrams, and other associated artifacts that create the models in a software project. In our case, the Unified Modeling Language provides the standard for modeling notations and diagrams. While the UML is getting accepted over a large number of different types of projects, and is a de facto standard, it is yet to be stamped by the International Standards Organization (ISO). Alternatives to the UML have been Data Flow Diagrams, Entity Relationship Diagrams, and even the humble flowchart. Nonetheless, the current UML 1.4 of the Object Management Group continues to provide the prime modeling standard for modern software projects.

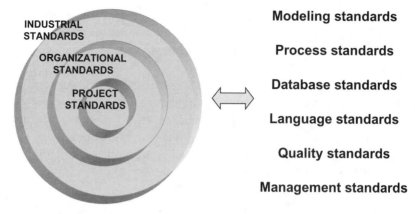

Levels of Standards   Areas of Application of Standards

Figure 2.11 *Applying standards: levels and areas*

- Process standards. These dictate the manner in which processes are put together and deployed. Processes need to be presented in an acceptable notational form, described and specified in a standard format, and deployed with associated training and support. This includes formal descriptions of the activities and tasks within a process, description of the roles that carry out the tasks, and templates for the deliverables that are produced as a result. There are a number of processes that support UML-based development, as discussed earlier and shown in Figure 1.8. An attempt to unify these processes is going on at the OMG,[6] and the hope is that we will have a common process standard that will be configured to suit different project types and sizes. In addition to unifying the notations and description of a particular process, it is also important to measure the repeatability and maturity of a process. This measure is provided by the Capability Maturity Model (CMM) . The CMM provides the measures that inform the maturity of the process in enactment. The CMM may also influence what else gets measured in the project by influencing the creation of a metrics program. Such a metrics

---

[6] See some recently published works such as *UML and the Unified Process: Practical OO Analysis and Design,* Addison-Wesley, 2002, and *The Unified Process Explained,* Addison-Wesley, 2001.

program would very much be a part of the process standards within the organization.

- Database standards. As with almost all tool vendors, database vendors are keen to promote their own individual view of standards. Nonetheless, relational database modeling and relational schema generation benefited greatly by the standards followed in drawing Entity Relationship Diagrams, as well as by normalization of relational tables. Furthermore, for data warehousing projects, Kimball et al. [1998] mention two standards: those for database object names and those for physical file names and locations.

- Language standards. These are decided at all levels, namely, project, organizational, and industrial. Modern projects tend to bring together a variety of programming languages (for example, a server-side component written in C++ or even a full development environment like JADE that can provide support for a Java applet running on the client machine). Because of these varieties of mixing and matching, it is important to follow standards in coding. Having the same (or similar) standards across languages is better than having widely varying standards for say, Java versus C++. This comes in very handy when the same programmers are working in different environments, reading and maintaining codes in Java and C++. Internal project and external industrial standards make the code more readable and easily maintainable. However, project standards, even for languages, must be agreed upon earlier in the project. Names for classes, attributes, operations, as well as formatting of classes and components, are an important part of language standards. Practical experience suggests, though, that programmers shun formal language standards that run into hundreds of pages. Also, standards without at least a brief justification are also not always popular.

- Quality standards. These standards, such as the ISO9001 quality standards, mandate what constitutes a quality environment, but leave the implementation of such standards to the individual projects and organizations. They can affect all other standards because they provide templates and guidelines for quality management documents and quality plans, and they specify the need for and the organization of quality personnel.

- Management standards. These can be derived from standards such as those of the Project Management Institute (PMI). Project management standards, like quality standards, can influence all other standards. However, they are particularly close to, and at times intertwined with, the process standards. For example, creation of an iterative and incremental process is a part of the process standards, but in practice its enactment is the responsibility of project management and can be dictated by the project management standard.

2.7.2   Project, Organizational, and Industrial Standards

In the previous section we described the various areas of standards in software (particularly UML-based) projects. These standards are created and applied at different levels, as shown in Figure 2.11.

- Project standards. This is a mutually agreed-upon set of standards that project members decide on early in the software lifecycle. Examples of project-level standards include naming conventions for use cases and classes, creation and application of stereotypes, and usage of relationships in creating UML-based models. While these project standards can be based on organizational and industrial standards, they can also be created for the purpose of the project—for example, templates for project documents or emails. These are the standards that change from project to project, depending on the type of a project and its needs. At the modeling level, an example can be a project that uses only the <<includes>> relationship between use cases. People with UML modeling experience know it is possible to create a use case diagram with only the <<include>> relationship. The decision not to use other relationships can be restricted to a particular project. Another example would be whether a particular class should be named as a noun starting with a capital letter and whether an attribute should be stereotyped as <<data>>. Stereotypes can change from project to project, as well. A data warehousing project will have a need for quite a few stereotypes related to data items and tables, whereas a project that integrates a legacy application will have to consider stereotyping its interfaces to the application.

- Organizational standards. Dictated by the organization, these are the standards that affect the enterprise architecture and all other artifacts at the enterprise level. For example, an organization may mandate the use of the UML in all its projects—a standard for all projects within the organization, but something that can change from one organization to another. The same can be true of documents and templates for reports, use of a process, and use of CASE tools. Corporate head offices are particularly responsible for dictating organizational standards across their offices—and if it happens to be a global organization, it leads to an interesting situation. For example, an organization may globally dictate the use of a particular Web application server that may have a high level of security encryption, which may not be allowed outside the U.S. Even at the modeling level, I have recently come across an organization that wants to use UML for modeling but is constrained by the fact that corporate standards have not yet changed (they are still dictating the use of Data Flow Diagrams and flowcharts!).

- Industrial standards. Typically the ISO standards, which do not change from organization to organization but are standards applied across the entire software industry. UML modeling standards and the XML schema standards derived from the OMG's Meta Object Facility are examples of industrial standards (albeit still waiting for recognition from the ISO). Nonetheless, these are the OMG standards that apply to at least the 800 organizations that are the members of OMG, and many more, which follow the standards. It is worth noting that there can also be some legal requirement for standards at the industrial level; for example, the need for designing certain user interfaces with a minimum font size for the screen. This is a workplace safety requirement, and as such there is a need for all software developers to follow this standard to ensure that a readable font is provided to all users of a banking or insurance application.

In creating an understanding of these various types and levels of standards, it is important not to lose sight of the purpose of the standards—to create an understandable environment by facilitating easier communication. If standards are followed in modeling, the models become understandable far more than if no standards are followed—and so on with all other artifacts created in a software project. Kimball et al. place the importance of standards in the right context when they state, "It is more important to have standards and follow them than they be perfect." There is no point in having reams of paper that dictate standards for modeling or languages that no one ever looks at or uses. This requires standards to be succinct, as well as easily deployed. It is hard to imagine only paper-based standards in modern software projects—they have to be deployed electronically either on the company's intranet, or interwoven electronically in the quality process itself. For example, it is easier to ensure that a deliverable or work product in a quality process gets produced based on a template that is electronically available every time a new deliverable has to be created within the project.

Finally, it is also important to have and perform activities in a quality software process that relate to creation and maintenance of standards within the quality-assurance process-components. These process-components result in the production of a few pages of directly applicable project standards that are followed by everyone within the project. For example, the quality-assurance process-component will update and fine-tune the checklists of UML-based deliverables (as suggested in the accompanying CD, and further enhanced by the practitioners).

2.8   Process Maturity: The CMM Standards

Having given detailed thought to the soft factors in IT, we build an argument for measuring the maturity of a process. In order to improve on the process, it is important to have some measure of the capability of the process. In subjecting our Quality Software Process to the malleability checks mentioned in Section 1.8.3, the measures of the process discussed here can be invaluable.

2.8.1   The Capability Maturity Model

The CMM provides the most widely accepted guidelines for improving a software process. The reason why the CMM plays a significant role in our discussion is because of its ability to provide software process measures and improvements. While the quality checks for the UML-based models focus on the quality of the diagrams produced, the CMM helps us with the quality and maturity of the process itself.

Currently the Software Engineering Institute (SEI; www.sei.cmm.edu) of Carnegie Mellon University professes a number of software process improvement models, including SW-CMM (for software development), SE-CMM (for systems engineering), and IPD-CMM (for integrated product development). An equally popular model at the Personal Software Process (PSP) level is P-CMM (Personal Capability Maturity Model).

Currently, the SEI is working on the integration of these models into a comprehensive CMM Integration production suite, or simply CMMi.

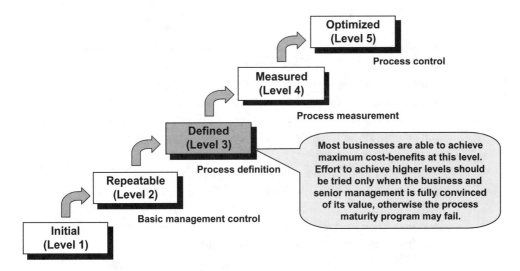

Figure 2.12 *The five levels of the Capability Maturity Model (adapted from Carnegie-Mellon University's Software Engineering Institute)*

Once again, the importance of CMMi is its potential to integrate the underlying structure of all process models—resulting in a framework against which process maturity is measured. More importantly, this can be a framework for the creation of appropriate instances of processes, resulting in substantial time and costs savings for organizations that adopt these measures.

In the context of our discussion on quality and processes, the five levels of maturity of software processes can be used to identify the current state of process discipline within the project and the organization, and the transition that needs to be brought about as the organization progresses to higher levels of CMM maturity. The SEI mandates the following five levels of software process maturity:

- Initial. At Level 1, work progresses in an ad hoc way, with some disparate attempts made by the organization to implement process discipline.
- Repeatable. Level 2 is achieved when not only are the elements of a process implemented in the organization but those process elements are also repeated with confidence.
- Defined. Level 3 provides the maximum cost-benefits to business organizations using information systems (as against, say, defense and health systems that may need much higher process maturity). Every element of the process is properly defined at this level. This means

the "what," the "how," and the "who" and the supporting guidelines of "when" are all defined and formally documented.

- Measured. When the process elements mentioned in CMM Level 3 can be measured in terms of their quality and contribution to the process, as well as the contribution of the process to the overall quality within the software development environment, the organization is said to be at Level 4.

- Optimized. Once we can measure something, the opportunity to improve on it becomes apparent. When the organization starts to fine-tune process elements, resulting in an optimization of activities and tasks, then the process discipline in the organization can be said to be fully matured. This is Level 5 maturity.

Figure 2.13 shows the practical application of these five levels of the CMM. Jalote [2000], in his book *CMM in Practice,* shows how these CMM levels can be applied in practice to take an organization to Level 4 on the process maturity scale. Each of the key process areas of a project, affected and improved by this change, is shown within the relevant rectangles in Figure 2.13.

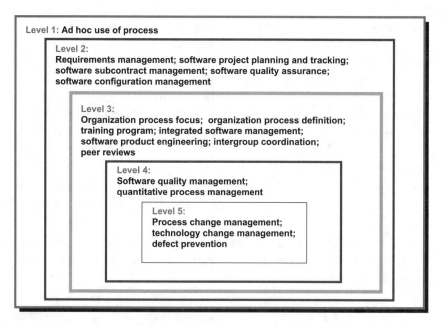

Figure 2.13   *The practical key process areas for each of the five CMM levels (adapted from Jalote 2000)*

2.8.2 Personal Software Process Maturity

In considering the soft factors in software development, it is not sufficient to give credence to these factors only at the project or organizational level. It is also important to consider their impact and their measurement at the personal level. The framework to measure the desire of individuals to strive for excellence and their personal motivation to achieve it is provided by Humphrey [1995] and is implemented as P-CMM by the SEI.

The PSP approach takes the following progression:

- The baseline process, which includes simple measurement of time and defect recording in personal performance.

- The planning process, which deals with estimating the size of programs and the time taken by individuals to develop them; the planning and scheduling of tasks in the future.

- The personal quality management process, which deals with code and design reviews of individual work and strategies to manage them.

- The cyclic personal process, which enables a complete software development cycle of designing, coding, compiling, and testing on a base module of a very large piece of software.

This process maturity measure provides guidelines to organizations in addressing their people issues. Establishing the maturity of individual workers, their goals and aspirations, and their continuous development are some of the things that are addressed by P-CMM. This provides organizations that want to transition to quality processes with valuable information on the readiness of their employees to do so. As this is being written, the first P-CMM certification at the highest maturity level is being reported.[7]

2.8.3 Applying CMM in UML-Based Projects

The UML, together with a process, provides substantial support for organizations to achieve a certain amount of process maturity. For example, the notations of the UML provide standard ways to create and maintain diagrams. Since these diagrams form the basis for creating models of

---

[7] QAIindia carried out the certification of WIPRO, in India, that has reached Level 5 for their Personal CMM processes in 2001. Visit *www.qaiindia.com* for further details.

requirements, solutions, and architecture, they provide great support in taking an organization to the defined level of process maturity.

In Chapter 3, we define the activities and tasks that need to be performed, the deliverables that need to be produced, and the people or roles that will produce the deliverables. These definitions are at the core of process maturity. The definitions of the deliverables use the UML notations, providing the required standards for what is being produced. However, a process is more than the UML, and therefore additional definitions (or descriptions) of the activities, tasks, and roles in the next chapter provide the necessary ingredients for process maturity in software projects.

It is interesting to note how a fully defined process at Level 3 on the CMM scale satisfies most of the definition needs of the three dimensions of a process—the technological, the methodological, and the sociological.

2.9   Process Checks

Quality environment facilitates checking the syntax, semantics, and aesthetic aspects of models and other deliverables in the project (as was shown in Figure 1.13). These checks ensure the correctness, completeness, and consistency of the models. These models, in our UML-based discussions, were MOPS, MOSS, and MOBS. Quality management deals with the "how to" of conducting these checks. And a crucial aspect of this how to is the process. What is even more important is checking the steps of the process itself. This can be further explained by an example. If a semantic check for a class diagram is to ensure that the class represents the correct business entity from the problem space, then it is necessary for that to be performed in a satisfactory manner. The necessity of this step is a quality check itself—but a check of the process rather than the deliverable. We discuss the practical issues of process checks in the context of quality environment.

2.9.1   Checking What Is Necessary

First we need to decide whether a particular process-component (defined in Section 3.2.7) is necessary. Having short-listed the relevant process-components, the next level of process checks is for the necessary activities, followed by necessary tasks. Tasks are the atomic level of process checks. This can be done as follows.

Step through the task plan for the project. Tick off the necessary steps. Interact with the users for what they consider necessary in terms of the tasks and deliverables. The deliverables (MOPS, MOSS, MOBS) will be verified through the model checks. But the steps for those checks will be a part of the process. These checks will then be carried out in a quality workshop.

2.9.2   Checking What Would be Sufficient

Checking the sufficiency means checking what else in addition to necessity should be performed as a part of the process. This can change slightly depending on the type and size of projects discussed in Chapter 1. For example, large projects will have some of the steps of a process as necessary, rather than sufficient.

Sufficiency of process checks does not merely deal with the ticking off of a set of activities or tasks. More importantly, it deals with how many times a particular activity or task gets iterated. Thus, sufficiency of process checks also represents the depth of quality checking.

For example, documenting a use case is a task that is repeated many times in a project, until all use cases have been documented. However, repetition of the task document in a use case happens after many other tasks (like creating a use case diagram and analyzing a use case documentation) have been performed.

Sufficiency of checks means that a particular activity or task has been repeated enough times to provide confidence in the project team that the deliverable resulting from that activity task is as complete and correct as possible.

2.9.3   Checking the Malleability of a Process

While checking the necessity and sufficiency of a process can be outlined as a set of checks, the malleability of a process is involved more with its inherent characteristics than an external check. The science of methods underlying a process seems to imbibe this dichotomy within a process: the repeatability of the process resulting from its rigorous definition versus the ability of the process to suit various development environments such as the six different types of projects and their three different sizes discussed in Chapter 1.

Malleability attempts to ascertain the ability of the process to adapt to different development environments. Furthermore, malleability implies the ability of the instance of the process to adapt to the changes in the project itself, as the development progresses. For example, if a process mandates the creation of state chart diagrams for a class, but after two attempts at doing so the project team—and in particular the process engineer—realizes that for this particular project it's more beneficial to create the state chart diagrams directly from the use case descriptions and to use those diagrams to update class operations, the change in the process should be immediately reflected in the process description in the relevant process-components. Use of process-based CASE tools makes this much easier to accomplish. However, this is the malleable aspect of a process, and is crucial to the overall quality of the development.

A process tool should enable a feedback mechanism for the process users, and this feedback should be incorporated in (a) construction of the process instance, which is the area of process architecture, and (b) usage of the process, as the development progresses, which is the dynamic aspect of the process enactment itself. The measure of how easy it is to change the process during a project—during or at the end of each iteration—indicates the malleability of the process during enactment.

2.10   The Planning Deliverables

The process defined and described in the next chapter is made up of a number of deliverables. These include the UML-based deliverables that are produced as a part of any UML-based project. However, UML-based deliverables are not the only deliverables in a process. Of substantial importance are the planning deliverables, made up of the project organizational plan, the quality plan, and the test plan, which are worth discussing in this quality environment chapter.

2.10.1 Project Organizational Plan

What is usually referred to as a project plan, containing a list of tasks and corresponding resources, is actually a task plan. While a project task plan is an important deliverable and a project management tool, the project organizational plan is an equally important document. This is not merely a list of tasks, but a detailed and descriptive document containing the objectives and goals of the project, its risks, its resource strategy, and many other organizational issues. The project manager is responsible for creating and maintaining the project organizational plan. A typical project plan that describes the organizational aspect of a project contains the following:

- Objectives of the project, as discerned from the steering committee and the project sponsor
- Risks and their grading; these are identified from the project sponsor and the users and domain experts
- Categorization of project types and sizes
- People and roles (discussed earlier)—important to assign people to roles
- Procurement of hardware and software
- Reuse strategy

2.10.2 The Quality Plan

A quality plan describes the specific organizational needs of a quality software development environment. While a quality plan can be made a part of the project plan, it need not be. A quality plan categorically deals with issues such as:

- Quality approach and selection
- Environment (e-factor)—creation of the physical seating arrangement, emails, and other communication mechanisms

Creating an Iterative, Incremental, Parallel (IIP) development and integration plan provides a major impetus to real-life projects. Quality plans help to create such IIP plans. It is also essential to incorporate the IIP aspect in a project task plan. A starting template for such an IIP plan based on the process-components described in Chapter 3 is provided on the accompanying CD.

2.10.3 Test Plan

A test plan deals with the organizational aspect of quality control or testing. Once again, it can be a part of the quality plan, and therefore part of the overall project plan, because the organizational needs of resources, hardware, and tools for testing must be reflected in the project plan somehow. However, it is better to keep the test plan separate to enable focusing on the important activity of organizing testing, getting the resources, training the testers, conducting the testing, collating the results, and conducting regression tests. These issues are discussed in detail in Chapter 6, but the deliverable of the test plan is mentioned here because it remains the responsibility of the management team in the project.

2.11   Bibliographic Notes

I first came across TA in my management study in 1984. Objects, at that time, were not heard of except in research and educational projects. With the emancipation of the project management discipline, I looked around and was reacquainted with the techniques of TA, and applied them in practical projects. I found them deceptively simple yet profoundly effective. I have used them not only in project management, but also in my training sessions and modeling workshops.

The CMM has a wide acceptance, globally. The largest number of CMM Level 5 organizations is in India—not surprising, considering the fact that the IT industry is at the heart of the country's economy. No wonder the software development organizations have realized the importance of CMM maturity and have put their money where their mouth is, by going through the rigors of deploying a process, and getting its maturity certified by an external party. The programmers of such organizations, though, consider it less fun and more bureaucracy.

2.12   Frequently Asked Questions (FAQs)

Q1: How does CMM relate to a process?

A1: The Capability Maturity Model provides guidelines related to maturity of a process. These guidelines can be applied to any process, including any in-house process that the organization uses. CASE tool-based processes, such as RUP[8] and MeNtOR,[9] need relatively less time to reach a desired level of CMM.

Q2: My organization has a project office. Where does it fit in with the roles described here?

---

[8] *www.rational.com*, Rational Unified Process from Rational.
[9] *www.processmentor.com* from Object-oriented Pty. Ltd.

A2: The project office is an administrative part of the project. What are described here are the actual working roles within the project. For example, this chapter has not described the role of a system administrator, but that role is crucial when the system goes into operation. The project office can be used to provide project-related information such as the project brief, total number of projects existing within the organization, their costs, and schedules. A quality manager and a project manager are the two main roles described here that would deal with the project office.

Q3: Why should I consider the soft factors described here separate from the standard project management approach?

A3: Because they are the often-neglected subtle factors that influence the outcome of a project—especially its quality. In fact, the soft factors described here are based only on the author's knowledge and experience. Practical project managers should keep an eye out for many more soft factors influencing their project teams, and actively work toward solving these soft issues.

Q4: How much time and effort do I need to understand the concept of Transactional Analysis, and apply them when managing my projects?

A4: TA is an extremely simple yet effective socio-psychological technique that is valuable to a project manager who does not have sufficient time to learn detailed psychology in project management. It usually takes a project manager two hours of training, and a few more hours of reading on the practical aspects of TA, and she is prepared to apply them to work straight away. The idea, as described in this chapter, is to start handling the counter-productive games as soon as possible—other techniques can follow.

Q5: We have no desire to get our processes assessed to the CMM levels. How much assistance does process maturity give us in this case?

A5: Irrespective of the need for formal process maturity, considering and using a formal software process has a positive impact on both quality and productivity. It is essential to at least consider the guidelines provided by the CMM in all process related work.

2.13 Exercises

E2.1: Name and describe the single most important role in each of the three modeling spaces.

E2.2: What is CMM? Discuss the importance of the CMM guidelines at each of five levels of process maturity.

E2.3: Describe how the Personal CMM can benefit a programmer working in a CRMS implementation project.

E2.4: Describe how the game of meetingitis harms the project. Describe how good meetings can be carried out.

E2.5: How do the four-team models of Constantine relate to the four life positions of TA?

E2.6: Describe how each of the three levels of standards can be applied to modeling work in a UML-based project.

E2.7: What is the difference between process standards, modeling standards, and programming standards? How do they help each other?

E2.8: When would you, as a quality person, recommend an inspection as opposed to a walkthrough?

E2.9: Workshops are an ideal quality technique when a review is warranted. Comment.

E2.10: A checklist can be used in a walkthrough, inspection, review, or audit. Comment.

2.14 References

Beck, K., *eXtreme Programming Explained: Embrace Change,* Reading, Mass.: Addison-Wesley, 2000.

Berne, E., *Games People Play,* Penguin, 1964.

———, *What Do You Say after You Say Hello?: The Psychology of Human Destiny,* Corgi, 1972.

Brown, W., et al., *Anti Patterns: Refactoring Software, Architectures, and Projects in Crises,* John Wiley and Sons, 1998.

Constantine, L., *Constantine on Peopleware*, Yourdon Press Computing Series, N.J.: Prentice Hall, 1995.

————, and L. Lockwood, *Software for Use: A Practical Guide to Models and Methods of Usage-centered Design*, Reading, Mass.: Addison-Wesley, 1999.

Cox, B., "What if there is a silver bullet?" *Journal of Object-Oriented Programming*, 1992, 5(3): 8–9, 76.

DeMarco, T., and T. Lister, *Peopleware: Productive Projects and Teams*, New York: Dorset House Publishing Company, 1987.

Dodani, M., "Archaeological designers," *Journal of Object-Oriented Programming*, May 1994.

Fowler, M., "The new methodology," *Software: The Journal of Software Engineering Australia*, April 2002, pp. 41–46.

Goldberg, A., and K. Rubin, *Succeeding with Objects: Decision Frameworks for Project Management*, Reading, Mass.: Addison-Wesley, 1995.

Graham, I., *Migrating to Object Technology*, Reading, Mass.: Addison-Wesley, 1994.

Hammer, M., and J. Champy, *Reengineering the Corporation*, Allen and Unwin, 1994.

Harris, T., *I am OK, You are OK*, London and Sydney: Pan Books, 1973.

Henderson-Sellers, B., *Book of Object-Oriented Knowledge*, 2nd ed., Upper Saddle River, N.J.: Prentice Hall, 1997.

————, and Y. Pant, "When should we generalize classes to make them reusable?" *Object Magazine*, 1993 3(4): 73–75.

————, and M. Serour, "Creating a process for transitioning to object technology," *IEEE 2000*, pp. 436–440, 00896731; also presented at *TOOLS USA 2001*.

Humphrey, W., *A Discipline for Software Engineering*, Reading, Mass.: Addison-Wesley, 1995.

Jalote, P., *CMM in Practice: Process for Executing Software Projects at Infosys*, Boston: Addison-Wesley, 2000.

James, M., and D. Jongeward, *Born to Win,* Reading, Mass.: Addison-Wesley, 1971.

James, M., *The OK Boss,* Reading, Mass.: Addison-Wesley, 1975.

Kimball, R., et al., *The Data Warehouse Lifecycle Toolkit,* Wiley, 1998.

Kriendler, J., "Cultural change and object-oriented technology," *Journal of Object-Oriented Programming,* February 1993, 5(9): 6–8.

Lim, W. C., "Effects of reuse on quality, productivity, and economics," *IEEE Software,* September 1994, 11(5): 23–30.

Meyer, B., *Object Success,* Prentice Hall, 1995.

———, Presentation at the Object-Oriented Special Interest Group of the Australian Computer Society (New South Wales Branch), Sydney, October 21, 1992.

Morrison, J., and J. O'Hearne, *Practical Transactional Analysis in Management,* Reading, Mass.: Addison-Wesley, 1977.

O'Hara-Devereaux, M. and R. Johansen, *GlobalWork: Bridging Distance, Culture & Time,* San Francisco: Jossey-Bass Publishers, 1994.

Thomsett, R., "Managing implications of object-oriented development," *ACS Newsletter,* October 1990, pp. 10–12.

———, "When the rubber hits the road: A guide to implementing self-managing teams," *American Programmer,* December 1994, pp. 37–45.

Unhelkar, B., "Developing the vital leadership skills required of an IT project manager," *Proceedings of IT Project Management by AIC conferences,* Auckland, New Zealand, April 1996.

———, "Transactional Analysis (TA) as applied to the Human Factor in object-oriented projects," *Handbook of Object Technology,* Saba Zamir (ed.), Boca Raton, Fla.: CRC Press, 1999, Chapter 42, pp. 42–1 to 42–12.

———, and G. Mamdapur, "Practical aspects of using a methodology: A Road Map approach," *Report on Object Analysis and Design (ROAD),* 2(2): July–August 1995, pp. 34–36, 54.

Weinberg, G., *The Psychology of Computer Programming,* 1971.

chapter

The Quality Process Architecture

The change from craftsmanship to industrialization does not come with the change to a new technique. The change must come on a more fundamental level which also includes the organization of the complete development process.

—Jacobson [1992]

Putting This Chapter in Perspective

The previous chapter focused on creating the right environment, and eliciting management support for necessary quality-assurance activities and tasks. A crucial aspect of that quality environment is a quality process. In this chapter we discuss what constitutes such a process, and how it helps to enhance quality in a UML-based project. This chapter does not propose a new process, but discusses the most commonly used activities and tasks that should be present in all processes. These activities and tasks and their related roles and deliverables are described with the aim of improving the discipline in a process, resulting in the enhanced quality of UML-based deliverables and, eventually, the software product.

This chapter starts by mapping the three dimensions of a process (the what, how, and who as mentioned in Chapter 1) to the corresponding examples in UML-based projects. Unlike the UML metamodel, though, we do not yet have an officially standardized process metamodel. Therefore, to simplify our process discussion, we develop the mapping of the three dimensions of a process into an unofficial metamodel for processes.

Various process-components are then derived from this metamodel. In identifying and describing the process-components, we consider the most basic or core elements of a process. Furthermore, we consider in greater detail the methodological or "how to" aspect of the process-components (their activities and tasks). Relevant deliverables ("what") and roles ("who") are also mentioned in the process-components. This is followed by descriptions of the necessity and sufficiency aspects of quality of the process-components. Malleability is part of process enactment and therefore not discussed separately for each process-component. Thus, this chapter deals with the construction of a process. Once a quality-conscious process is created, it is ready for deployment and enactment—topics dealt with in Chapter 4.

The Prime Reader: Process Engineer, Quality Manager

3.1   The Process Backbone

In Sections 1.4.2 and 1.4.3, we considered the three dimensions of a process and discussed a simple baking example to demonstrate them. Here, we begin the discussion of a process by extending that example further, in order to put it in a process metamodel. This will help us immensely as we construct the quality software process-components later in the chapter. We will also use that understanding to facilitate the creation of a process metamodel.

3.1.1   The Three Dimensions of a Process

The first dimension of a process develops an understanding of the materials on which the actions are performed, as well as the tools that help to perform those actions. This forms the technological dimension of a process. In the example of baking a cake, the activities related to this technological dimension are the evaluation of the dish, the ingredients, and the equipment. This constitutes the "what" of a process.

The second dimension of a process is the step-by-step guide to "how" a particular process is conducted. The discipline of conducting a process comprises a sequence of well-defined activities and tasks that are organized in a specific order. This discipline, or *method* of working, constitutes the methodological dimension of a process. Some activities corresponding to this dimension in the baking example are recipe, cookbook, and timing. This constitutes the "how" of a process.

The third dimension of a process deals with the people who are going to take responsibility for the actions, and carry them out by following the prescribed methodology. An understanding of the dimension of a process that deals with the people who carry out the tasks, and the environment or the organizational context in which those tasks are carried out, results in the sociology of a process—the sociological dimension. In the baking example, the sociological aspect is comprised of the cook, the kitchen environment, and the "soft" issue of cake presentation.

Quality assurance, although a part of the overall process, has a separate set of deliverables, activities, tasks, and roles. Therefore, these elements of the process are separately defined—focusing on the quality management, quality assurance, and quality control suite of activities. These quality-related activities continue to influence the rest of the process. They are also self-influencing in the sense that each quality activity can be used to perform quality assurance on itself. For example, an activity of workshopping in a quality-assurance part of the process can be used to verify the process of conducting workshops in a process. Understanding these three dimensions is crucial to understanding the logic behind the metamodel for a process.

3.1.2 "What" of a Process

The "what" of a process is the technological dimension of the process that answers everything related to the physical things in the process. This primarily includes the raw material with which the process is executed, as well as the deliverables. It is concerned with the technology of the process. Many factors from the technological dimension influence the overall output of a process. These factors include the quality of material that is used, the availability of the material, and the appropriateness of the tools that are used in the process. Thus, everything that deals with the "what" in a process plays a part in influencing its deliverable. Examples of some of these technological factors in a UML-based project are summarized in Table 3.1.

Table 3.1 *Influence of technology factors (what) in a UML-based project*

	Model (components, other deliverables)	Tool (TogetherSoft or ROSE, for example)
Availability	Problem statements, existing applications, MOPS, MOSS, and MOBS	Is TogetherSoft available, or is ROSE better? Consider other options
Standards	UML as a standard for modeling; documentation of project standards	Compliance of TogetherSoft to UML standards
Appropriateness	Is MOPS the right thing to create a model in problem space?	Is TogetherSoft the right tool for modeling? (for example, it can't be used for a process)

3.1.3 "How" of a Process

The "how" or the methodological aspect of the process deals with the steps you follow to produce the deliverable. It is essentially a glossary of the distilled experiences of numerous project managers. The "how" of a process is instrumental in conserving effort when the process is enacted. Taking the cooking example further, the "how" of the process is the recipe book for the baking process. A description of the activities and tasks using suitable notations and language is essential to expressing the "how" of a process. In the case of UML-based projects, examples of the methodological dimension of the process are as follows:

Table 3.2 *Influence of methodological factors (how) in a UML-based project*

	Requirements Modeling Process-component (and others, as described later in this chapter)
Notations	UML notations for models; process notations, as described later in this chapter.
Language (description)	The actual description of the methodological aspect (the how)—by using the building blocks of a process. These are the process-components described later in this chapter.
Documentation	This is the accompanying standard for process, models, the description of how to use them, and their acceptance criteria.

3.1.4 "Who" of a Process

Simply following a method, as described in a recipe book, does not produce the desired deliverable. Application of the methodology is the purview of the person who is applying it. Success depends on the skills and experience of the person, as well as the environment in which she is working. Thus skills, experience, and environment form the sociological factors, or the "who" of a project. These are also called soft factors, as they deal with the softer or human-relations issues of a process. Refer to Chapter 2 for further discussion of soft (not easily quantifiable) factors.

Skills, one of the factors influencing the final outcome of a process, require regular training—especially when new ways of doing things and new equipment become available on a daily basis. Experience comes from practicing developed skills in a real environment. In addition to the skills and experience, it is also important to consider the motivational factors and their influence on the process. These are some of the sociological factors that continue to influence the final outcome of the project. For a UML-based project, some of these sociological factors are summarized in Table 3.3.

Table 3.3 *Influence of sociological factors (who) in a UML-based project*

	Business Analyst (and so on with other roles)
Skills (role description)	The title and description of the role is described here. Also, the relevant skill set needed for this role is described here. A business analyst must have good business domain knowledge, familiarity with UML notations, comfort with use case and activity diagrams, and good interviewing and workshopping techniques.
Experience	A minimum of two years of business analysis experience might be considered essential for a person to be able to "get up to speed" in week one of a project. However, business analysts with less experience can also provide significant input into the project, provided they have had additional training in both UML techniques and the process.
Environment	The sociological factor or e-factor, as described in Chapter 2, should be handled here. Proper working environments (desks, phones, email facilities, decent meeting areas, and so on) are physical considerations that should be addressed in a UML-based project.

3.2   The Process Metamodel

3.2.1   Describing the Process Metamodel

In order to better understand the three dimensions of the process described above, and to further describe the various elements of a process as applicable to UML-based software development, we created the metamodel shown in Figure 3.1. It is not a formal metamodel, but one created to explain the process-components described later in this chapter. A metamodel is a succinct and helpful way of understanding things. For example, the UML has a metamodel that encapsulates the rules that govern the creation of UML diagrams. A look at the UML metamodel can tell us how a class relates to the attributes and operations inside of it.

The purpose of the process metamodel, as shown in Figure 3.1, is to provide the underlying rules for how the process elements connect to and relate with each other. Discussions on formalizing a process metamodel are underway at the OMG. In the meantime, this simplistic process

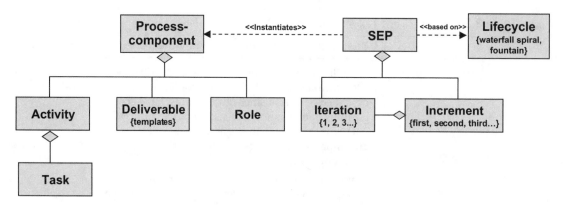

Note 1: This is an informal process metamodel created by me. It is not an OMG standard!

Note 2: The process-components provide the building block. They are put together in a SEP. Eventually, they have to be enacted (enactment is not shown here).

Figure 3.1   *A Quality Software Process Metamodel (using UML notations)*

metamodel serves our purpose of discussing and creating a Quality Software Process (QSP). The metamodel shown in Figure 3.1 uses the UML's class diagram notations, which readers should know. It can be interpreted as follows:

The *process-component* is shown as the building block for the process. This process-component is made up of *activities*, *deliverables*, and *roles*. Activities associate with *tasks*. The *lifecycle* provides the philosophical background for construction of a process. Examples of software lifecycles are shown as waterfall, spiral, and fountain models. A Software Engineering Process (SEP) is based on this lifecycle. In order to create a SEP, the process-components are instantiated. The SEP is made up of *iterations*, which can be 1, 2, 3, and so on. Similarly, a SEP is also made up of *increments*, which are first, second, and third (and can be many more). Increments are made up of iterations.

Each of these elements, appearing in the process metamodel, is further described with their corresponding notations.

3.2.2 Process Ingredients

Figure 3.2 shows the notations that are used to describe a process. These notations represent the elements that constitute the "what," "how," and "who" of the process. Some of these notations are UML-like, such as the role. Others, like deliverables, are needed to express the process aspect. These notations are also simple. They can be easily written on whiteboards, facilitating process-based discussion and leaving the opportunity open for other uses of these process elements, such as describing processes in a typical business exercise. These process elements can also be inserted in a process-based CASE tool that in medium to large projects will greatly ease their enactment. Each of the process elements shown in Figure 3.2 is described in the subsequent sections.

3.2.3 The Role Element in a Process

The *role* provides a descriptive profile of the person who is involved in executing the process. In a quality-conscious process, this role is properly defined and documented. A person will fulfill the description of the role provided here. The person playing the given role is responsible for carrying out the process. He or she can also be the recipient of the process. If use case proponents wish to use the term actor, they may—despite the fine

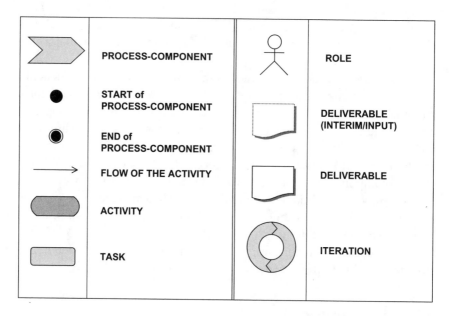

Figure 3.2   *Notations used to describe various process ingredients*

difference between actor and role. Some of the characteristics of a good quality role are:

- The role is well defined and is understood by the person who is responsible for the role.

- The person playing the role should be able to understand the activities that he is responsible for.

- The role must be assigned the suite of activities and tasks that the role player is capable of performing.

- Depending on the scope of the process, the actor element can have multiple instances. For example, a large development process may have 20 programmers but a small-scoped process may have only two.

- Examples of roles defined for a UML-based project include Project Manager, Business Analyst, System Designer and Tester, and Developer/Programmer.

3.2.4   The Activity Element in a Process

The *activity* is the description of the responsibility of the role in the process. The activity element is shown with an elliptical rectangle, and it describes in general what the role encompasses. Activities have a sequence or dependencies. Some activities can also be performed in parallel by more than one role. The activity element in a process is the controlling element for a set of tasks within the process. Therefore, the activity element on its own doesn't have the same concrete existence as the tasks. Actors playing the roles described above carry out the activities by performing a sequence of tasks within the activities. Some of the characteristics of an activity element are:

- Activity is the overall controlling element for a set of tasks.
- It is helpful in understanding the flow of events.
- Some activities may begin before others end. Thus, activities may be carried out in parallel.
- Activities are accomplished by completing the set of tasks which they encompass.
- It is not essential for all tasks within an activity to be accomplished in a single iteration.
- Example activities within UML-based projects include storyboarding, business class modeling, use case modeling, operational analysis, advanced interface design, quality resourcing, and test execution.

3.2.5   The Task Element in a Process

The *task* element in a process discipline is the atomic element in the working of a process. As shown in Figure 3.2, tasks are rectangles with rounded edges. Tasks are carried out under the umbrella of the encompassing activity. Thus, the purpose of the well-defined tasks is to complete the activity under which they fall. Some characteristics of the task element include the following:

- They are the performing elements in a process; that is, they don't need to be further subdivided before they are performed.
- A set of tasks belongs to an activity.
- In the overall process, these tasks are usually carried out in a specific sequence. The designer of the process usually specifies the sequence.
- However, since activities may sometimes be performed in parallel, so can tasks.

- The result of the execution of tasks in a sequence is the completion of an activity.
- Tasks have a concrete existence of their own. This implies that when a task is completed, it is effectively an incremental completion of the activity under which the task is performed.
- Tasks are what the project manager puts in a project plan. Thus, they can be assigned a time for completion and resources to complete them.
- Examples of tasks in a UML-based project are draw a business class diagram, conduct research, apply equality review, and execute a prototype.
- Techniques for carrying out a task may be described.

3.2.6   The Deliverable Element in a Process

A *deliverable* is the final output or result of the process. The roles (actors) are involved in performing various activities, which are carried out by executing a set of well-defined tasks. These tasks result in creating and upgrading what are called deliverables. Since deliverables are the result of work carried out by the roles, they are also called "work products." Deliverables can be concrete, as in a set of documents, or they can be abstract, as in a motivated work force (which results from work performed by a project manager). In our cooking example, the final deliverable is a baked cake. Deliverables in a UML-based project are usually produced iteratively. That means, even if a deliverable is shown as being produced as a result of activities, only some of the tasks within the activities will result in a partial completion of the deliverables. Eventually, more activities and tasks within the activities will be performed to complete the deliverable. This deliverable and its corresponding notation are shown in Figure 3.2.

3.2.7   A Process-Component

A *process-component* is a collection of a subset of the activities, tasks, roles, and deliverables in a process. Thus, a process-component indicates a logical collection of process elements that combine to accomplish a sizeable chunk of the process. The term process-component signifies that a suite of process elements is treated as a component, having a common set of roles working on a logically cohesive set of activities and tasks, resulting in a significant deliverable within that area of the process. Examples of process-components in a UML-based project are Business Evaluation, Requirements Modeling, System Architecture, and Quality Control.

3.2.8   Iterations

An *iteration* signifies an execution of a sequence of process-components, but with varying intensity. For example, some process-components related to evaluating the business proposal for a project are performed with high intensity in the first iteration, but the process-components dealing with requirements modeling are performed with high intensity in the second iteration. An iteration in a medium-sized project may last for about three months, at the end of which reviewable deliverables should be produced. Larger projects will need more time to complete iteration.

3.2.9   Putting Together a Process-Component: A Baking Process

Once the notations are described and understood by the process participants, the representation of the process by means of a diagram plays a significant part in conveying the activities, their sequence, the final deliverable being produced, and the roles responsible for producing those deliverables. Figure 3.3 shows graphically, by using the notations described in detail in the previous section, the simple baking process that we have been using as an example.

- There are three formal roles that are involved in this process-component. They are the chef, the food inspector (quality manager), and the consumer.

- The process is made up of a series of activities: environment creation, baking, quality checking, and consuming. Each of these activities has a set of tasks to go with it. For example, environment creation will have the tasks of procuring the raw materials, like sugar and butter, and preparing the kitchen. The activity of baking includes tasks like mixing the batter, preheating the oven, putting the pan in the oven, and taking the cake out of the oven at the right time. For a large cake (for example, a wedding cake) the activity of quality checking will come into play, followed by consumption. Consumption activity is shown as iterative, and it may be performed numerous times. The consumers of the cake will be multiple people filling the role.

- The final deliverable is shown as a baked caked. If necessary, the raw materials going into the process-component can also be shown (they are not shown here).

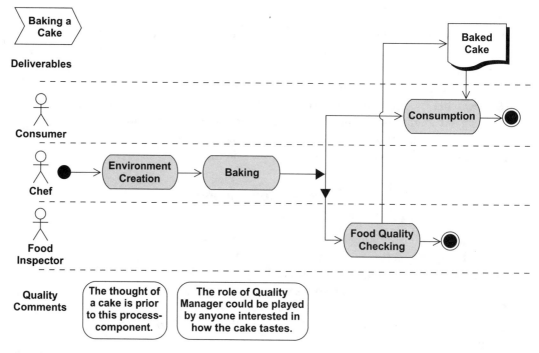

Figure 3.3 *Putting together an example baking process-component*

3.3   Quality Software Process

3.3.1   The Software Process

A software process has process-components that provide help and guidance to produce the models of problem, solution, and background space and the corresponding software. The quality process is made up of process-components that follow the actual software process-components like background shadows—providing the role descriptions, activities, tasks, and deliverables that are the end result of the activities carried out within the quality process.

Thus, an overall Quality Software Process includes process-components not only for development but also for quality assurance. A quality process is not necessarily a totally independent process but can be comprised of a set of process-components that are configured depending on the needs of the project to ensure the quality of the actual software development process. Each process-component within the software process is subject to the criteria of necessity and sufficiency—with the third criterion of malleability being applied in the configuration of the process-component itself. A necessary checklist can be applied to the process-components, followed by the sufficiency checks, to ensure that the basic steps or tasks within a process not only have been followed but they have also been followed in the best possible way and with sufficient depth. Finally, the malleability of the process is provided by the process feedback loop and the ability of the process to change itself, not only for the next project but also during the project's execution.

3.3.2   The Quality Process

While the *software process* described above is a generic term that deals with the process of development (or integration or data warehousing, and so on), the term *quality process* describes the subprocess that accompanies the software process. This quality process is made up of the quality management, quality assurance, and quality control process-components discussed later in this chapter.

3.3.3   Rigorous Process

The extent to which a process is enforced depends on a number of factors. For example, a large project will have sufficient resources and process management skills to follow the iterative and incremental aspect of the process in great detail. In situations where the budgets are tight, or the skills are lacking, projects can still try to follow the process but the rigorousness with which they follow the process (sufficiency or depth) will be much reduced. Understanding the necessary and sufficient aspect of a process is extremely beneficial in balancing the rigor of the process.

3.3.4   Process Maturity

Judging the quality of process requires measuring its maturity. The Capability Maturity Model is the most popular and most accepted form of measurement of process maturity and subsequent quality. The CMM levels and their applicability in measuring processes, as discussed in the previous chapter, are crucial when measuring the maturity of the QSP. The process discussion in this chapter is aimed at helping organizations climb up the CMM maturity scale.

Furthermore, it is also worth considering CMMi as an integrated measure of the process. For example, in describing the six different project types for UML-based projects, we consider Internet-based development or e-development as a default. For each of the UML project types, the process-components are still described in a common format here, as process-components for development. This is because these process-components are relevant to new development as well as to most other project types. Variations to these process-components are permitted before the project starts, especially if we have a vastly different project type. Some changes to the way the process-components are executed should also be allowed. This is the malleability aspect of a process, as discussed next.

3.3.5   Malleable Process

We can judge the quality or the value of a process by its ability to configure these process-components. This is what I have called malleability of the process (see Section 1.8.3). Consider the differences of various UML-based projects in terms of their process requirements. For example, a straight development project uses certain process-components that directly provide development support. In that project we configure a set of process-components together and create a Software Engineering Process. That SEP is an instantiation of a process for new development. Once that SEP is created, we will still need to change it, particularly during the initial iteration of the process. This is malleability. It is an aspect of process not yet fully discussed within CMM.

3.3.6   Process Timing

Furthermore, note that a quality process or process-components that deal with quality first deal with the goals of an organization, followed by the goals of the project. Therefore, many times quality process-components in both instantiation and their enactment may start before a project starts. There are also some management-related process-components, which are included in most software processes. This management-related work usually starts before the project begins. These can be process-components that deal with the investigation, comparison, and analysis of the problem scenario to make the "Go/No Go" decision. They include numerous aspects related to cost, budget, marketing, and sales. The chance of identifying newer opportunities also comes into the picture given these process steps. Note once again these steps have to be taken before the project begins.

3.4   The Software Process

In this area we discuss the process-components that are responsible for software development. The other area containing three process-components is the quality process. (Please refer to the accompanying CD for a tabular list of the following process-components and a starting project plan based on them.)

3.4.1   Business Evaluation Process-Component

Figure 3.4 describes the process-component of business evaluation that describes the part of the process that deals with the prime reason why the project exists. This process-component also presents the very early approach

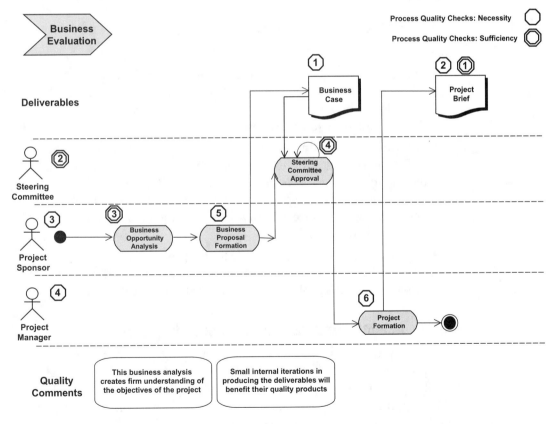

Figure 3.4   *Process-component for business evaluation*

to organizing the project. This is undertaken by the project sponsor, who starts with the activity of a business opportunity analysis. This is followed by a business proposal formulation. The steering committee performs the activity of project approval in an iterative fashion; the project manager handles the responsibilities of the project once the project is formed.

This process-component is important when undertaking a formal evaluation of the business reasons why a software project should proceed. Not only does this argument help those who are going to manage the project, but it also helps to confirm, in the minds of the project sponsor and the eventual end users, the goals and objectives of the project. Because this process-component deals with the initial understanding of the business problem, the deliverables produced here form part of the Model Of the Problem Space (MOPS). They are the *business case* and the *project brief*.

3.4.2   Roles in Business Evaluation

The roles in business evaluation are as follows:

- The steering committee deals with the highest-level management of the project. It brings together expertise from various domains including technology, business, human resources, accounting, finance, and legal, to name a few.

- The project sponsor initiates the project, benefits from it, and pays for it. The project sponsor is the chief person who must be satisfied with the quality of the end product. Therefore, the project sponsor (also known as the business sponsor) is the one who should be involved in documenting the project objectives, identifying the risks, and establishing the priorities.

- The project manager is responsible for the project once it has been evaluated and approved by the business. Therefore, in a way, the project manager's goal is more operational in nature than strategic.

3.4.3   Activities and Tasks in Business Evaluation

Figure 3.5 describes the activity-task mapping within the process-component of business evaluation. This activity-task mapping is also available on the accompanying CD for creating a project plan based on this mapping. The activities and tasks of this process-component play an important role in evaluating the business case and ensuring the project objectives within the business context.

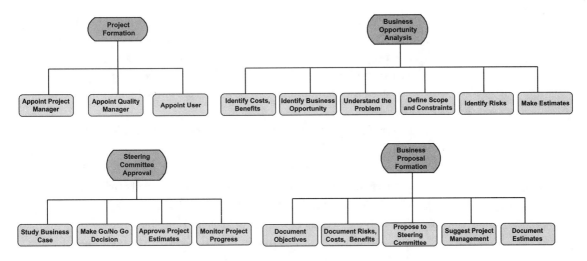

Figure 3.5 *Activities and tasks in business evaluation*

3.4.4   Deliverables in Business Evaluation

- Business case. The business case deliverable contains the arguments for why the project should go ahead. It also documents the cost-benefit analysis for the project. The scope of the project, its risks, and the related project estimates are all documented in the business case. This is the document presented to the steering committee.

- Project brief. Typically, the project brief is a two-page document describing the project; it outlines the objectives of the project, the relevant project numbers, and the project schedule. The project manager and the quality manager are named in the project brief.

3.4.5   Quality Comments on Business Evaluation

Necessity

1. The business case should be carefully prepared to justify the need for a project. This document ensures that the purpose of the project is clear to all parties involved.

2. The project brief is the second mandatory part of this process-component, ensuring that the details of the project are succinctly summarized and available for reference throughout the project.

The project brief also describes the type and size of the UML-based project.

3. The project sponsor is the main role in this process-component, ensuring that the business opportunities are properly analyzed and documented, and that the business proposal has considered all options.

4. The project formation is the starting point of the project manager's project responsibilities.

5. The activity of formulating the business proposal is crucial to the process-component of business evaluation. Results from this activity formally complete the deliverable of the business case.

6. The activity of project formation, through the tasks of the appointments of project manager and quality manager, literally *forms* the project.

Sufficiency

1. The project brief may not be produced in just one iteration. It will, perhaps, need to be updated based on the discussions during the steering committee approval. However, having the project brief deliverable provides the sufficiency, in terms of quality, in this process-component.

2. The steering committee also provides the criteria of sufficiency for this process-component. In small projects, the steering committee may play a notional role, but for medium and large projects, the committee brings in expertise from varying domains within the organization. The steering committee can also help to categorize the project into its respective type (for example, data warehousing, integration, or outsourcing). Having a steering committee for the project satisfies the sufficiency criteria of quality.

3. Business opportunity analysis provides the sufficiency in rigorously analyzing and questioning the need for the project.

4. Steering committee approval will easily iterate twice, if not more, before it provides sufficient rigor in deciding about the project. The steering committee members may ask the project sponsor to further investigate, collect, and collate the information—and only then will they approve the project.

3.4.6 Project Management Process-Component

The project management process-component deals with all activities and tasks that are carried out (primarily by the project manager) in managing the project. Project management is an extremely important process-component that includes understanding the technology, methodology, and sociology of the project. Therefore, this process-component interacts with the process-component of process configuration. The primary purpose of project management is to organize and track the project. Tracking involves risk management; therefore, project management also deals with

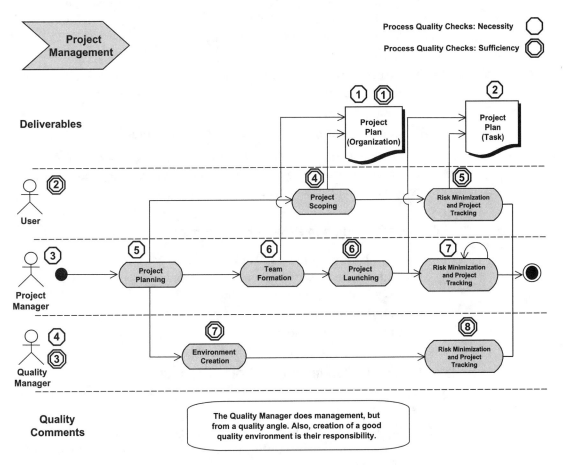

Figure 3.6 *Process-component for project management*

risks and their prioritization. Project management provides feedback on the status of the project to various stakeholders including the user, the steering committee, and the project sponsor.

3.4.7   Roles in Project Management

- The project manager is the primary role in this process-component of project management. This role is responsible for dealing with the activities of planning for the project, forming teams, launching the project, and continuously monitoring the risks.
- The quality manager accompanies the project manager when performing her responsibilities but, at the same time, provides the independent crosscheck on the activities and tasks performed by the project manager.
- The user continues to help the project manager by scoping the project, prioritizing the risks, and helping to minimize them.

3.4.8   Activities and Tasks in Project Management

Figure 3.7 shows the mapping of activities to tasks in the process-component of project management, which helps to create a good quality project plan and the management of the overall project.

3.4.9   Deliverables in Project Management

- Project plan (organizational). The organizational project plan provides the detailed description of the category and type of project, its resources, and its approach to quality.
- Project task plan. The project task plan is a task list with corresponding resources assigned to it.

3.4.10   Quality Comments on Project Management

Necessity

1. The organizational project plan descriptively documents the planning process for the project. It is necessary to cross check its accuracy with the users, the project sponsors, and the steering committee.

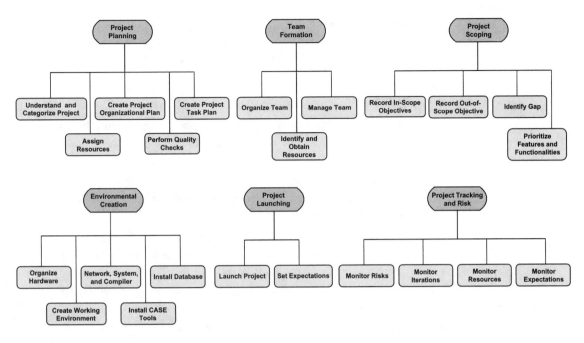

Figure 3.7   *Activities and tasks in project management*

2. The project task plan lists the tasks to be performed in the project and maps them to the corresponding resources. This is a necessary part of the process and requires an inspection to verify its quality.

3. The project manager, as the primary role in this process-component, should be checked for the correctness of the role description and the ability of the person playing this role to fulfill it.

4. The quality manager is necessary for the quality of the overall project. Creating a good quality environment is the responsibility of this role.

5. Project planning is a necessary part of the process-component, resulting in an organizational plan.

6. The activity of team formation should be checked to ensure that it provides all necessary guidelines in identifying team members and their formation into the right team. This is followed by ongoing management of the team.

7. Risk minimization and project tracking is an ongoing activity that is performed, in parallel, by all three major roles in this process-component. The project task plan is updated and fine-tuned with this activity.

Sufficiency

1. The organizational project plan should be updated with the soft issues related to team formation, to satisfy the criteria for sufficiency.

2. The user, another sufficiency criterion, is preferably onboard, as a part of the project team, to ensure the quality of project scope and risk minimization.

3. The quality manager not only performs the activities of environment creation and risk minimization as necessary, but also organizes and performs the quality tasks of inspection, walkthroughs, and reviews (described in the quality process-components), to ensure sufficient checking.

4. Project scoping is performed more than once to satisfy the sufficiency criteria.

5. Risk minimization, a responsibility of the user, will have to be performed to provide sufficient quality for the project.

6. Project launching is a formal activity in a large project, but may not be necessary in small projects.

3.4.11 Process Configuration Process-Component

Figure 3.8 shows the process-component of process configuration, which deals with understanding the process-related needs of the project, putting the process together, and later, enacting it in practice. If an organization is already process based, and the project is provided with a configured process to follow, then there is no need to undertake an extensive process survey. Initiating a process, customizing it, deploying it, and transitioning the people and the current style of working to the process style are critical for quality. Not only does this help to jump-start a situation where people working on the project do not spend or waste a lot of time deciding what to do, it also puts rules, standards, and templates in place that ensure the necessary steps within the process to produce the models in the various modeling spaces. Process configuration is also important in an iterative and

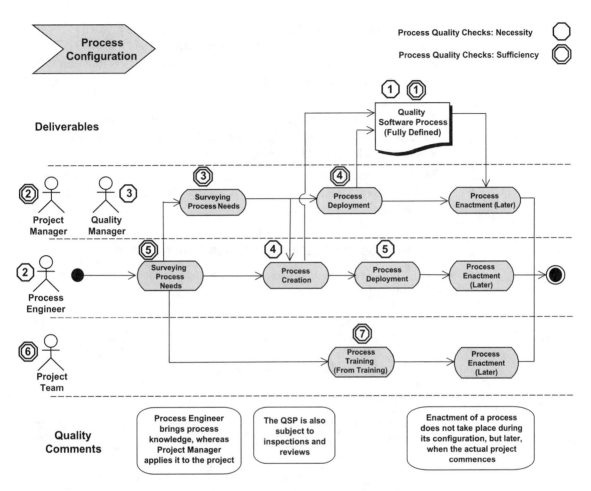

Figure 3.8 *Process-component for process configuration*

implemental process because the need to identify the extent of iterations
and the things that should be included in the increments are all important
to the success of the quality of the project deliverables.

3.4.12 Roles in Process Configuration

- The process engineer is the primary role in this process-component,
  responsible for the important activities of surveying the needs of a
  process within the project and creating a suitable SEP to satisfy it. It is

not necessary for this role to be a permanent role in the project, because once the SEP is created by this role, the project manager is able to enact it. However, large process-conscious projects that need to handle the malleability of the process benefit by having this role on a long-term basis.

- The project manager and the quality manager facilitate the work of the process engineer by providing the necessary needs of the process, and later deploying and enacting the process.

- The project team has to understand and follow the process. They also have to provide feedback for the process, to enable its change and fine-tuning.

3.4.13 Activities and Tasks in Process Configuration

Figure 3.9 describes the activities and tasks of the process-component of process configuration.

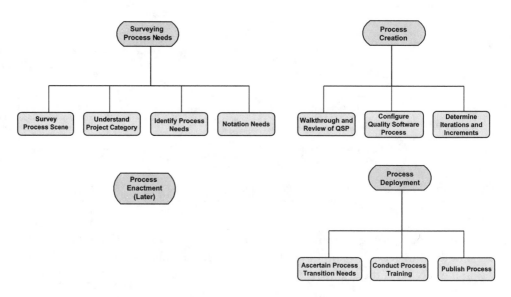

Figure 3.9 *Activities and tasks in process configuration*

3.4.14 Deliverables in Process Configuration

- The Quality Software Process is the repository of all process-components in the process. The QSP is configured to create an instance, which is the SEP to be followed in the project.

3.4.15 Quality Comments on Process Configuration

Necessity

1. The Quality Software Process with definitions of all process-components is the basic necessity of this process-component. The QSP itself is subject to quality checks, ensuring that it covers all areas of development.

2. The process engineer, also called the process consultant (due to the temporary nature of this role), is necessary for the process.

3. The quality manager focuses on the quality aspect of the process and the process aspect of quality—both of which are necessary for a good quality product.

4. Process creation is the activity of putting together a process, based on the process-components defined here.

5. Process deployment is sending the fully configured process out in the project, for use.

Sufficiency

1. The QSP is checked, rechecked, and brought to a level where it is acceptable to all stakeholders in the project, especially the project team.

2. The project manager provides the supporting role to the quality manager in organizing the process and ensuring it is the correct process for the project on hand.

3. Surveying the needs of a process is significant in a large, high-ceremony project.

4. The responsibilities of the process deployment, as handled by the project manager and quality manager, provide the sufficiency criteria to send the process out in the project.

5. Surveying the process needs by the process engineer is also part of a large, high-ceremony project. It is not necessary, in small projects, to undergo the detailed rigors of process surveys.

6. The project team must undergo sufficient training and should have the necessary buy-in, to derive the advantage of process deployment.

7. Process training is sufficient criteria, from the training process-component, to configure and deploy a process.

3.4.16 Requirements Modeling Process-Component

Figure 3.10 shows the requirement modeling process-component that deals with the actual capture, engineering, and analysis of the requirements of the business in the project. This process-component uses the primary mechanisms of use case modeling and activity diagramming to

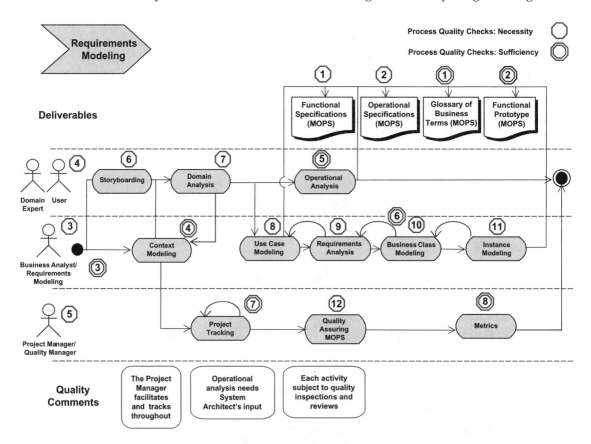

Figure 3.10 *Process-component for requirements modeling*

capture and document the problem that the business is trying to solve. Because quality is such a subjective phenomenon, it is absolutely crucial that those who will ascertain the quality (users and project sponsors) are involved as extensively as possible in this process-component.

The quality techniques of interviews and workshops are very helpful in executing this process-component. In addition to documenting the functional requirements in the problem space, this process component also encourages the user to provide the operational needs of the system. The user of the system or the businessperson who is involved in the project is ideally placed to provide the information on the expected volume, performance, and security needs of the system from an operational or nonfunctional viewpoint. This is all documented as a result of requirements modeling. Prototyping is also used in order to extract further requirements and refine the requirements already captured.

3.4.17 Roles in Requirements Modeling

- The business analyst (also called the requirements modeler for most of this process-component) is the primary role here, and is responsible for understanding and documenting the requirements.

- The domain expert and the user provide the information that the business analyst is trying to document.

- The project manager, together with the quality manager, facilitates the process of requirements modeling. They also monitor and track the progress of the requirements-modeling exercise and report to the steering committee on this crucial process-component.

3.4.18 Activities and Tasks in Requirements Modeling

Figure 3.11 describes the activities and tasks of the process-component of requirements modeling. Refer to the accompanying CD for a tabular form of these activities and tasks to enable you to create your own customized project plan.

3.4.19 Deliverables in Requirements Modeling

Functional specifications containing the use cases and activity diagrams that make up the model of the problem space are the main deliverables coming out of this process-component. Additional UML-based diagrams, namely the class diagrams, sequence diagrams, and state chart diagrams,

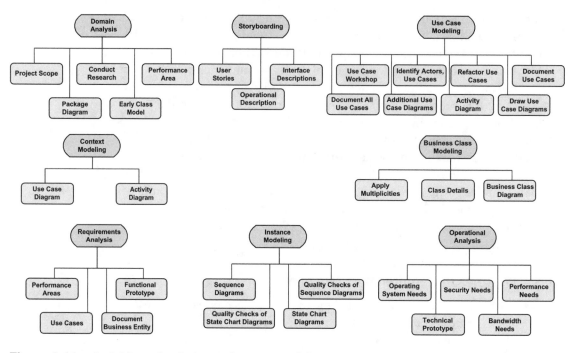

Figure 3.11   *Activities and tasks in requirements modeling*

also form part of the functional specifications. While a part of the model will usually be put in a CASE tool, some specifications (such as the use case documentation or the class responsibilities arrived at using the CRC techniques) may be outside the CASE tool.

Operational specifications document the requirements of the system when it goes out in operation. Therefore, these requirements are stored mostly in a document that describes the stress, volume, and performance requirements. Additionally, these requirements are provided using the deployment diagrams of the UML.

A glossary of business terms helps to record confusing or important terms. For example, terms like cover, policy, and insurance may mean the same thing for most people, but may have interpretation variations for the insurance domain modelers.

Functional prototype, as mentioned in the discussions on prototype, enables the extraction of complete and correct requirements.

3.4.20 Quality Comments on Requirements Modeling

Necessity

1. Functional specifications are a necessary deliverable of the process-component and should be produced iteratively with quality checks being applied to the diagrams inside them.

2. Operational specifications are an equally important and necessary part of this process-component. Without good quality operational specifications, the system may not succeed when it is deployed.

3. The business analyst is a necessary part of this process-component and must be checked for the accurateness of its role description and understanding of that description by the person performing the role. A business analyst is similar to the requirements modeler, except that the latter focuses only on creating the model (as opposed to the BA, who looks at the broader picture).

4. The domain expert and, more importantly, the user, are absolutely necessary in order to create a good requirements model. By participating in the MOPS creation process, they also firm up their own objectives and purposes for the project. This has a valuable quality connotation, as the user is eventually going to judge whether the product has quality or not.

5. The project manager, supported by the quality manager, provides the background organizational support for the process of requirements modeling.

6. Storyboarding is increasingly considered an important technique in discovering the correct and complete requirements with substantial participation from the user.

7. Domain analysis, particularly with the help of the domain expert, provides a much broader view of the requirements—not limiting them to a single project. This is very valuable in a reuse program.

8. Use case modeling, by far the most revolutionary approach to requirements modeling, is primarily performed by the business analyst—with considerable input provided by the user/domain expert. This is a necessary activity and should be performed iteratively to produce a good suite of use cases and use case diagrams, together with the activity diagrams.

9. Requirements analysis is necessary to understand whatever has been documented in the use cases, and to extract correct business entities from that documentation in order to produce business class diagrams.

10. Business class modeling, also occasionally known as business domain modeling or business object modeling, is the creation of class diagrams at the business level, and should be checked as a necessary step in this process-component.

11. Instance modeling is necessary to correctly identify the way in which instances like objects on sequence diagrams or state charts behave. Documenting this behavioral aspect of this process-component is vital for quality MOPS.

12. Quality assurance of the entire MOPS, by conducting extensive inspections and reviews, is a necessary quality check, and should be performed following the quality techniques described in Chapter 6.

Sufficiency

1. The glossary of business terms is very helpful, if produced in a project where the team members are new to the domain.

2. A functional prototype, although not necessary for every project, is sufficient for a good quality requirements modeling exercise.

3. The roles of business analyst and requirements modeler should also undergo process sufficiency checks to ensure that they are properly defined, are staffed in the right numbers, and have sufficient understanding of the uncertainties around this process-component.

4. Context modeling, through the use of case diagrams at an abstract level with a boundary and activity diagrams at an abstract level, can provide the context of the system. Performing this activity satisfies the sufficiency criteria of quality.

5. Operational analysis should be performed with sufficient depth—otherwise, the operational specifications will end up getting produced through the other activities of domain analysis and use case modeling—not an ideal situation.

6. The business class modeling should be iterated sufficiently before a good class model at business level emerges.

7. Project tracking, an ongoing activity, satisfies the sufficiency criteria of a quality process.

8. Measurements and metrics provide the additional benefits of process maturity to a project, if desired.

3.4.21 Interface Modeling and Design Process-Component

The process-component of interface modeling provides guidance for modeling and designing the important interface aspect in a system—the GUI, printing interface, and interfaces to other devices. The GUI and

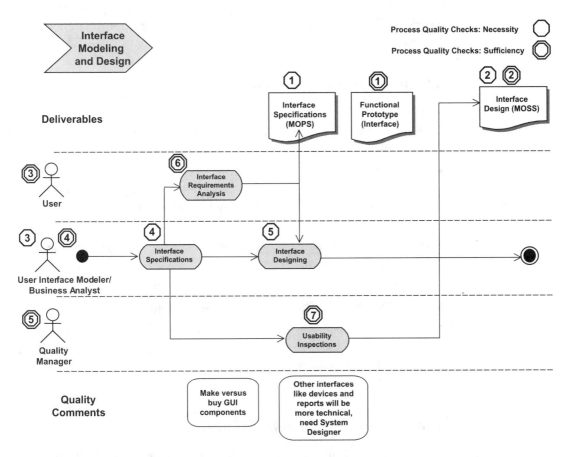

Figure 3.12 *Process-component for interface modeling and design*

printer interfaces are essential, not only for the performance of the system, but also for the way it is perceived by the users. In all e-business applications, this particular process-component takes an even more crucial role. It is not enough to provide just a good-looking interface; it should be designed as a system on its own—with sufficient discussion and modeling on the navigational aspects of the interface. Availability of the interfaces across geographical and time boundaries is vital. Issues of language and notation (as in Chinese, Hindi, or French and corresponding cultural notations) relating to widely dispersed user groups are important in Web interfaces. Furthermore, providing feedback to the user through legible messages, sound, and related mechanisms is vital for a good user interface. Thus, the interface modeling process-component should encompass prototyping, navigation diagrams, site maps, sketching, play acting, and other appropriate techniques to create a quality-conscious interface.

3.4.22 Roles in Interface Modeling

- The user interface (UI) modeler and the business analyst play the primary roles in this process-component; the BA specifies the requirements of the interface and the UI modeler designs it.

- The involvement of the user in interface modeling and design is of interest both to the user and the UI modelers. Quality perception is positively affected by the involvement of the user in this process-component.

- The role of quality manager facilitates the activities and tasks within the process-component.

3.4.23 Activities and Tasks in Interface Modeling

Figure 3.13 describes the activities and tasks of the process-component of interface modeling. Refer to the accompanying CD for a tabular form of these activities and tasks to enable you to create your own customized project plan.

3.4.24 Deliverables in Interface Modeling

- Interface specifications document the requirements of the interface and are mainly driven by the needs and desires of the user.

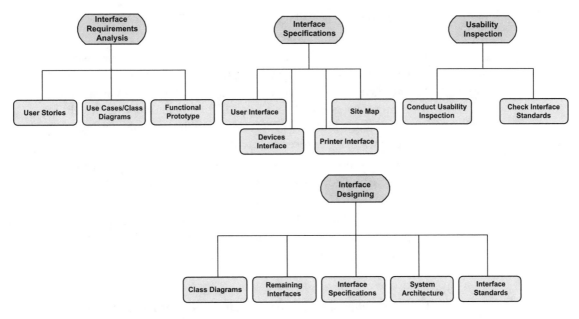

Figure 3.13 *Activities and tasks in interface modeling and design*

- Interface design is a deliverable containing details of the design that implement the GUI. It contains solution-level class diagrams that also include reusable user interface libraries and so forth.
- Functional prototype (interface) optionally adds value to the interface specifications and designs in this process-component.

3.4.25 Quality Comments on Interface Modeling

Necessity

1. Interface specifications are a necessary part of this process-component. The quality of the final interface depends on specifying, in detail, what users want and how they want it. Therefore, this specification document relates to the use case specifications, associated use case diagrams, and activity diagrams.

2. Interface design is a deliverable produced in the solution space. It is the design of the interface and a system on its own. Therefore, it contains all the necessary checks for a good design, including

checking the class diagrams that mainly have their stereotypes as `interface` or `boundary`.

3. The user interface modeler and the business analyst are necessary parts of this process-component and should be checked for their understanding of the requirements from the user's viewpoint. Therefore, a good BA and a good UI modeler work iteratively, by showing the interface progressively to the user and getting their feedback before proceeding with more designs.

4. Interface specifications are necessary before a good design can be produced. They are also checked for their ability to satisfy the requirements described in the use cases.

5. Interface designing is the activity that ensures that the results of the interface specification activity are taken down close to low-level design, wherein they can be easily implemented.

Sufficiency

1. The functional prototype provides additional criteria for quality, as it enables better documentation of the interface.

2. The interface design is also sufficiency criteria. It is possible to jump directly from interface specifications straight to implementation, but it's not advisable. Therefore, the interface design is provided as sufficiency criteria, as well.

3. The user should be sufficiently involved in the interface specifications by analyzing the interface requirements.

4. The business analyst, in particular, provides the quality criteria for sufficiency by providing the link between the modeling done by the UI modeler and relating it to the user.

5. The quality manager is involved in this process-component by providing sufficient support and coordination—especially when usability inspections are formally conducted.

6. Interface requirements analysis provides the background to perform the user stories, the use cases, and the functional prototypes, in order to understand the interface requirements fully before designing them.

7. Usability inspections are along the lines of Constantine's Collaborative Usability Inspections (CUIs) and provide a formal review of interface quality, in the presence of the user and the developers.

3.4.26 System Design Process-Component

The process-component for system design produces the system design deliverable. The system design deliverable has the low-level designs that contain classes and class definitions that deal with the language of implementation and the databases. Solution-level design includes solution-level class modeling and instance modeling.

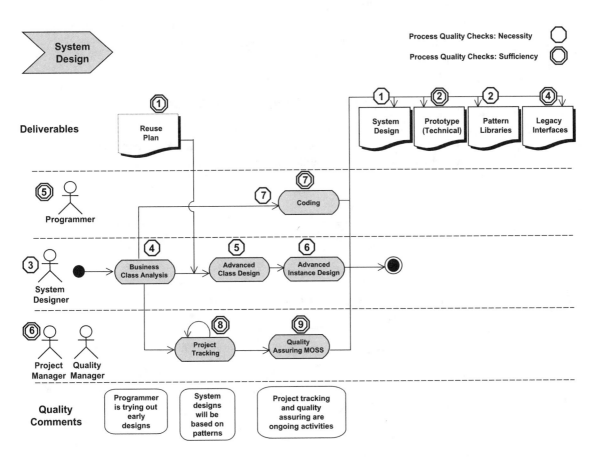

Figure 3.14 *Process-component for system design*

3.4.27 Roles in System Design

- The system designer is the main role in this process-component. The system designer must have enough information about the implementation language and the environment for implementation to perform this role successfully. Quality in this process-component comes not only from the experience of the designer but also from his/her technological knowledge.
- The programmer continues to assist the system designer, checking on the feasibility of the designs by trying them out in code.
- Project manager/quality manager

3.4.28 Activities and Tasks in System Design

Figure 3.15 describes the activities and tasks of the process-component of system design. Refer to the accompanying CD for a tabular form of these activities and tasks to enable you to create your own customized project plan.

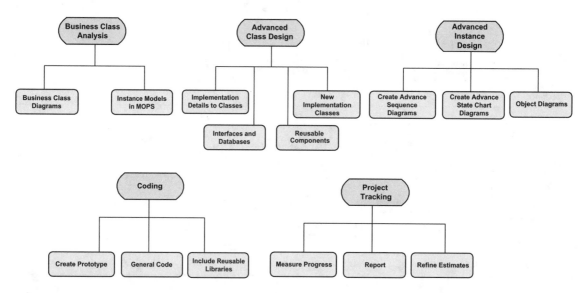

Figure 3.15 *Activities and tasks in system design*

3.4.29 Deliverables in System Design

- The system design contains the details of the technical design that form part of MOSS.
- The prototype (technical) is a code-level prototype that helps when trying out a few code examples.
- The pattern libraries may be directly inserted in the system designs or may be newly created for local project or organizational-level patterns.
- The legacy interfaces (especially in integration projects) are considered at the design level. We think of all the necessary issues of implementation, including legacy interfaces, before a system can be fully implemented.
- The reuse plan (input), if produced, provides the background support for reuse in the designs.

3.4.30 Quality Comments on System Design

Necessity

1. System design is a necessary part of the system design process-component and should undergo the quality checks using the techniques of interviews and reviews in workshop format.

2. Using the pattern library, or at least giving patterns serious consideration, is necessary for good quality.

3. The system designer is the primary owner of this process-component. The role should be well-defined and understood by the person performing it.

4. Business class analysis requires understanding the class diagrams drawn by the BA in the requirements modeling process-component. Therefore, this is a necessary starting point for any work that takes place in the design.

5. Advanced class design, as shown in Chapter 4, is necessary for this process-component. It deals with creating classes that are very close to implementation.

6. Advanced instance design is a necessary step in system design because the sequence and state chart diagrams ensure that the

classes drawn in the class diagrams are complete and correct. This is done by cross checking the sequence and state chart diagrams with the classes in the class diagrams.

7. The coding activity provides the necessary support for creating the prototype and verifying the designs. It may be undertaken quickly by the system designer herself.

Sufficiency

1. Check the availability of a reuse plan and incorporate the suggestions and standards from the plan into the design.

2. Check to determine if the technical prototype is necessary—it should be created to test out the validity of the designs and will satisfy the sufficiency criteria.

3. Pattern libraries should also be sufficiently considered in the system designs.

4. Legacy interfaces, for a legacy integration project, are created to satisfy the sufficiency criteria.

5. The programmer, if available, is sufficient for the quality system designs. If not, the cursory programming work is carried out by a system designer.

6. The project manager/quality manager provides the background support and coordination activities.

7. Coding may be attempted a few times, in creating prototypes, reusing libraries, or simply creating earlier cuts of the code.

8. Project tracking is an ongoing activity, which may be undertaken at the completion of major activities in this process-component.

9. Quality assurance of MOSS will have to be performed a few times, iteratively, to satisfy the sufficiency requirements of the project.

3.4.31 Persistence Design Process-Component

Persistence design, another term to describe database design, is treated as a separate process-component because of its importance—not only in storing standard relational data, but also in storing a variety of content in today's Web applications. The need to interface with existing legacy systems, store and massage audio and video contents, convert data, and pro-

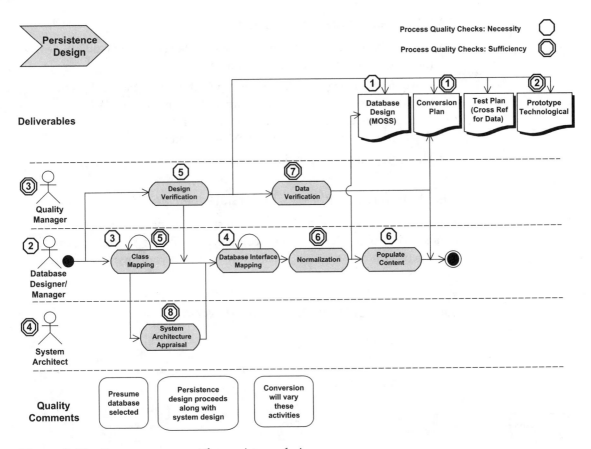

Figure 3.16 *Process-component for persistence design*

vide reuse and multidimensional drilling into the data are some of the reasons database design is important and is treated as a separate process-component.

While using the capabilities of the UML to represent the databases in class diagrams, it is also important to use sequence diagramming techniques in order to document the access to the databases, the security to the databases, and the consistency requirements. Prototyping from an operational viewpoint can also provide valuable information during the database-design phase.

3.4.32 Roles in Persistence Design

- The database designer/manager creates database schemas, strategies for conversions, and population of data.
- The quality manager facilitates the environment for the creation of the databases and ensures the quality of the schemas created. Thoughts are also given to the population of the databases, especially if data is to be converted from an existing system.
- The system architect provides operational input.

3.4.33 Activities and Tasks in Persistence Design

Figure 3.17 describes the activities and tasks of the process-component of persistence design. Refer to the accompanying CD for a tabular form of these activities and tasks to enable you to create your own customized project plan.

3.4.34 Deliverables in Persistence Design

- Database design
- Conversion plan
- Prototype (technical)

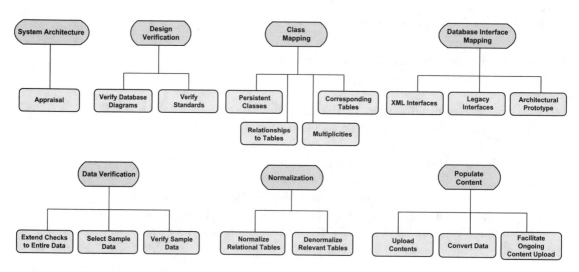

Figure 3.17 *Activities and tasks in persistence design*

3.4.35 Quality Comments on Persistence Design

Necessity

1. Create the database design based on the persistent classes from the MOSS class diagrams.

2. Ensure that the person playing the role of the database designer understands both the UML modeling techniques and the capabilities of the database in implementation. Conversion requires additional skills in understanding the structure of the existing database.

3. Class mappings require mapping the class diagrams in the solution space to the database tables. Relationships between classes in the class diagrams are translated to relationships between database tables using the primary and foreign keys of relational database designs. Multiplicities also provide additional and valuable information.

4. Database interfaces include interfaces to front-end Web interfaces (using, say, the XML), or back-end legacy interfaces. Prototypes are created to investigate these interfaces and produce designs.

5. Design verification is a formal activity, following the review techniques, to ensure the consistency of the new database schema.

Sufficiency

1. A conversion plan is required only when data has to be converted into the new system. Alternatively, for a Web application, contents might be required.

2. Prototypes provide sufficient details in creating a good database design—not only from the structural viewpoint, but also from the population and performance viewpoints.

3. The quality manager provides the organizational support and applies the quality techniques of inspections, reviews, and workshops to the designs.

4. The system architect ensures that the database design is in accordance with the overall system architecture.

5. Class mapping has to be double-checked for sufficient compatibility of the classes and the corresponding relational tables.

6. Normalization may be attempted in practice and will be influenced by the multiplicities in the class diagrams.

7. Data verification follows some of the testing techniques of equivalence partitioning and boundary value (as discussed in Chapter 6).

8. System architecture appraisal ensures that the database design does not transgress the architecture of the system (for example, the bandwidth limitations of the architecture will influence the database design).

3.4.36 Implementation Process-Component

The process-component for implementation deals with coding. While all other process-components deal with understanding the problem in managing the project, this one deals extensively with implementation of the models using the available technology. Thus, the designs created during the system design, database design, and interface modeling are implemented during enactment of this process-component. Implementation deals with understanding both the requirement models and the designs.

Before creating the actual code it is necessary to incorporate the reusable libraries (already done in the system design process-component). This is followed by creating the implementation classes and compiling, linking, building, and testing them. Testing includes the creation of test harnesses within the code itself, as well as conducting unit tests and stepping through the created code. Occasionally, if processes like eXtreme Programming are followed in the project, the results from the implementation effort can be immediately showed to the users with a very short turnaround time.

3.4.37 Roles in Implementation

- The programmer implements the designs iteratively. Many people play this role in a project; they interact with each other in the roles of programmer and, when the need arises, with other roles such as system designer and business analyst.

- The system designer supports the programmer by explaining the designs created in the MOSS.

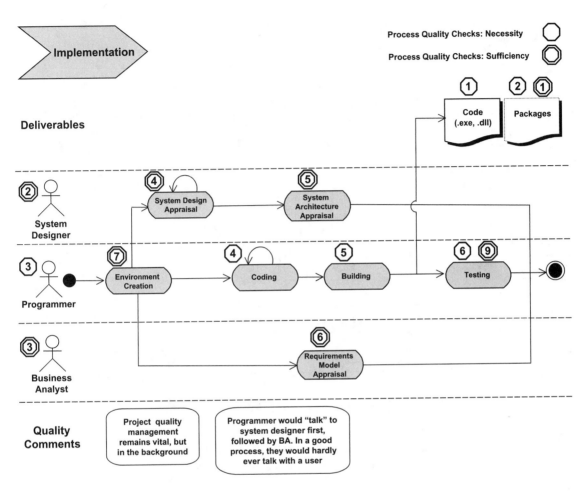

Figure 3.18 *Process-component for implementation*

- The business analyst supports the programmer by ensuring that the requirements are properly understood and met.

3.4.38 Activities and Tasks in Implementation

Figure 3.19 describes the activities and tasks of the process-component of implementation. Refer to the accompanying CD for a tabular form of these activities and tasks to enable you to create your own customized project plan.

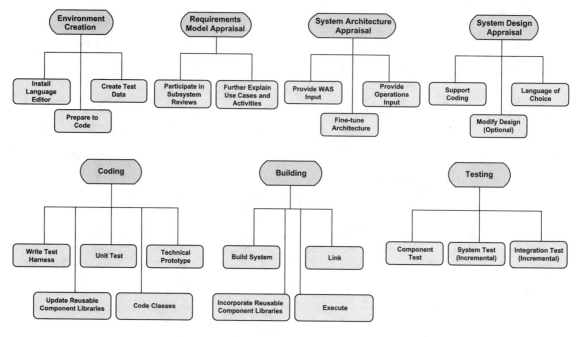

Figure 3.19 *Activities and tasks in implementation*

3.4.39 Deliverables in Implementation

- The code (executable) is the final software deliverable resulting from the modeling effort. This executable may not be a single file; it may be comprised of a number of executables spread over the system architecture.

- Reusable libraries (components and packages). In addition to the final code produced, there should be a provision, in a good process, to produce and store reusable components for future use. This reusable library deliverable enables the creation and storage of reusable code, typically made up of components and packages.

3.4.40 Quality Comments on Implementation

Necessity

1. Executable code, including dynamic libraries, is the primary product of this process-component. While this is produced iteratively, eventually it is the product deployed. In outsourced

projects, this deliverable is produced by an external (outsourcing) organization.

2. The reusable library deliverable is almost an integral part of code production because it can be termed an interim deliverable before the final product is produced. This is because most object-oriented/component-based systems are not built as systems but, rather, as reusable components, which are then assembled to create the product.

3. The programmer is at the core of this process-component. Her profile, job description, skills, and experience should be well coordinated and a match with the project technology. Furthermore, it is vital that the programmer is able to converse with the system designer to determine that the designs are properly understood. In a small project this role may merge with the design role.

4. Coding is the primary activity of this role. It is performed by the programmer in an iterative and incremental manner. This activity requires that the programmer writes classes, tests harnesses, conducts unit tests, and updates the reusable class libraries with the created components.

5. As required by most programming environments, the activity of coding is followed by the detailed activity of building the software. This requires the programmer to integrate the code written with associated libraries in order to make it runnable.

6. Having written the code and built the executable, it is necessary for the resultant module within the product to be tested in detail. This testing ensures that the testing progresses incrementally from component to system to integration tests. Incremental testing implies creating a component and testing it first. This is followed by creating another component (perhaps by another programmer) and testing it. Once the second component is created, it may be necessary to test them together. Once a significant number of components are created, they will have to be integrated with other systems (for example, legacy systems). Thus, the incremental creation and addition of components to the system is what is described in the testing activity.

Sufficiency

1. Reusable class libraries need additional checks in terms of generalization of code. When the classes and components are created, they need to be generalized incrementally. This generalization may happen in the second or third iteration of the current development, or in subsequent projects.

2. The system designer provides the sufficiency of process by supporting the programmer. The necessary aspect of the system designer role is discussed in the system design process-component. Here, he is supporting the programmer, thereby satisfying the sufficiency criteria in the process.

3. The business analyst, similar to the system designer, provides the sufficiency aspect of the process by supporting the programmer in explaining the requirements on a "need to know" basis.

4. The activity of system design appraisal provides information to the programmer on the languages and middleware recommended by the system designer. Optionally, the activity of coding influences the system design as well.

5. Similar to the influence of system design on coding and vice versa, there is influence of the architecture on coding and vice versa. This means the architectural decisions taken in the system architecture process-component provide the boundaries for coding.

6. The requirement model's appraisal may also be necessary, optionally, for the programmer who is trying to understand and keep in mind the use cases at the highest level. Although the activity of coding is driven by class diagrams in the MOSS, the influence of requirements should be considered, wherever relevant.

7. Environment creation, if treated separately, ensures that the development environment is given its due and separate importance. For small projects, however, it may not be necessary to treat this separately, and the activity may be performed by the programmer as a part of coding.

3.4.41 Prototyping Process-Component

The process-component for prototyping combines skills of requirements modeling, system designing, and programming in order to create prototypes; it also benefits the creation of models in the problem, solution, and

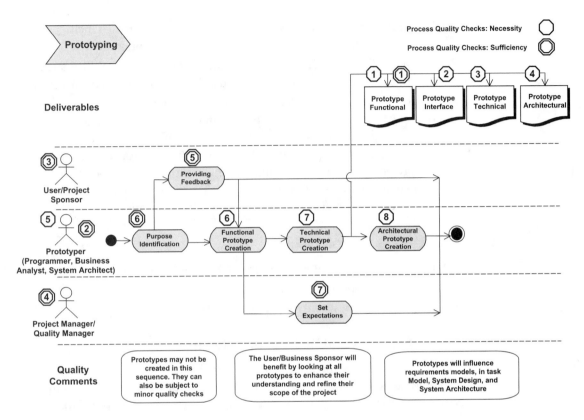

Figure 3.20 *Process-component for prototyping*

background spaces. Since this process-component for prototyping enhances the quality of all other deliverables, prototyping does not stand on its own. I have treated prototyping as a separate process-component because of the need to understand it on its own before using it to improve the quality of deliverables in the other process-components.

While prototypes enhance the overall quality of the system, they themselves should adhere to some quality requirements. For example, prototypes should not give the wrong impression of what can be achieved. This happens most commonly when a highly sophisticated prototype is produced in order to gain project approval; the implementation may not be able to sustain the promises of the prototypes.

In most practical software projects, the process-component for prototyping potentially produces three prototypes:

- The first deals with the functional needs of the users, which includes the needs for the interface, navigation, and overall functionality.
- The second deals with the selected technology and its suitability, such as languages, language compilers, reusable libraries, and databases.
- The third one is the architectural prototype, which deals with issues of security and performance. This architectural prototype also experiments with technologies such as Web application servers, e-services, and mobile services, to consider their appropriateness in the project or the overall organization. Therefore, in addition to the knowledge of the languages and databases, there is also a need to understand the overall environment for implementation.

3.4.42 Roles in Prototyping

- Prototyper (programmer, business analyst, system architect)
- User/project sponsor
- Project manager/quality manager

3.4.43 Activities and Tasks in Prototyping

Figure 3.21 describes the activities and tasks of the process-component of prototyping. Refer to the accompanying CD for a tabular form of these activities and tasks to enable you to create your own customized project plan.

3.4.44 Deliverables in Prototyping

- Prototype (functional)
- Prototype (interface)
- Prototype (technical)
- Prototype (architectural)

3.4.45 Quality Comments on Prototyping

Necessity

1. The functional prototype is a necessary aspect of any process because it helps set and manage expectations of users and business sponsors.
2. The interface prototype is usually a GUI prototype that may be produced along with the functional prototypes. It provides the

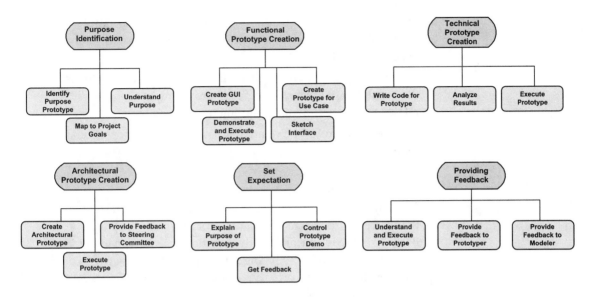

Figure 3.21 *Activities and tasks in prototyping*

"look and feel" of the system and should be attempted after at least some part of the functionality is clear. Otherwise, there is a risk that the functional requirements will be sidestepped for discussions related to the interface.

3. The technical prototype provides information to the system designer and the data modeler on the capabilities of the solution. It is important that this prototype is produced, however briefly, before the actual solution is implemented.

4. The architectural prototype provides information related to the architectural capabilities that already exist in the organization, its limitation, and how the system architecture fits with the overall enterprise architecture. For large projects, information and security architecture have separate influence and, therefore, benefit by creation of a prototype.

5. The role of a prototyper can be played by any of the other roles shown in Figure 3.20, depending on the type of prototype being created.

6. Functional prototype creation provides the necessary input into the requirements modeling exercise. However, this may not be an executable prototype.

7. Technical prototype creation usually has an executable that tests the capability of the technologies in providing the solution; it relates to the operational requirements.

8. Architectural prototype creation also relates to the operational requirements.

Sufficiency

1. The functional prototype needs to be iterated and checked more than once in order to reach a satisfactory level of acceptance. Because of the importance of the functional prototype in the project—especially in reducing misunderstandings between users and developers—this prototype should be carefully created and agreed upon for sufficient quality.

2. Prototyper is not just one person playing one role but, perhaps, more than one person playing multiple roles. While a prototyper is necessary in this process-component, it is the variation to this role that satisfies the sufficiency criteria.

3. The user or project sponsor provides sufficient depth to the prototyping exercise by providing detailed feedback to the prototypers on their requirements, as well as getting a good understanding of their own expectations.

4. The project manager or quality manager also provides the additional support in understanding the user expectations correctly.

5. Providing feedback is an activity that enables the prototypers to understand their own prototypes and iteratively improve them to enable the users to express their needs correctly.

6. Purpose identification helps to focus on the purpose of the prototype. It is only when the question "Why are we creating this prototype?" is answered that the prototyper can be comfortable with his work.

7. While a prototype is created for numerous purposes, setting the expectations of the users is one of the most important aims of prototype creation. This check provides the sufficiency criteria of rightly setting the expectations of the users.

3.4.46 Change Management Process-Component

The process-component for change management supports all the changes that occur in the project. In addition to the sociological aspect of change, this process-component also deals with the critical job of providing support for the configuration and version management needs of the project. Versioning and version release is important in an IIP process. This is where the configuration management part of change management helps to put together the product releases. Therefore, this process-component is closely associated with that of process configuration and

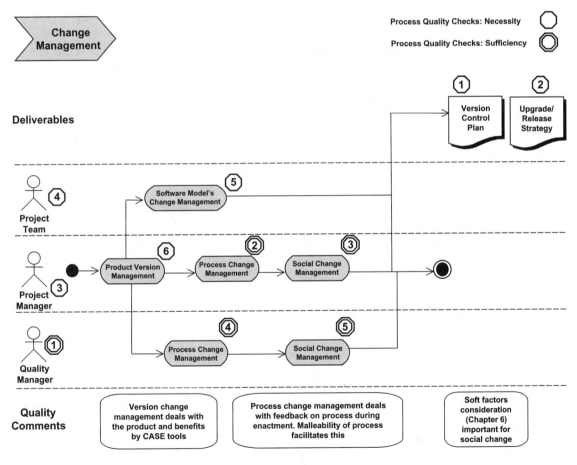

Figure 3.22 *Process-component for change management*

project management. Once an item such as a UML model or a class has reached a stable situation it should be placed under the change management process-component.

3.4.47 Roles in Change Management

- Project team
- Project manager
- Quality manager

3.4.48 Activities and Tasks in Change Management

Figure 3.23 describes the activities and tasks of the process-component of change management. Refer to the accompanying CD for a tabular form of these activities and tasks to enable you to create your own customized project plan.

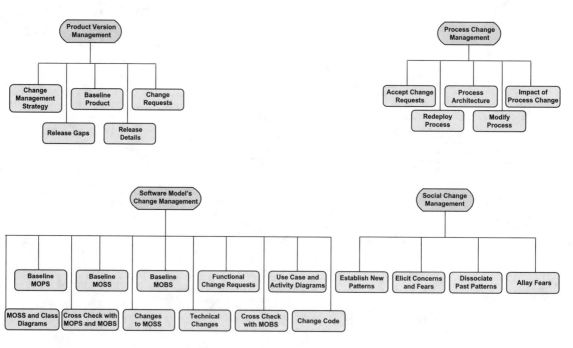

Figure 3.23   *Activities and tasks in configuration management*

3.4.49 Deliverables in Change Management

- Version control plan deals particularly with the software product version control. This is either a separate deliverable or part of the change management plan.

- Upgrade/release strategy is the end result of the effort made in change management. It deals in general with any upgrade to the software, environment, or teams. In particular, though, it deals with upgrades to the software models and products.

3.4.50 Quality Comments on Change Management

Necessity

1. The version control plan deals with the versioning of software releases. This is a necessary part of a good process because this plan decides on the version numbering and deployment of the software product.

2. Upgrade/release strategy is the result of the activities in change management. While mostly it affects a software model or product, this upgrade/release strategy can also be a change in team structure, organizational structure, and so on.

3. The project manager effectuates the change.

4. The project team undergoes the change in most cases.

5. The software model's change management will likely be the most important aspect of change management.

6. Version management ensures that the changes and upgrades brought about in the software are appropriately released in the user community.

Sufficiency

1. The quality manager provides additional support to the project manager in bringing about the changes. In some cases, though, the quality manager herself may bring about the change.

2. Process change management provides sufficiency in terms of process steps when change is brought about.

3. Social change management is usually associated with product change management, although the way in which it is dealt with is different from the product change management approach.

4. Process change management is supported by the quality manager.

5. Social change management is supported by the quality manager.

3.4.51 Enterprise Architecture Process-Component

The enterprise architecture (EA) process-component deals with the overall enterprise modeling and ensures that the system produced as a result of the project under consideration is able to operate with the existing systems of the enterprise. At a project level the activity of creating the enterprise architecture is limited, but ensuring that the system architecture conforms to the EA (resulting potentially in an EA Integration) is high.

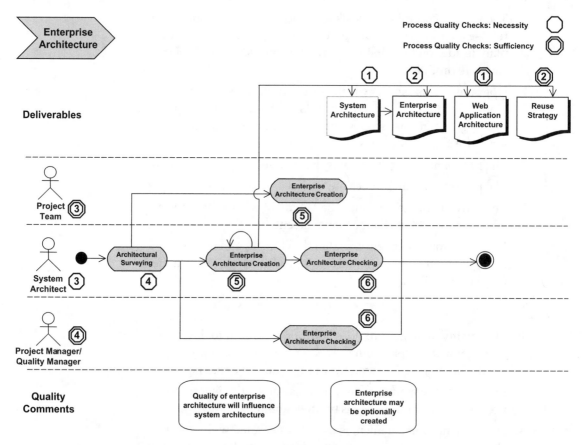

Figure 3.24 *Process-component for enterprise architecture*

3.4.52 Roles in Enterprise Architecture

- System architect provides expertise and experience in producing a good, robust enterprise architecture.

- Project team interacts with the architect to ascertain the mechanism to implement the architecture and highlights the possible limitations of the existing technical environment.

- Project manager/quality manager organizes and manages the creation of the enterprise architecture.

3.4.53 Activities and Tasks in Enterprise Architecture

Figure 3.25 describes the activities and tasks of the process-component of enterprise architecture. Refer to the accompanying CD for a tabular form of these activities and tasks to enable you to create your own customized project plan.

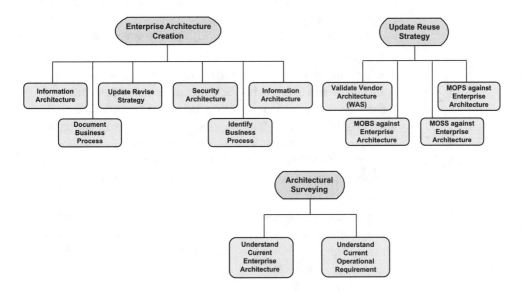

Figure 3.25 *Activities and tasks in enterprise architecture*

3.4.54 Deliverables in Enterprise Architecture

- Enterprise architecture is made up of the actual enterprisewide architecture and the document that outlines that architecture.

- System architecture is produced during the system architecture process-component and embellished here. Alternatively, creation of the initial system architecture may start here, followed by its rigorous upgrade in the system architecture process-component.

3.4.55 Quality Comments on Enterprise Architecture

Necessity

1. A primary necessity check ensures that the system architecture is iteratively cross checked against the enterprise architecture. This results in compliance of the system architecture with the enterprise architecture.

2. In most projects, the opportunity to create enterprise architecture is limited. However, each project influences the overall architecture of the enterprise, and may incite rethinking on the part of the architects in terms of, say, bandwidth requirements or database capacity.

3. The system architect is the primary role in this process-component, in terms of checking the influence of enterprise architecture on the system architecture. When decisions related to the enterprise and all its related systems and architecture are to be made, the role of system architect may be played by a senior technical person well versed in the enterprise architecture. The system architect ensures that the architecture of the system conforms to the enterprise architecture.

4. Architectural surveying deals with understanding the existing enterprise architecture to ensure that the system architecture is created within the bounds of the enterprise architecture. Operational requirements are also considered in surveying the overall architectural needs.

5. It is important to perform the activity of enterprise architecture checking while keeping in mind its potential effect on the project and the quality management aspect of the project.

Sufficiency

1. With the advent of Web-based solutions in almost all modern-day projects, it is important to consider the Web application architecture in overall enterprise architecture. Web architectures have the ability to influence, and many times change, the manner in which solutions are provided.

2. Reuse strategy is important at the enterprise level in terms of its influence on creating architecture versus buying middleware and Web architectures off the shelf. The reuse strategy influences the system architecture as well.

3. Some senior project team members will be involved in the creation of part of the enterprise architecture. Other team members should be aware of the enterprise architecture.

4. The project manager and the quality manager play supporting roles in ensuring that the enterprise architecture is cross checked against the architecture of the system. The project manager is involved, in particular, when there is a conflict between the system, enterprise architecture, and the ramification of this conflict on project cost and time estimates.

5. Creation of enterprise architecture is not a singular activity with a set completion time. Instead, enterprise architecture is created based on a number of projects, with each project improving and adding to the existing architecture. Sometimes, though, when not only the software system is newly built, but also the organization itself is new, there will be an opportunity to create completely new enterprise architecture. While the system architect is primarily responsible for this enterprise creation, the project team also joins in discussing and understanding the architecture.

6. Enterprise architecture is checked for its completeness and consistency by the system architect. The project manager and the quality manager must facilitate this checking and will have to be fully aware of it as the project progresses.

3.4.56 System Architecture Process-Component

System architecture deals with the architectural work in the background that ensures that the requirements and the designs are in accordance with the overall needs and availabilities of the project. The activities and tasks in the system architecture process-component take a "bird's-eye" view of the requirements and design, ensuring the consistency and completeness of the MOBS.

3.4.57 Roles in System Architecture

- System architect
- System designer
- Project manager/quality manager

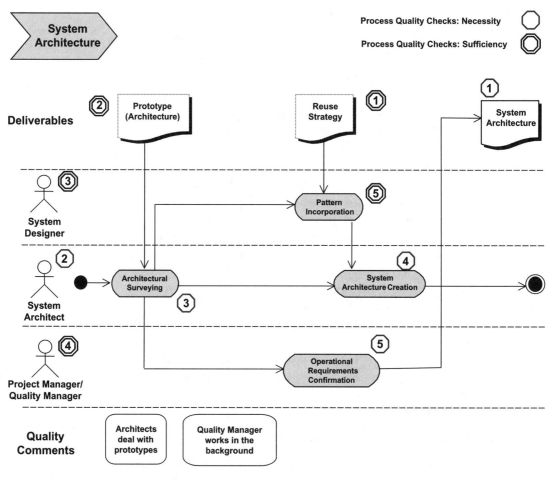

Figure 3.26 *Process-component for system architecture*

3.4.58 Activities and Tasks in System Architecture

Figure 3.27 describes the activities and tasks of the process-component of system architecture. Refer to the accompanying CD for a tabular form of these activities and tasks to enable you to create your own customized project plan.

3.4.59 Deliverables in System Architecture

- System architecture (solution architecture).
- Reuse strategy. As seen in the system architecture process-component diagram, the reuse strategy facilitates the incorporation of reusable architectures and designs in the architecture of the current system.
- Prototype architecture also provides valuable input into the system architecture.

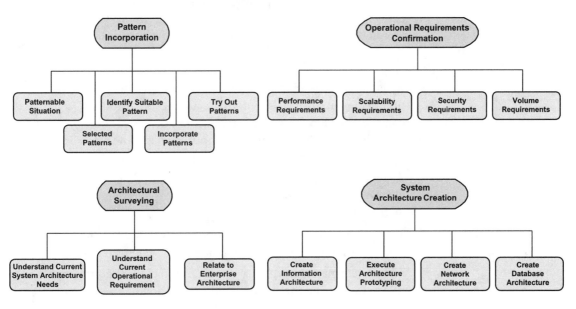

Figure 3.27 *Activities and tasks in system architecture*

3.4.60 Quality Comments on System Architecture

Necessity

1. System architecture is the main deliverable of this process-component. It is either a document outlining the architecture of the system or, especially in large projects, a suite of libraries and patterns on which the actual system is built.

2. The system architect plays the primary role of creating the system architecture.

3. Architectural surveying is an activity that takes stock of the existing enterprise architecture before relating it to the system architecture.

4. The creation of a system architecture deals with information, network, and database architectures, to name but a few. This activity results in the system architecture mentioned in step 1 above.

5. Operational requirements confirmation ensures that all operational requirements are formally incorporated in the system architecture. While other activities in this process-component continue to take input from the operational requirements, this specific activity is intensely focused on ensuring that the system architecture can handle the operational requirements.

Sufficiency

1. Reuse strategy is an iteratively produced deliverable that is updated even during the enterprise architecture process-component. Here, in system architecture, the reuse strategy provides valuable and sufficient input to enable the reuse of patterns and designs.

2. Architectural prototype, created in the prototyping process-component, is used here to help create and verify the system architecture.

3. The system designer plays the supporting role to the system architect in verifying the implementability of the system architecture.

4. The project manager/quality manager also plays the supporting role in facilitating the creation and verification of the system architecture.

5. The pattern incorporation activity provides sufficient depth to the system architectural work by enabling identification, experimentation, and adoption of known patterns. These known patterns are

not restricted to published patterns. They can also include patterns that were discovered and documented in previous projects within the organization.

3.4.61 Deployment Process-Component

See figure 3.28.

3.4.62 Roles in Deployment

- The project manager organizes the deployment and release of the product after taking input from the change management process-component.

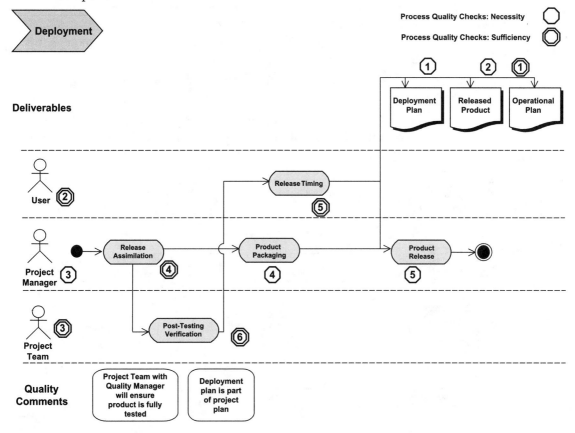

Figure 3.28 *Process-component for deployment*

- The project team participates in deployment and post-deployment reviews.
- The user is involved in ensuring that the deployment of the system is smooth, especially from the sociological angle.

3.4.63 Activities and Tasks in Deployment

Figure 3.29 describes the activities and tasks of the process-component of deployment. Refer to the accompanying CD for a tabular form of these activities and tasks to enable you to create your own customized project plan.

3.4.64 Deliverables in Deployment

- The deployment plan deals with the strategies of sending the product out in the real world. This deployment plan also deals with issues related to switching the business over from one product to another. It may be a part of the overall project plan.
- The released product is the final software product that is released to the users.
- The operational plan provides important information in deployment, as it contains details of the system's requirements when it goes out in operation.

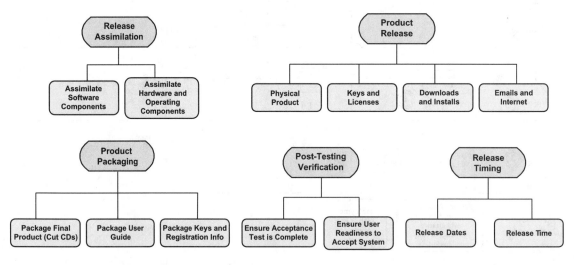

Figure 3.29   *Activities and tasks in deployment*

3.4.65 Quality Comments on Deployment

Necessity

1. It is necessary to ensure that the deployment plan is in accordance with the expectations of the users. This plan must consider the issues of new deployment as well as of switching over, when a replacement product is introduced. It is also necessary to consider supporting materials such as help and user manuals and initial training to support the product being deployed.

2. Check that the released product is in a fully deployable format. This means that not only is the product fully tested in the development environment, but it is also litmus-tested in the production environment before being deployed.

3. The project manager is in a continuous coordination role in this process-component.

4. Product packaging is important in cases where the product is released in physical forms such as CDs and Zip disks. In these cases, packaging of the product, its associated licensing, and so on, is crucial.

5. This is the activity of actually releasing the product to the users.

Sufficiency

1. Check the operational plan for additional information on the system in terms of its operations. For example, backups and mirroring are common requirements of a system in operation and should be specified and adhered to for the system to be of good quality in operation.

2. The user representative facilitates deployment of the system, especially socially, wherein it is made acceptable and promoted within the larger user community.

3. The project team is involved in getting the product ready for release. While there will be very little programming or design-related activities here, the technical aspect of the deployment is still critical and is handled by the project team.

4. Release assimilation becomes important in cases where the product has to be physically sent to the users or when the product is packaged and put on shelves for sale (for example, shrink-wrapped software).

5. Release timing provides for the sufficiency of release by ensuring that the release is properly coordinated. This becomes important when a new module or system is released to replace an existing system that is working on a 24×7 basis (online and available all the time).

6. Post-testing verification ensures that the integration and acceptance testing is complete and that the users are ready to accept the system.

3.4.66 Training Process-Component

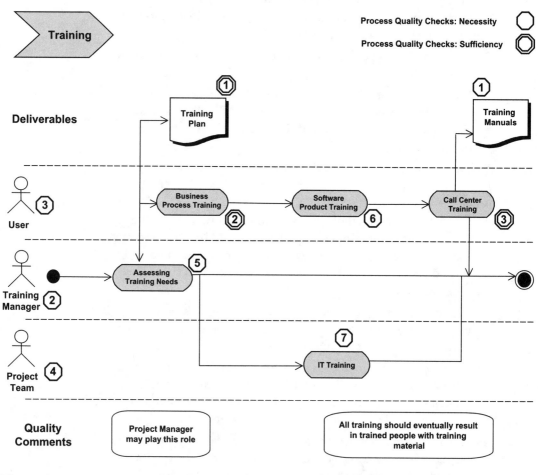

Figure 3.30 *Process-component for training*

3.4.67 Roles in Training

- Training manager, who organizes the training. This role may be played by the project manager or a member of the project team.
- Project team plays a dual role here. Initially, the project team needs technical and other related training. Later, during the deployment of the product, this team is also responsible for creation of a training mechanism for the user. Selected members from the project team can be made responsible for creation of appropriate training packages. User representatives on the project can provide invaluable assistance in creating such training packages.
- Users, who will undergo training and learn to use the system effectively.

3.4.68 Activities and Tasks in Training

Figure 3.31 describes the activities and tasks of the process-component in training. Refer to the accompanying CD for a tabular form of these activities and tasks to enable you to create your own customized project plan.

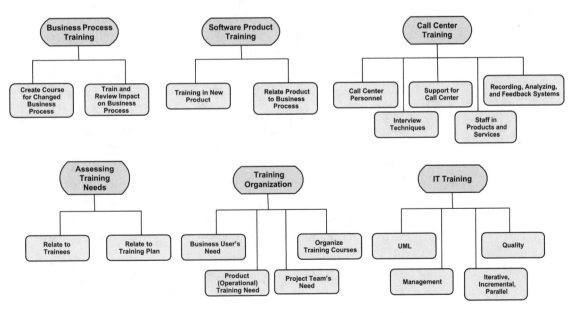

Figure 3.31 *Activities and tasks in training*

3.4.69 Deliverables in Training

- The training plan contains descriptions of what type of training is required, who are the target participants of the training, and most importantly, when the training is conducted.

- The training materials are the handouts or other accompanying materials provided to the participants of a training course. This training material need not be printed paper only, as it is common to have CDs and videos accompanying training courses. These additional tools containing training materials are especially helpful in conducting user training in the software product delivered.

3.4.70 Quality Comments on Training

Necessity

1. The training material is the prime material accompanying a training course. This step ensures that such material is readily available and is provided in a format acceptable to the users.

2. The training manager should be fully aware of the training needs of the organization, the suppliers of the training needs, and the timing of the training. In small projects the project manager may also play this role; large projects will greatly benefit if this responsibility is assigned to a separate individual.

3. Users will have to be trained not only in the use of the new system but also in the altered business procedures as a result of the new system.

4. The project team undergoes training depending on its skill levels and needs. In a large project, it is important to train the team in relevant modeling (UML) and processes early. The project team will also deliver relevant training on their product to the user.

5. Assessing the training needs of all players in the project should be done carefully to ensure that the training relates to the needs of the trainees. It is also important to ensure the support of the management by referring to the training plan.

6. Software product training is undertaken to enable the user to start using the system.

7. IT training is aimed at the project team to equip them with their needs for modeling, process, and technical skills.

Sufficiency
1. The training plan is part of the overall project plan, and describes the training needs of the project. This includes a range of training needs from technical training to be provided to the technical team through end user training on the software product.
2. Business process training ensures that the users are able to carry out the changes in conducting business.
3. Call center training is required if the new system requires the organization to provide that support.

3.4.71 Reuse Process-Component

The process-component for reuse provides the crucial background set of activities and tasks that actively encourage reuse at all levels within the project. This includes not only the well-known code level reuse (through

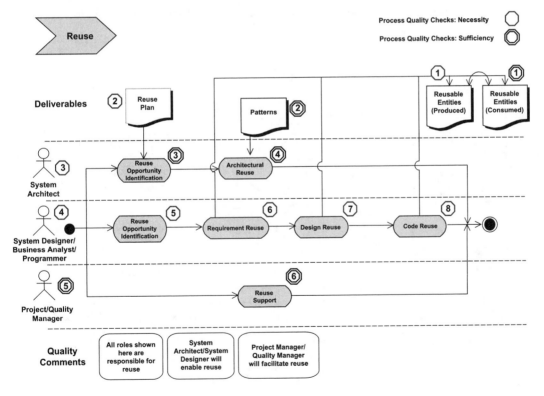

Figure 3.32 *Process-component for reuse*

classes and components in the domain of object technology) but also includes the reuse of requirements, architecture, design, and testing.

3.4.72 Roles in Reuse

- System architect, who knows enough about the overall technical environment to facilitate both creation and consumption of reusable components.
- System designer/business analyst/programmer
- Project manager/quality manager

3.4.73 Activities and Tasks in Reuse

Figure 3.33 describes the activities and tasks of the process-component in reuse. Refer to the accompanying CD for a tabular form of these activities and tasks to enable you to create your own customized project plan.

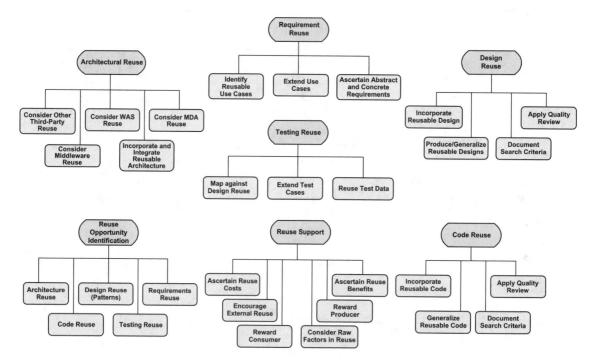

Figure 3.33   *Activities and tasks in reuse*

3.4.74 Deliverables in Reuse

- The reuse plan helps to organize the process-component of reuse within the project.
- Reusable entities (consumed) are models and documentation of reusable components that have been inserted in the architecture and the software design within the current project.
- Reusable entities (produced) are models and documentation of potential reuse components produced by this project for future use.

3.4.75 Quality Comments on Reuse

Necessity

1. Reusable entities are produced by the project.
2. The reuse plan iteratively provides input into enabling reuse opportunity identification.
3. The system architect provides necessary support in terms of enabling reuse strategies by identifying opportunities for reuse and actually reusing the architectural aspects of the system.
4. The system designer, business analyst, and programmer are involved in their respective aspects of reuse.
5. Reuse opportunity identification is an activity carried out by people of relevant roles.
6. Requirement reuse is important and is easily facilitated by the UML's use case-based approach.
7. Design reuse is also facilitated by the object-oriented aspect of the UML and, in particular, design patterns and class diagrams. It is important to note that both production and consumption of reuse is encouraged in design reuse.
8. Code reuse is well known and the first attempt at reuse by the software community.

Sufficiency

1. Reusable entities consumed by the new projects provide for the sufficiency aspect of reuse.
2. Patterns—both published and internally created—are crucial for analysis- and design-level reuse in any project.

3. Reuse opportunity identification is additionally carried out by the system architect.

4. Architectural reuse enables reuse of Web application servers and other middleware-type architectures.

5. The project manager and quality manager facilitate reuse and work on the reward structures supporting reuse.

6. Reuse support deals with the managerial activities of rewarding reuse and also promoting the policy of "reuse rather than build."

3.5   The Quality Process

3.5.1   Quality Management Process-Component

The quality management process-component strives to bring together the social and methodological aspects of the project with a focus on quality. Some of the responsibilities of this process-component are planning for the project while keeping quality in mind, identifying the standards (including the UML standards for modeling), setting the expectations of the users, and, most importantly, getting the right people together for the quality work.

3.5.2   Roles in Quality Management

- Quality manager organizes and manages the quality function including creation of the quality environment.

- User highlights the quality expectations and provides feedback on the product/team's ability to meet those expectations.

- Quality team/quality analysts carry out the quality functions.

3.5.3   Activities and Tasks in Quality Management

Figure 3.35 describes the activities and tasks of the process-component in quality management. Refer to the accompanying CD for a tabular form of these activities and tasks to enable you to create your own customized project plan.

3.5.4   Deliverables in Quality Management

- The quality plan handles the overall approach to quality within the project.

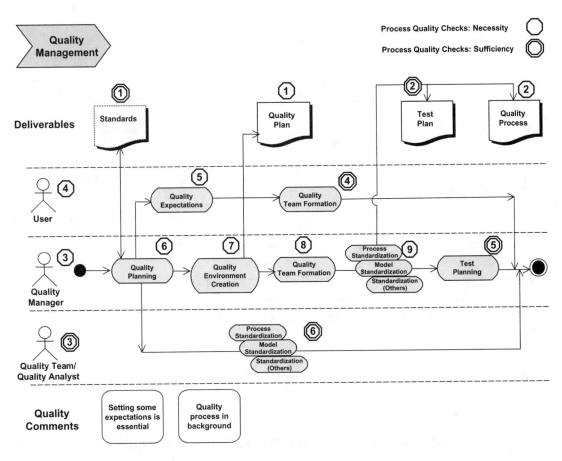

Figure 3.34 *Process-component for quality management*

- The test plan handles the management aspect of testing within the project.
- The Quality Software Process describes the software process that can be customized and followed by the project members.
- The standards (interim/input) exist at all levels within the project, including design, documentation, coding, and testing standards, to name but a few.

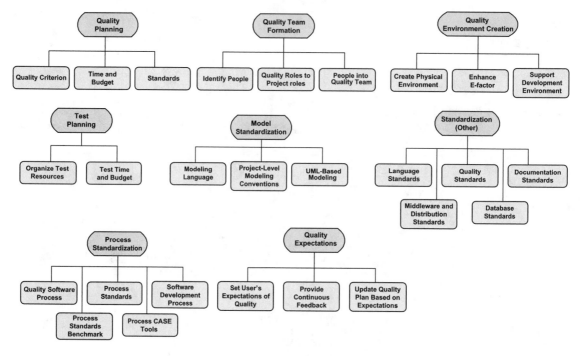

Figure 3.35 *Activities and tasks in quality management*

3.5.5   Quality Comments on Quality Management

Necessity

1. The quality plan includes all documentation related to organizing the quality function. This includes all resources and schedules related to quality management, as well as to the project itself. This can be considered the main controlling deliverable for all quality-related activities in the project.

2. The quality process is part of the overall QSP, but specifically deals with the process-components related to quality.

3. The quality manager is responsible for overall planning, execution, and tracking of the quality functions—supported by the project manager.

4. The user participates in explaining her quality needs and expectations, as well as providing input into quality activities.

5. The quality expectations are created and continuously updated by the user with the quality manager.

6. The quality planning activity undertakes planning and documentation of all quality functions.

7. The quality environment creation deals with the creation of the physical and technical environment for quality activities.

8. The quality team formation includes staffing, organizing, and motivating the people who perform quality roles in the projects.

9. The process/model/other standardizations deal with creation and implementation of all relevant standards within the project.

Sufficiency

1. The standards document provides a reference point for all standards within the project. In addition to the process and model standards, there are standards related to languages and databases, which are referred to in this iteratively produced standards document.

2. The test plan deals with the quality control aspect of testing. It is created here especially from the resourcing point of view.

3. The quality team and quality analyst are responsible for following the standards. At this stage, though, they provide input into the project and the organizational-level standards.

4. The quality team formation is achieved by users who may decide to become part of the quality team, facilitating direct and continuous input in terms of quality expectations.

5. The test planning activity creates and updates the test plan.

6. The process/model/other standardizations are updated and followed by the quality team.

3.5.6 Quality Assurance Process-Component

Quality assurance follows the process-component of quality management and it undertakes the actual effort of assuring the quality of the models and processes in the project. As with most other process-components, the quality assurance process-component is not an independent process-component, but rather is intertwined with the process-components that

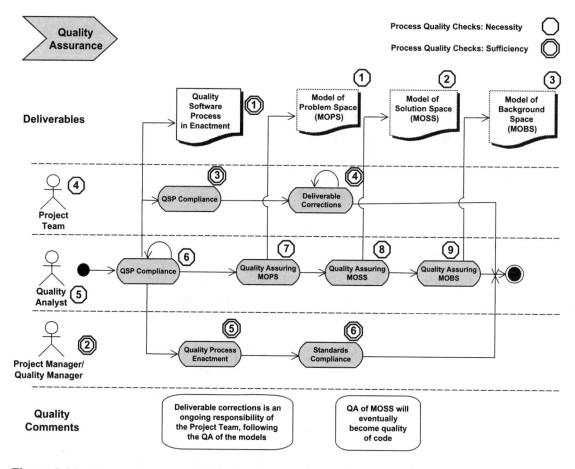

Figure 3.36   *Process-component for quality assurance*

produce the MOPS, MOSS, and MOBS. The project manager and the quality manager play key supporting roles in the execution of this process-component.

3.5.7   Roles in Quality Assurance

- Quality analyst
- Project team
- Project manager/quality manager

3.5.8   Activities and Tasks in Quality Assurance

Figure 3.37 describes the activities and tasks of the process-component in quality assurance. Refer to the accompanying CD for a tabular form of these activities and tasks to enable you to create your own customized project plan.

3.5.9   Deliverables in Quality Assurance

- Quality Software Process in enactment. The QSP provides the basis for enacting the quality aspect of the project. This is made up of the templates, deliverables, activities, and tasks (including the ones mentioned here) that focus on quality.

- MOPS. The Model Of Problem Space is subject to the rigors of quality assurance activities and tasks.

- MOSS. The Model Of Solution Space is subject to the rigors of quality assurance activities and tasks.

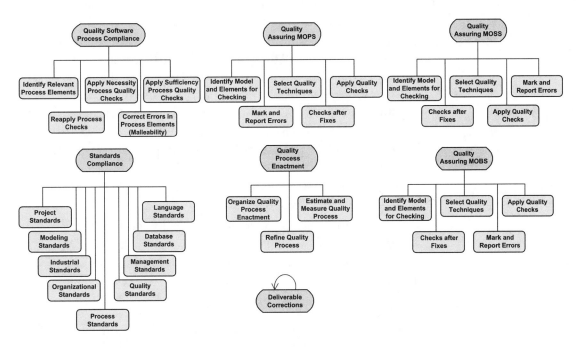

Figure 3.37   *Activities and tasks in quality assurance*

- MOBS. The Model Of Background Space is subject to the rigors of quality assurance activities and tasks.

3.5.10 Quality Comments on Quality Assurance

Necessity

1. The MOPS contains the relevant UML diagrams, descriptions, and specifications that are subjected to the quality checks. It is essential that this model is at a suitable level of completion (ideally at the end of an iteration) before quality checks are applied to it. As a result of the quality activities, the MOPS is updated.

2. The MOSS contains the solution-level UML diagrams. This model is iteratively produced; therefore, its quality checks also iterate with the other two models.

3. The MOBS is also subject to quality checks (a list of suggested quality checks appears in the accompanying CD for all three models including MOBS).

4. The project team plays the supporting role to the quality analyst in his attempts to ensure quality of the models.

5. The quality analyst is the primary role in this process-component. This role ensures that all the quality-related activities and tasks are carried out at the correct time and by the right people. In large practical projects, more than one person plays this role.

6. Quality Software Process compliance ensures the compliance of the process as it is enacted. The necessary, sufficient, and malleable aspects of the process itself are assured here. This activity is carried out by the quality analyst.

7. Quality Assuring MOPS undertakes the quality checks for MOPS as suggested on the accompanying CD.

8. Quality Assuring MOSS undertakes the quality checks for MOSS as suggested on the accompanying CD.

9. Quality Assuring MOBS undertakes the quality checks for MOBS as suggested on the accompanying CD.

Sufficiency

1. The Quality Software Process in enactment is not a document-based deliverable but rather represents the entire QSP in enactment.

2. In addition to the necessary roles played by the quality analyst, project manager, and quality manager, these managerial roles provide the organizational support for the quality effort.

3. Quality Software Process compliance is supported by the project team.

4. Deliverable correction is a reminder activity. It reminds the project team that they will continue to make corrections to the models, executables, and other deliverables in the project.

5. In the quality process enactment, the project manager and the quality manager enact the process configured earlier in the process-configuration process-component.

6. The standards compliance is also organized by the quality manager, but may be enforced by the quality analyst.

3.5.11 Quality Control Process-Component

While the process-component for quality control is mentioned here as a part of the overall quality process, it is discussed in great detail in Chapter 6.

3.5.12 Roles in Quality Control

- Tester
- Modeler/programmer/user
- Quality manager

3.5.13 Activities and Tasks in Quality Control

Figure 3.39 describes the activities and tasks of the process-component in quality control. Refer to the accompanying CD for a tabular form of these activities and tasks to enable you to create your own customized project plan.

3.5.14 Deliverables in Quality Control

- The test plan contains the organizational aspect of testing. This includes details of the people and the schedules of testing, as well as what is expected of the testing process.
- The test design provides a more tactical view of testing. Test designs can be organized around subsystems or packages.

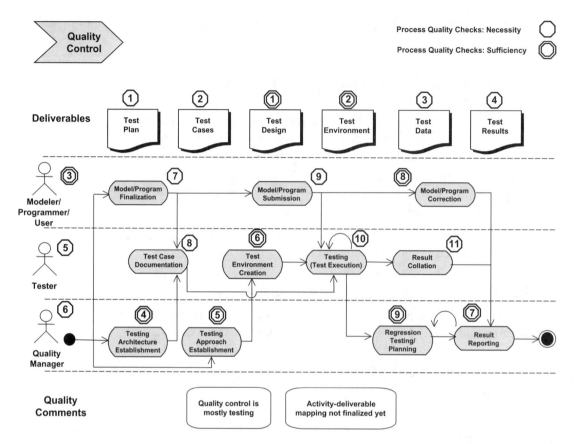

Figure 3.38 *Process-component for quality control*

- The test environment is the physical environment that needs to be created before testing can begin. It is also the software environment (like the test databases and machines) that needs to be created for testing.

- Test cases are the basic units of tests. They can be technical or business test cases. They contain, in addition to the steps to be executed in testing, inputs and expected results.

- Test data is created, based on the sampling mechanisms (discussed in detail in Chapter 6), to ensure correct execution of tests—especially the ones with dependencies on another.

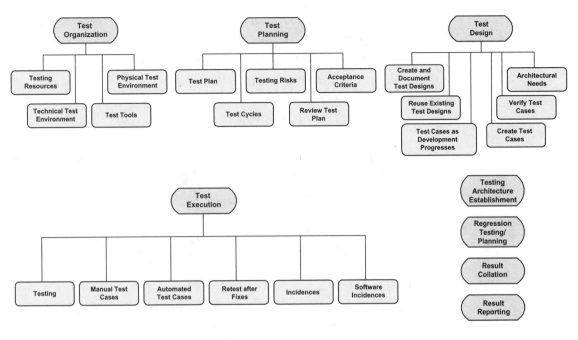

Figure 3.39 *Activities and tasks in quality control*

- Test results are documented, collated, and used for reporting purposes. They can also be used to anticipate areas of the system that need more corrections, or even rewrites.

3.5.15 Quality Comments on Quality Control

Necessity

1. The test plan is necessary for proper testing organization.

2. Test cases are the basic units of tests and have to be created by users, testers, and programmers.

3. Test data is the data on which tests are carried out. This is either the input in a test case or the test database.

4. Test results should be carefully documented and analyzed.

5. The tester is the primary actor in this process-component. The tester is played by more than one person, and depending on

whether it is a technical or business testing, this role is played by a programmer, a business analyst, or a user.

6. The quality manager supports the quality control activities.

7. The model/program finalization is necessary before proper testing commences.

8. The test case documentation must be carried out before testing can proceed.

9. The model/program submission is made to the test manager, who then proceeds with the testing.

10. The test execution is the testing of the model, executable, or whatever artifact is submitted for testing.

11. The result collation is achieved preferably by using a tool to analyze the result, collate, and report.

Sufficiency

1. The test design provides the sufficiency criteria, as good test designs based around the system design ensure that the testing is modular.

2. The test environment focuses on creating a good test environment. It ensures that testing progresses in an orderly manner and takes less time than testing without the proper environment.

3. The modelers, programmer, and user provide all necessary support to the programmer or, at times, play the tester role, as well.

4. Testing the architecture establishment provides the additional impetus to testing by providing a well-organized basis for conducting the tests. This means organizing the databases, software, and operating systems for testing to commence.

5. Testing the approach establishment ensures that all participants in the test teams are aware of the testing approach. This can be, at a high level, a decision to intensely test data, but not functionality, and vice versa.

6. Test environment creation supports the physical creation of the environment.

7. Reporting results is further analysis and reporting of the results from tests carried out.

8. Model/program correction is correcting whatever has been found in error.

9. Regression testing/planning is redoing tests after the corrections have been made by the developers/modelers.

3.6   Bibliographic Notes

The use of process CASE tools is invaluable in deploying a process in a large organization. Check UML CASE Tools for some popular process-based CASE tools.

Most process CASE tools provide their own variation to the process-components as well as the ability to maintain the process. This is done by taking the feedback from the developers and other users of the process, considering the type of the project, and then customizing the process.

Proponents of eXtreme Programming and Agile methodologies may not fully concur with what has been described in this chapter. But this description is scalable and works effectively with a large number of individuals in a project. Combining the nimbleness of Agile methodologies with the process-components described here is my most judicious and favored approach.

3.7   Frequently Asked Questions (FAQs)

Q1: Are there aspects in a process apart from the "what," the "who," and the "how"?

A1: Yes, and they are related to the timing of execution of the process—in other words, the "when." I have described the three parts of a process in order to simplify the understanding of a process. They are not the only aspects in a process. Furthermore, the issues of creating a process environment itself, the corresponding process-based CASE tool, along with the issues of transitioning to a new process, are some important practical considerations to consider. These practical issues are discussed in Chapter 4.

Q2: Is understanding the process metamodel important for process-based work in a project?

A2: The metamodel I have described in Figure 3.2 is only to create a theoretical understanding of how process-components are put together. You can work a process without worrying about the logic behind the metamodel. However, if your role in a project is that of a process engineer, then this understanding of a process metamodel is invaluable in your work of creating a SEP and adopting it. The same applies to the role of a process CASE tool developer.

Q3: How do I apply the process-components?

A3: You don't apply the process-components as they are described in this chapter. Rather, you create a project task plan based on the requirements of your particular project, its size and type, and how you want to iterate within the project by taking help and guidance from the process-components. This is also described in Chapter 4.

Q4: How do the process-components described here relate to the Agile methodologies like eXtreme Programming and Crystal?

A4: Agile methodologies eschew the formal descriptions and possible bureaucracy of complete process. However, in practice, I find it highly advisable to combine the process-components described in this chapter with the principles of Agility.

3.8   Exercises

E3.1: How does a software process differ from a quality process? Describe how together the software process and the quality process form a good QSP.

E3.2: Which process-components would you use in creating the MOPS?

E3.3: Describe the relevance of prototyping process-components in MOSS.

E3.4: Describe why the project management process-component applies to all modeling spaces.

E3.5: Name two important deliverables produced by the business analyst.

E3.6: Name two important deliverables produced by the test manager.

E3.7: Name all the tasks involved in the activity of use case modeling.

E3.8: Name all the tasks involved in the activity of business class modeling.

E3.9: To which activity does the task of "create state chart diagrams" belong? Why, according to you, is the activity named as such?

E3.10: In which process-component is the system actually produced?

E3.11: How does the reuse process-component apply to other process-components where reuse takes place?

E3.12: Where is the incremental and iterative aspect of a process handled?

E3.13: Describe the responsibilities of a training manager.

E3.14: In which types of projects would you not envisage a steering committee?

3.9   References

Jacobson, I., et al. *Object-Oriented Software Engineering: A Use Case Driven Approach,* Reading, Mass.: Addison-Wesley, 1992.

chapter

Enacting the Quality
Software Process

All projects are behind schedule—it's just a question of when you discover that fact and
how the project team will respond to the discovery. So you might as well plan for it: Create
an extreme artificial crisis in the early days of the project and observe what happens.
—Ed Yourdon [1998]

Putting This Chapter in Perspective

In this chapter we discuss the enactment of an example process whose
architecture was discussed in Chapter 3. We explore the practical issues
of configuring an Iterative, Incremental, and Parallel project plan based on
the process-components discussed in the previous chapter. We also discuss the practical issues of tracking the progress of a project and modifying the project plan based on that tracking. An IIP project plan facilitates
better absorption of changes than a sequential project plan. Creation and
management of such a changing plan, derived from the malleability
aspect of the process, is also discussed here.

Furthermore, when the sufficiency aspect of process checks was discussed in the previous chapter, it also implied sufficiency of depth—how
intense or deep a particular activity should be. That depth of checks is a
practical issue of application of the process-component. These are the
issues that relate to the usage of a process in practical projects and are
called the *enactment* of a process. This chapter discusses what happens
when the "rubber hits the road" in terms of application of a process.

Chapter 3 dealt with the concepts of a process through its building
blocks called process-components. Creating the process-components is the

job of a process-thinker, as shown in Figure 4.1. This thinking, however, must further evolve in order to make the processes applicable in practice. This requires the process engineer, with support from the project manager, to bring together the process-components in a suitable Software Engineering Process (SEP). The SEP has to be stepped through together with the application of the quality-assurance principles in practice. This is ensured by applying the quality criteria of necessary activities and steps that are also sufficiently iterated in practice. Thus, the evolution of process-components in practice must consider three major areas (also shown in Figure 4.1):

- Configuration of a process. This means putting together a practical project task list based on the iterative and incremental lifecycle. The process-components described in the previous chapter are put together in a project plan, the activities and tasks repeated sufficiently, and resources assigned to roles.

- Adoption (or deployment) of a process. This involves sending the process out in the field. We need to know the current state of process discipline within the organization, the readiness of the project team to accept a new process, the training associated with the process, and the type of project best suited for the first deployment—all this leads

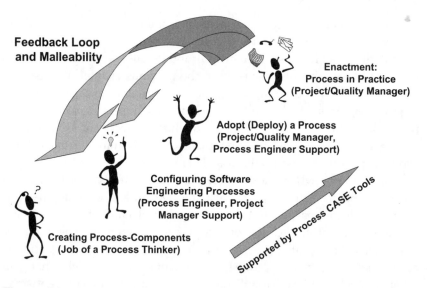

Figure 4.1   *Process in practice: From process-components to enactment and feedback*

to the process being configured and readily available for use as the project kicks off.

- Enactment of a process. This is the actual *usage* of the process. As project teams start stepping through the activities and tasks, they perform quality checks on UML diagrams, followed by checks of the process steps themselves. This leads to fine-tuning of the process steps.

This chapter focuses on the practical application of a quality process *as the project progresses.* During enactment, a good process enables the provision for feedback. This feedback, as the enactment proceeds, fine-tunes the process itself—this is the malleability of a process, shown as a feedback loop in Figure 4.1.

The Prime Reader: Project Manager, Quality Manager

4.1   Configuration of a Process

The process-components in the previous chapter provided the process building blocks. While these building blocks provide the necessary theoretical background for a process, they cannot be used directly in practice. The process-components must be combined or configured into a real Software Engineering Process before they can be used by a project manager. Configuring the process achieves the job of creating an executable process from the given process-components. This work is done by the process engineer together with the project manager and the quality manager. The activities and tasks related to this configuration of a process are also process based, and are described in the previous chapter under the process configuration process-component. Activities of process deployment and process enactment are also described in Chapter 3 as part of the dual responsibilities of a process engineer and the project managers.

Figure 4.2 [Henderson-Sellers and Unhelkar 2000] shows how a SEP is created from the process architecture. On the left side of the figure are the four major process elements (activities, tasks, roles, and deliverables). These process elements are described as cohesive components of a process in the previous chapters. These process elements, based on their process-components, are brought together in a complete process, or SEP.

Occasionally, techniques for performing tasks (or the guidelines that might be provided with a task) are shown separately. This is because in a high-ceremony process, external guidelines and techniques may deserve a

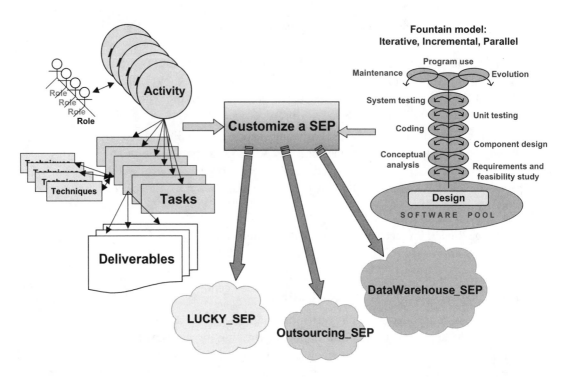

Figure 4.2   *Configuring Software Engineering Processes*

separate discussion. Alternatively, the techniques are part of the tasks to be performed.

The right side of Figure 4.2 shows the fountain model that represents the iterative and incremental nature of the process (discussed later in this chapter). The job of a process engineer, together with the project and quality manager, is to bring the process elements and the iterative and incremental lifecycle together to configure a practical process. Such practical processes may be preconfigured for direct usage, or they may be created on a project-by-project basis. Examples of creating SEPs are shown in Figure 4.2 (for a problem statement on the Lucky Insurance case study, please see the accompanying CD). A LUCKY_SEP is created for Lucky Insurance's CRMS implementation. Other examples shown are the creation of a SEP for data warehouse implementation and one for an outsourced project.

The sample SEPs shown in Figure 4.2 are also made readily available by process tool vendors. In that case, they are called "off-the-shelf" processes. The architecture of these processes is prefabricated, making them available for use in practical projects. The current IT scene has a few off-the-shelf Software Engineering Processes that claim to provide the necessary support for object-oriented development that is iterative and incremental. They also claim to facilitate UML-based development. They include Rational's Unified Process (RUP), which is based on Jacobson et al.'s work [1999], also succinctly described by Kruchten [1999]. The *OPEN* Consortium has also put together a rigorous process [Graham et al. 1997] whose practical application is shown by Henderson-Sellers and Unhelkar [2000]. Other commercial processes include *ICONIX* and *MeNtOR*.[1] The lightweight programmer-centric process called *eXtreme Programming* [Beck 2000] also deserves attention in any process talk, as it tries to kowtow to programming as the core activity of a project team.

In fact, numerous methodological approaches centered on programming and considered "light" by the methodology purists are now under the umbrella of "Agile" methodologies [Fowler and Highsmith 2002]. Despite differing weightings accorded by processes to programming and modeling, they all recognize the need to create some form of models before coding. Processes recognize what Barry Boehm [1981] noted two decades ago:

> Only about five percent of the difficulty in software development lies in the code itself, with much more of the difficulty in specification and design.

These ready-made processes have their own strengths and weaknesses, which should be carefully considered by the process engineer, together with the project manager and the quality manager, before a process is procured and adopted. For example, some processes, like MeNtOR, are strong in the areas of requirements modeling, providing benefits in package-implementation projects that have relatively limited lower-level design activities. Rational's RUP, on the other hand, is tightly integrated with its UML CASE tool ROSE, providing the advantage of seamlessness between the deliverables produced by a process and the UML diagrams.

The type of project plays an important role when deciding which commercial off-the-shelf process should be procured. For example, a data

---

[1] MeNtOR is available on *www.processmentor.com* as well as on the owner company's home site on *www.oopl.com.au*. Currently, MeNtOR remains a pure practical process (as opposed to theoretical research and/or support of a published book).

warehousing project requires a process that focuses on multidimensional drilling of data and data conversion; not all ready-made SEPs can satisfy these special requirements.

Once the SEPs are created, they are able to outline the path to be followed during the enactment of the process. With UML-based projects in particular, the SEP, based on the activities and tasks belonging to the process-components, can guide the sequence of creating the UML-based diagrams. Creation of UML diagrams needs to follow certain steps. The UML standard itself, and eventually the quality checks of these diagrams and their models (available in the accompanying CD), do not discuss the sequence of creating these diagrams. A SEP provides that missing guidance in practice.

The project team has a number of choices when deciding the sequence of creating UML diagrams. For example, it is possible to start the process of software development with use case diagrams, which are then followed by the sequence and class diagrams, usually resulting in a GUI. This is shown

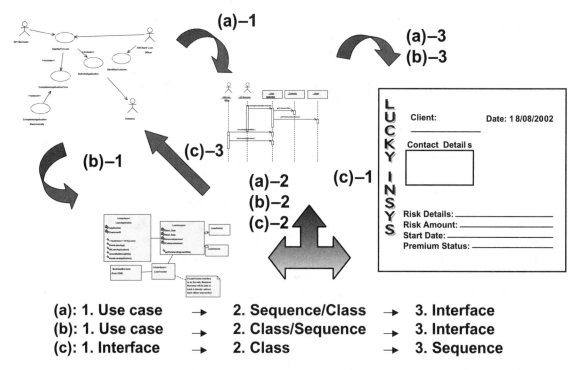

Figure 4.3 *Practical options in configuring a Software Engineering Process (based on Henderson-Sellers and Unhelkar [2000])*

as option (a) on Figure 4.3. Options (b) and (c) show different combinations and sequences of UML-based diagrams. On their own, these options are not good or bad—it all depends on which type of project will apply these SEPs.

In addition to putting together a full process based on the process-components, a SEP must consider the important aspect of the software development lifecycle (SDLC) on which it is based. We discuss these SDLCs briefly, before proceeding with configuring the process.

4.1.1   The Waterfall-Based SDLC

A waterfall lifecycle represents a linear phased approach to software development [Sommerville 1989]. A process based on this approach produces deliverables such as the analysis model, designs, code, and tests, which are sequentially dependent on the previous deliverable. For example, design, in such an approach, does not proceed until the analysis model is signed off, and coding proceeds only after the design is signed off. And just as a waterfall travels in one direction only (from top to bottom), similarly, software development proceeds in one direction with no opportunity of going back to correct or improve on the work done in the earlier phase.

Although the waterfall lifecycle itself does not prescribe ordering of the UML diagrams, any software-development process based on the waterfall approach can still be used in UML-based projects. For example, a process based on such a sequential approach and using the UML would perhaps recommend the creation of all use cases up front, followed by all the activity diagrams, and then the class diagrams and so on. Drawing of the class diagrams, in a waterfall lifecycle, does not proceed until all the use cases have been signed off. Such a process supports the production of one deliverable at a time, and is not able to facilitate user feedback and changes to the completed deliverables.

The quality-assurance activities in a waterfall lifecycle follow the production of the deliverables, and therefore focus heavily on quality control. The risks to quality are not so much the correctness of the deliverables produced at the end of each phase, but the appropriateness to the purpose for which the users want the system.

4.1.2   The Spiral-Based SDLC

Barry Boehm's view of software development was that it proceeds in ever-expanding spirals [1986]. He divided the software scene into four quadrants, namely:

- Determine objectives, alternatives, and constraints
- Evaluate alternatives; identify and resolve risks
- Develop and verify
- Plan next phase

Software development starts with activities in one quadrant, and follows in a spiral fashion, passing through other quadrants in expanding spirals. UML-based projects that follow this model produce deliverables at the end of each quadrant of activities. These quadrants within the spiral model provide the basis for repetition. However, the approach focuses more on how systems are implemented rather than providing a full iterative support in dealing with the needs of the users. Therefore, the quality risks, although mitigated compared with the waterfall approach, still exist.

4.1.3   The Fountain-Based SDLC

If water-based models are indeed considered appropriate to depict the software development lifecycle, then none come closer to showing it more faithfully than the fountain model [Henderson-Sellers and Edwards 1993]. Just as a water fountain rises to a height and then comes down again, similarly software development proceeds in an iterative fashion—reaching a certain height in terms of requirements, design, implementation, and testing, and then falling back into the development pool.

A software process based on the fountain model provides feedback to the users and, in fact, to all other players in the project throughout the development and across all deliverables. Such a software process incorporates the concepts of iterations and increments. Development in such an iterative and incremental process, even if following the phases, does not aim to produce a complete deliverable in one hit. Project managers accustomed to sign-offs at the end of each software phase have to readjust their views on sign-offs when they start following the iterative and incremental approach to software development.

Processes based on the fountain model mitigate the risks by ensuring that the development in the solution space is in accordance with the needs expressed in the problem space. Furthermore, the initial work in the solution space is used to influence the thinking in the problem space. This is made possible by demonstrating a small part of the solution to the modelers and the users in the problem space (by either actually developing that small solution, or by creating a prototype, or both) and receiving their feedback.

4.2 The Iterative, Incremental, and Parallel Development Process

4.2.1 Need for Iterations and Increments

A sample development process can be configured to start with the first process-component of business evaluation and end with the last one—deployment. However, a good iterative software process does not perform the process-components in a sequential fashion. Instead, the activities and tasks within the process-components are performed in a collaborative fashion, with the relevant activities, tasks, and deliverables feeding off each other. As discussed in the earlier section on fountain models, these iterations provide a feedback mechanism to the user and modelers in the problem space, enabling them to provide a complete and consistent model of what the system should do.

Figure 4.4 shows the iterations on our example Lucky Insurance system's development process. Consider the development of the Client package. It is developed in three iterations, and each of these iterations derives its activities and tasks from the process-components described in Chapter 3. Figure 4.4 further suggests that an increment can be the complete delivery of one cohesive functionality of the system. Each additional slice of the functionality of the system provides the basis for a full increment of the system, resulting in an executable deliverable of direct benefit to the business users.

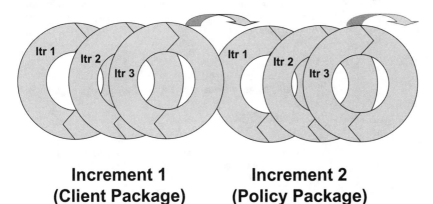

Increment 1 (Client Package)   Increment 2 (Policy Package)

Figure 4.4 *Iterations and increments*

Typically, each increment also has a release number, and is placed under change-control mechanisms within the project. The iterations and the increments, in practice, tend to merge with each other, and are not as clearly separated as shown in Figure 4.4 (although, even in that illustration, we see how the first iteration of the next increment almost merges with the third or last iteration of the previous increment).

As shown in Figure 4.4, there are usually three iterations in delivering an increment, although more are possible. These iterations can be called the initial, major, and final iterations. A small project may encompass all iterations in one, and may be delivered in one go rather than incrementally. A large project based on the waterfall lifecycle also does not have the increments and iterations—all activities and tasks are completed in one attempt. However, for large and complex development following a high ceremony process, all three iterations are formally needed.

Furthermore, the process-component that deals with the creation of iterations and increments within a SEP is itself kept outside the iterations.

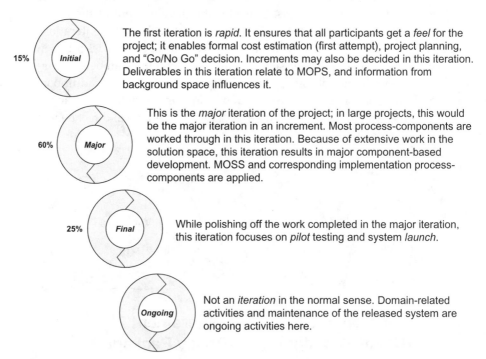

15% **Initial** — The first iteration is *rapid*. It ensures that all participants get a *feel* for the project; it enables formal cost estimation (first attempt), project planning, and "Go/No Go" decision. Increments may also be decided in this iteration. Deliverables in this iteration relate to MOPS, and information from background space influences it.

60% **Major** — This is the *major* iteration of the project; in large projects, this would be the major iteration in an increment. Most process-components are worked through in this iteration. Because of extensive work in the solution space, this iteration results in major component-based development. MOSS and corresponding implementation process-components are applied.

25% **Final** — While polishing off the work completed in the major iteration, this iteration focuses on *pilot* testing and system *launch*.

Ongoing — Not an *iteration* in the normal sense. Domain-related activities and maintenance of the released system are ongoing activities here.

Figure 4.5 *Time and effort per iteration in an IIP process*

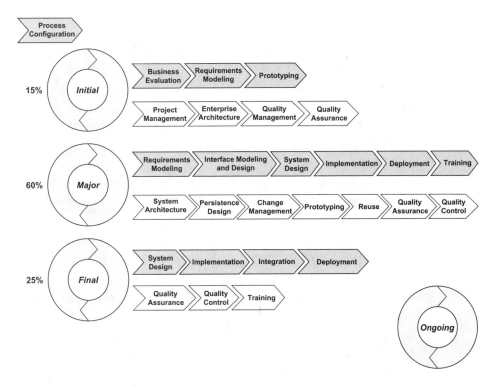

Figure 4.6   *Adopting process-components in process iterations*

This is shown in Figure 4.6, where the process configuration process-component happens before the formal project iterations begin. This figure shows the distribution of the process-components over one major increment. The distribution still holds true beyond one increment. Let us consider in greater detail the three iterations in terms of time and effort spent, and deliverables produced.

4.2.2   Initial

The initial iteration usually involves 15 percent of the overall effort (time and budget) of the project. During the initial iteration, the following should be reasonably achieved:

- A complete evaluation of the business goals of the project
- A final "Go/No Go" decision by the steering committee on the project
- Full understanding of the scope of the project and the creation of project teams with necessary skills

- Adoption of a process (either preconfigured, off the shelf, or config-ured in the context of the project)
- Fine-tuning of the process (depends on the malleability of the process)
- Creation of context diagrams, use case diagrams, and activity dia-grams to describe the requirements of the system
- Creation of early business class diagrams, state chart diagrams, and sequence diagrams
- Creation of prototypes to understand the requirements—prototypes may be extended to provide basic GUIs that are used to test some implemented classes
- Optional implementation of a class or two, to ensure the entire devel-opment cycle is covered once
- Documenting complete operational requirements
- Considering operational requirements in the context of the enterprise architecture
- Completing the organization of the quality management infrastruc-ture and applying quality-assurance principles and techniques

The activities and tasks that that are performed with high intensity in this iteration belong to the process-components shown in Figure 4.6:

- Business evaluation
- Requirements modeling
- Prototyping

The process-components that are performed in the background are:

- Project management
- Enterprise architecture
- Quality management
- Quality assurance

4.2.3 Major

The major iteration comprises completion of three-quarters of the project, or 75 percent (including the 15 percent in initial iteration) of the overall effort needed for the project. A frequently asked question at this point in the discussion is, "How does one know the percentage completed, without knowing what the actual length of the project is going to be?" It is true that the project manager will not be able to state up front that she has completed

50 percent or 75 percent of the work allocated to the project. However, based on the experiences of past projects, it can be stated that 75 percent of work gets completed at the end of major iteration. A detailed discussion on this estimation aspect of the process follows in Chapter 5.

At the end of the major iteration, the following should be reasonably achieved:

- Completion of MOPS, with all its business class diagrams and associated UML diagrams
- Completion of most of the design-level classes
- Implementation of the system, with all classes completely designed
- Design of most of the interfaces
- Creation of system architecture
- Application of reusability at analysis, design, and code level
- First attempts to deploy part of the system (this not only makes a functional piece of software available to the user, but also tests out the process of deploying the system when it is fully developed— reducing the risks of last-minute surprises during deployment)
- Start organizing the releases of the system
- Mapping classes to database design
- Population of test beds

The process-components that are performed with high intensity in this iteration (as shown in Figure 4.6) are:

- Requirements modeling
- Interface modeling and design
- System design
- Implementation
- Deployment
- Training

Process-components in the background:

- System architecture
- Persistence design
- Change management
- Prototyping
- Reuse

- Quality assurance
- Quality control

4.2.4   Final

During the final iteration in a development process, all of the remaining activities are completed. This implies that all necessary elements of a process-component have been completed and have been sufficiently covered to provide a robust system (or increment of a system). The following should be reasonably achieved at the end of the final iteration:

- All three modeling spaces will have been completed modeled.
- All models will have been subject to quality checks.
- All classes will be completed designed, implemented, and tested.
- Packages have been integrated and users have tested them.
- The system has been released in planned increments to the users.
- User training on the product has begun.
- Help desk or other relevant support has been organized.
- Data conversion (if relevant and complete) and database are populated with relevant data for business usage.

The process-components that are performed with high intensity in this iteration (as shown in Figure 4.6) are:

- System design
- Implementation
- Integration
- Deployment

Process-components that remain in the background but continue to be performed with high intensity in this iteration are:

- Quality assurance
- Quality control
- Training

4.2.5   Parallel Developments within a Lifecycle

Parallel development takes the concept of iterative and incremental development further. By ensuring that the interfaces are first designed and then stabilized, it is possible for the vertically sliced packages, based on business functionality, to be developed in parallel. Until the system development reaches a stage where packages need to be integrated, there is no dependency between packages—enabling parallel development.

4.2.6   Maintenance or Ongoing Iteration

The initial, major, and final iterations of a process are completed, as discussed above, for a single increment of development. For multiple increments, these iterations are repeated. However, once all increments and iterations are complete, there is a need to maintain the system on a regular basis. Estimates on the costs associated with this maintenance lifecycle vary, but my practical experience, and that of many of my colleagues, has been that the maintenance costs of a system are usually equal to its development costs, over the life of the system. This happens to be true of good quality systems, as well. Systems lacking quality run into high maintenance costs over a short time, but good quality systems continue to exist and serve the business much longer, requiring an ongoing maintenance effort.

The kinds of activities that take place in the ongoing maintenance cycle include:

- Receiving requests for changes from users and business sponsors
- Receiving error reports from users and testers
- Considering enhancement requests from business sponsors
- Collating and prioritizing the requests for changes
- Updating the MOPS with the requests once requests for changes are accepted
- Adding new classes or modifying existing classes—for their designs in the MOSS as well as their code
- Considering reuse—both "for" and "with" reuse
- Quality control of data

4.3   Adoption of the Software Process

Adoption of the process (also occasionally called deployment) means bringing a fully configured process into the project. Furthermore, as correctly noted by Serour et al. [2002], for organizations with a procedural culture this transition to object technology using the UML presents an even bigger challenge in terms of culture change. If it is a process configured within a process tool, then this adoption process includes installation of the process and availability to all project-team members.

Adoption of a process encompasses sociological as well as methodological issues. Therefore, adoption of a fully configured process benefits by applying the soft concepts of quality and project management discussed in Chapter 2. The existing culture of the project team, the state of the project, the use of a process CASE tool, and the amount of training and mentoring required and made available to the project are all crucial issues in process adoption. They are considered in detail here.

4.3.1   Ascertain Current Process State

Ascertaining the current state of the organization and the project in terms of its process culture can be a formal activity as performed in the CMM type audits.[2] This ascertainment reveals whether the three dimensions of a process—the technical, methodological, and the social dimensions—are clearly defined, accessible, and followed. This reviewing of the process state should be carried out in the context of its IIP capabilities, because a UML-based project invariably needs and benefits by an IIP process.

The urgency of the need for a process and the type of process that is suitable for the project is highlighted as a result of this assessment. For example, some projects without processes benefit by the adoption of a process—any process. In such cases, the benefits from a slight introduction of discipline to the process far outweigh the effort to ascertain the state of the project. Therefore, any process (even in-house configured processes) should be introduced immediately. Other projects starting in organizations that have a history of good process usage (these organizations may be on Level 3 on the CMM scale) will need further investigation of their status and their particular needs before a process is adopted.

4.3.2   Crucial Pilot Project

Small projects, as described in Chapter 1, can be used as pilot projects. These pilot projects are very helpful in enabling organizations to adopt new ways of doing things. While not always mandatory, a pilot project

---

[2] For excellent empirical research in transition, see Serour, M., and B. Henderson-Sellers, "The role of organizational culture on the adoption and diffusion of software engineering process: An empirical study," presented at *http://www.ccc.newcastle.edu.au/ifip86/program.html*.

helps organizations to get a good feel for the process before it is adopted for a large, crucial, and sensitive project, and before it is adopted across the entire organization. Furthermore, it is essential that the pilot project runs on the full lifecycle of the process (although briefly) and not only on one aspect of the process such as requirements or testing.

4.3.3   Point of Adoption

An important aspect of adoption is the point at which a project starts to adopt the process. The questions that deal with the point of adoption are:

- When do we start adopting a process? (The beginning of the project is preferable.)
- Are we starting with a clean slate in terms of process adoption in this project? (This is the preferred scenario.)
- What happens to the existing process (if the organization has a standard process, but it is not IIP and not suitable for the project)?
- What happens if the project is already using a process, and the project is almost halfway complete in terms of its allocated time and budget? Process need is felt during the enactment of a "lack of process." In such a case, there is a need to identify the current activities going on in the project and map them to the activity within the process-component of a formal process. Backtracking of the activities is not always possible; therefore, it is necessary to start from a process-component that is also halfway in a formal process.

4.3.4   Separating UML from the Process

When organizations using traditional structured techniques for software development decide to move to an object-oriented software-development approach, they occasionally tend to treat the adoption of the UML and the adoption of the process as one and the same. Indeed, using the UML techniques on a project benefits by the use of a supporting process, but the process and UML are not the same thing. Therefore, the adoption of a process should be treated separately from that of the UML techniques.

4.3.5   Keeping All CASE Tool Implementations Separate

It is crucial for successful process adoption not only to keep the UML separate from the process, but more importantly to keep the adoption of all CASE tools separate from the processes and the UML. For example, the process-components discussed in the previous chapter should be presented to the project team and discussed in a project even before the first formal iteration starts. However, these same process-components can be configured in a process CASE tool, such as eTrack or RUP, or simply in Microsoft Project. If project-team members are new to these process tools, they should be trained in the use of these tools *after* they have understood the process-components in theory.

4.3.6   Training and Mentoring

Process training should form a totally separate area of work, including a separate budget. While the target audience of the process training includes the hands-on project-team members (for example, business analysts, system architects, programmers, and system designers), it is *more* important to train the project managers, the quality managers, and the project sponsors (with varying intensity). This is because following an IIP process is a project manager's job, and many project managers with traditional backgrounds find it difficult to adopt the IIP approach, where sign-off on a particular phase is not as formal as in the traditional waterfall approach.

Briefly training the project sponsors and the users on this approach to software development ensures that they understand and accept the iterative and incremental delivery of the software—as opposed to the delivery of completed software at the end of the development. In my experience, receiving the software before it is fully developed is a new thing to users and sponsors and they should be apprised of the iterative nature of the process.

As also mentioned earlier, training of the project team in process-components should be kept separate from their training in a process CASE tool and corresponding UML CASE tool. The theoretical part of process-component discussions should precede deployment of any tools in the project.

Use of process engineers as consultants or process mentors is highly beneficial in projects/organizations that do not have a process culture. If an organization has very little process discipline, it is difficult to find an internal person who has the knowledge and experience to provide process-related guidance. Furthermore, adoption of a process is an exercise fraught with much sociological and political friction. Having an external person who is deemed neutral is extremely beneficial to a project that is trying to transition to the new way of doing things.

4.3.7 Access to the Process

Providing ready access to the process is critical for the adoption of the process by a project team. Process elements in the three dimensions of the process, including the role definitions, the activities and tasks, and the templates for the deliverables, should be readily available to the project team.

Almost all practical processes are electronically deployed. This means that the process elements are available to the teams electronically—most probably over the company's intranet. This not only improves the access to the process, but also enables sharing of the process elements. For example, a process deployed electronically enables the business analyst and the user to share the same use case diagrams placed within the MOPS and to share a common template to create the glossary of business terms.

This "shareability" becomes especially important when the projects are outsourced. In outsourced projects, the process has to support the creation and documentation of requirements in a place geographically and temporarily separate from the place where the design and development occurs. Creation of satisfactory test plans, test designs, and test cases, and execution of acceptance tests, are further challenges that a process has to deal with when the development and testing are outsourced—making the electronic deployment of a process almost mandatory.

4.4   Enacting the Quality Process

In a quality process such as the one described here, checkpoints are needed at the end of each iteration of the process component. This is where we apply the process checks of necessity and sufficiency. They are followed by the ability of the development process to modify and change itself to suit the actual project or to map to the actual project. This is where the malleability aspect comes in.

4.4.1 Creating Iterations and Increments in Lucky Insurance's Development

An iterative and incremental project plan ensures that the user is continuously involved in the development process. Table 4.1 shows how a typical insurance system's development occurs in an iterative and incremental fashion. The left-most column in the table shows the actual release versions of the entire system. These releases are shown as versions 0.1, 0.5,

Table 4.1 *Mapping of the iterative and incremental lifecycle to the horizontal and vertical architectural slices in an IIP project plan*

Example Release Versions	New Lucky Insurance System	Client Subsystem	Policy Subsystem	Claims Subsystem	Marketing Subsystem
v 0.1 (initial)	Full scoping; layering	All use cases, activities, and business classes; prototypes; in MOPS some implemented	Some use cases and business classes identified in MOPS	Some use cases identified in MOPS	Exists only as a package name; no work thus far in MOPS
v 0.5 (major)	Reviews of MOPS with users MOSS with designers	Client package within MOSS complete; most classes implemented	All use cases, business classes documented some implemented; prototypes	All claims-related use cases complete; relating to client and policy in MOPS; initial classes	Sales and marketing research; some use cases and activities documented
v 0.9	MOPS MOSS, and MOBS complete for client	GUI, charts printing, and interfaces to legacy complete; testing started	Some interfaces completed; tested	Some classes implemented; no work on interfaces, printing; prototypes	Business-level classes identified; none implemented
v 1.0 (Final) Main release	First release (increment) deployed	Acceptance testing of client by users; possible deployment	Complete domain-specific underlying class library	Math models complete; generic for future reuse	Specific charting complete generic for reuse

0.9, and the first main release (1.0). Corresponding to each of the releases is a row indicating what is likely to be achieved in that release. The horizontal rows indicate the part of an iteration that is completed within the release. The vertical slices correspond to each of the subsystems or packages, and represent a physical increment.

As you will notice from Table 4.1, the client subsystem is part of the first increment of this project plan. Therefore, in the initial release of the system, the client use cases get completed first, along with their corresponding class diagrams and the solution design. The other increments are in the offing, and will perhaps follow the first increment. Some of the domain-level activities that deal with the entire insurance domain will continue to happen in the background across all iterations and increments.

Compare the approach outlined in Table 4.1 with a waterfall-based software development lifecycle. A waterfall-based approach completes all use cases and activity diagrams across all subsystems before proceeding with the business class diagrams, and so on. If, during the implementation of a suite of class diagrams, an error in understanding the requirements is discovered, then the analysis-level diagrams need to be changed, which is a very difficult undertaking.

In the iterative and incremental approach discussed here, risks are reduced by letting the users shape the requirements through an initial iteration within an increment of the system. Completing and correcting requirements and designs, even with this IIP approach, is difficult to achieve because the requirements change and because the users learn more about what they want as they see the output of each iteration. What can be said with confidence is that this is the ideal way to guarantee the least-incomplete and least-incorrect models. I take the humble view of least incompleteness and least incorrectness, because in practice, despite taking extra care and following the process precisely, I have always come across well-meaning users, architects, and designers who want to add "one more thing" to the requirements.

4.4.2   An Iterative Project Task Plan

The iterative and incremental approach outlined in Table 4.1 needs to be placed in a project task plan in order to enable a project manager to follow it. This requires the project manager to create a task plan that *repeats* the activities and tasks from the process-components. This project plan can incorporate all the increments at the outset, or one increment only with provisions for adding to and updating the project plan with additional increments.

Table 4.2 shows a small cross section of such a plan. As you will notice, the tasks related to requirements modeling (these tasks will be mostly derived from the process-components) are repeated for the subsystems. The essence of what is shown in Table 4.2 is that all practical project plans have sequential tasks, as shown by the task numbers in the first column. However, iterative and incremental development means that the project manager has to attempt to repeat activities and tasks at suitable intervals. Finally, although the tasks in Table 4.2 are repeated for different subsystems,

Table 4.2   *Section of an IIP project task plan*

Task No.	Tasks	Deliverables	Role
1	Identify actors	Requirements model (use case model)	BA, User
2	Identify use cases for client subsystem	Requirements model	BA, User
3	Document use cases for client subsystem	Requirements model (use case documentation)	BA, User
4	Create use case diagrams for client subsystem	Requirements model	BA, User
5	Complete actor list	Requirements model	BA, User
6	Complete use case diagrams for client subsystem	Requirements model	BA
7	Document most use cases for client subsystem	Requirements model (use case documentation)	BA
8	Identify initial test cases for client subsystem		Tester, BA, User
9	Identify use cases for policy subsystem	Requirements model	BA, User
10	Document use cases for policy subsystem	Requirements model	BA, User
11	Create use case diagrams for policy subsystem	Requirements model	BA, User
12	Complete actor list for policy subsystem	Requirements model	BA, User
13	Document remaining use cases for client subsystem	Requirements model	BA
14	Document most use cases for policy subsystem	Requirements model	BA, User

identification of these subsystems is not shown here. It can be assumed that these subsystems will have been identified earlier in the project plan.

4.4.3   Iterative Project Management Tools

The project plan in Table 4.2 would usually be created in a sequential task-based project management tool such as Microsoft Project. However, it is worth considering project-management tools that are iterative and incremental in nature themselves. That means these project-management tools use techniques to enable the project manager to manage the project *without* repeating the tasks (as was necessary in the sample project plan in Table 4.2). Examples of such process tools are discussed in Process Tools Using UML. These tools give due consideration to the iterative and incremental aspect of a process. This means these process CASE tools are able to take the activities and tasks of the process and place them within the context of a project-management framework that allows these activities and tasks to be performed again and again, a sufficient number of times, resulting in a complete and correct deliverable.

The iterative and incremental nature of process tools also helps to provide not only detailed cross-referencing on all activities and tasks within the process, but also excellent tracking mechanisms for the activities and tasks. Despite their growing importance, availability, and capability, in practical enactment of the process, these process CASE tools usually end up being used together with the sequential project-management tools such as Microsoft Project.

4.5   Tracking Quality throughout the Process

When the project team enacts the process, it follows the activities and tasks put together in a SEP and produces the UML-based deliverables. The quality techniques of walkthroughs, inspections, reviews, workshops, and so forth are applied as the process is enacted, ensuring the quality of the deliverables and guaranteeing that the necessary and sufficient aspects of the process-components have been fully enacted. Even if a process is successfully adopted, it is important for the project manager to enact it properly. This requires, in addition to project-management knowledge, practical experience in following a process. The importance of experience in enactment comes from the fact that there are many things happening in a project that are outside the process, and yet crucial to its enactment and to the ultimate success of the project. These issues, outside the process, are called driving conditions, and we discuss them next.

4.5.1   Importance of Road Factors in Process Enactment

The use of a process in software development is similar to the use of a street directory when planning a trip [Unhelkar and Mamdapur 1995]. A street directory helps when deciding which roads to follow to reach the destination using the shortest route and in the quickest time. A good street directory even indicates traffic signals, rotaries, and one-way streets. However, the directory is not blamed if a road is closed due to maintenance, if the journey is not completed due to an accident, or if the car breaks down because it hits a pothole.

As far as directories are concerned, they are used without complaining about the dynamic aspect of a particular road and address. However, software processes (and the corresponding process-components discussed in the previous chapter), which are akin to street directories of software development, are criticized for failing to handle the driving conditions.

A process provides guidance on a project's activities, tasks, roles, and deliverables. A fully configured process incorporates the concepts of iterations and increments. In practice, a process also assists in scheduling the overall development. But a process that deals with software development may not have inside it precise activities and tasks that help to handle issues like human-relations problems (see the discussion on games in Section 2.5.4), financial instability of the company, technical incompetence of programmers, and so forth. Factors such as these can and do contribute to the success or failure of a software project. These are called the driving conditions or road factors.

Processes, configured like street directories, provide direction to the project. Just as determining a good route is a lot more difficult without the street directory, similarly, processes help to determine the direction a project should take. However, processes hardly ever tell us about the driving conditions faced during their enactment. Therefore, it is important to look consciously for factors *outside* the process, which can and do influence the project. Thus, the process provides the *direction*, but the development process should not be limited to it.

Sometimes the process appears to be doing more than expected by providing a perfect road map to follow, whereas at other times the road factors may take over and it may become necessary to temporarily suspend strict adherence to the process while these factors are handled. Astute project and quality management combines adherence to a process in enactment with existing and new road factors, to ensure that while the project remains on track (in terms of following a process), the additional road factors are also handled and are not allowed to negatively influence the process enactment. Figure 4.7 shows this unnecessarily strict adherence to a process in enactment, and the loss of process discipline due to the influence of the road factors.

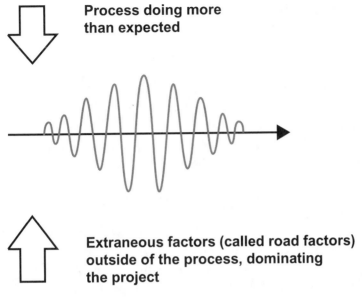

**Process doing more
than expected**

**Extraneous factors (called road factors)
outside of the process, dominating
the project**

Figure 4.7   *Practicality of process enactment: a street directory approach*

In small projects, with low-ceremony process, the street directory example can be further extended to argue how process is followed by the project manager in her head. For example, one would scoff at a person if she were to open a street directory every day in the evening while driving home from work. In spite of rain and closed roads, she is still able to reach home without referring to the street map lying in the glove compartment.

Similarly, good developers, who have gone through a certain development more than once, who know the project type and are comfortable with the project size assigned to their team, would not want to be forced to follow a high-ceremony process to do their development work. In these situations, where following the process may be more detrimental than not following it, it is suggested that the project and quality manager carry the process in their heads, and apply it in an informal manner. A variant of what I am suggesting is any of the Agile methodological approaches, wherein the process is applied from experience and mutual understanding, rather than deployed and enacted formally as one would in a medium to large project.

Having given due importance to the road factors in practical process enactment, let us now discuss the quality-specific activities that take place during and at the end of each iteration.

4.5.2 Quality Activities at the End of the Initial Iteration

The initial iteration ensures that the business objectives of the project are fully understood by all parties. This understanding is achieved by following the business evaluation process-component in great detail, supported by the requirements-modeling activities and tasks. Once the project type and size is ascertained, the process is configured and deployed. Some of the process-components may be configured beforehand, and may directly fit in the project requirements.

In the initial iteration, all UML diagrams of the MOPS are quality-checked and their dependency on each other is also thoroughly checked. Furthermore, the MOPS is developed with user involvement and user input on a regular basis. Workshops and interview techniques are heavily used in extracting complete and consistent requirements. Cross checking the technology, in terms of its capability to satisfy and influence the functional *and* operational requirements, also takes place here. Therefore, prototypes play a crucial role in quality enhancement in this iteration.

During the initial iteration, it is not only the user who is busy with the business analysts in terms of specifying the requirements, but also the project manager who is trying to organize his project by creating appropriate teams and assigning responsibilities to them. The best way to divide software-related work and assign it to team members is to create initial package diagrams of the UML. I create the high-level packages early on in the project (albeit taking input from the domain expert) and start assigning these packages to the teams within the project. Creation of packages, assignment of packages to teams, and resultant assignment of increments is considered as early in the project as possible and is certainly part of this initial iteration.

In some cases, quality activities at the end of the initial iteration may provide valuable information to the senior management in terms of the progress of the project. In such circumstances, the end of this iteration may be the end of the project—as management may realize that it is not possible for the project to fulfill the given objectives, or that the costs and timings are likely to blow out. While by no means a favored scenario, it should still be understood that if a project is doomed for failure, it is better to ascertain that information up front and act on it, rather than wait till the end of the project.

While paying attention to the actual software development (or any of its variations) it is also important to consider the issues related to the process itself. Malleability of the process or its ability to lend itself to fine-tuning is beneficial at this stage. This fine-tuning means not only updating the process steps (in a process tool) with the steps (tasks) completed, but also changing the sequence of activities and tasks, performing them with more (or less) intensity, and changing the templates for the deliverables to better suit the requirements of the project. For example, in a formal review at the end of initial iteration, the reviewers might realize that stereotyping use cases is not relevant. This task would then be dropped from the process's second iteration.

4.5.3   Quality Activities at the End of the Major Iteration

While we continue to apply the quality process during the development work, at the end of the major iteration we have the opportunity to apply formal quality techniques to the deliverables produced during the major iteration. It should be noted that at the end of this iteration the project would have spent more than half its time and allocated budget. Therefore, the deliverables are expected to be substantial in terms of designs, coding, and documentation.

The necessity and sufficiency of steps outlined in Chapter 3 should be satisfied when the project reaches the end of this iteration. Quality activities at the end of this major iteration ensure two separate aspects of development within the project:

- One that deals with the verification and validation of the models and code, ensuring that the models are syntactically and semantically correct and the code is bug-free.

- A second one that deals with ensuring that the steps needed to produce a deliverable have been met or have been conducted.

Quality workshops at the end of major iterations will check the MOSS deliverables to a large extent, requiring the quality personnel to ensure correctness and completeness of models as well as their corresponding implementation. Therefore, quality work includes testing, as discussed in the next chapter. Operational requirements, especially including requirements of performance and volume, *must* be validated and verified at this stage. Furthermore, issues related to training users on the product to be released should also be addressed during the quality checks at this stage. With the extent of quality work expected, the workshops of quality checks usually evolve into formal reviews and may include external parties (external to the project, that is). Accuracy and completeness of test beds are also included in the quality reviews at the end of this iteration.

In terms of process checks, the process-component of requirements modeling is complete, but those of interface modeling and design, system design, and implementation continue at a feverish pace. Similarly, the background process-component of system architecture, persistence design, change management, prototyping, and reuse is cross checked to ensure that the activities and tasks within these process-components are followed for their necessity and sufficiency. Other process-components like deployment commence their activities and tasks.

4.5.4   Quality Activities at the End of the Final Iteration

The end of the final iteration is where the outcome of following a quality process and modeling is evident. This is the quality work that not only ensures that the final product rolling out of the project is of the highest quality but also ensures the understanding and documentation of the lessons learned during the project.

During the final iteration in a development process, all outstanding activities are complete and, as relevant, satisfy the necessity and sufficiency criteria of the process. This is verified through a workshop environment, where the activities and tasks within the project plan are checked by the quality personnel together with the process engineer and the project manager. The quality workshops ensure that the process-components of system design, implementation, and integration are fully complete and deployment is in the process of being completed.

Training, especially related to the end user of the system, is handled by the process-component of training. Results of the quality-control process-component are of great interest to both the project members and the users. Therefore, the process-component of quality assurance and quality control is the subject of process checks during and at the end of this final iteration. If data conversion is involved in the project, this is also the iteration that undertakes the conversion. Therefore, the end of the iteration requires verification and validation of the conversion process.

Quality activities at the end of the final iteration may require external (third) parties to come in and audit the process and the deliverables. These can be internal audits, wherein auditors within the organization (but outside the project) come in to check the correctness and completeness of the deliverables as well as the process. There can also be external audits, especially in projects that are outsourced, and where there are legal ramifications for not delivering the required functionalities or not delivering them on time and within budget or even not following the activities and steps outlined in an agreed process.

Finally, the quality activities at the end of the final iteration can undertake a post-project review. In most projects, it is prudent for the project and quality managers, as well as the senior management, to find out what went wrong and, equally importantly, what went right in the project. The end of the final iteration is the ideal time to achieve this post-project understanding of the process, models, and implementation. Quality techniques of workshops and audits are heavily used at the end of this iteration.

4.6   Frequently Asked Questions (FAQs)

Q1: Is there a need to consider configuration, adoption, and enactment of a process separately? Is it possible for all of this to be one single enactment of process?

A1: Creation of a Software Engineering Process from given process-components is the job of a process engineer. If a ready-made SEP is available, then it can be immediately adopted and enactment can start. However, if a project has specific needs, which cannot be satisfied by a commercial off-the-shelf process, then configuration is required.

Q2: Does malleability of a process go against the fundamentals of process discipline?

A2: No. Malleability, in this context, is the ability of the process to lend itself to fine-tuning, after the project has started. More often than not, project managers realize during the project what they want from a process. If it is not a major change (for example, re-creation of an operational requirements template), the process should facilitate this. It is easily done in an electronically deployed process.

Q3: Why should I create an Iterative, Incremental, and Parallel project plan?

A3: To ensure that there is continuous feedback to all parties involved in the project on the way the project is progressing—particularly to the users. Component-based technology is well suited for this type of development, with the potential for incorporating components iteratively and incrementally in the project. However, the process that is based on the IIP lifecycle is helpful in such component-based development.

4.7   Exercises

E4.1: What happens *before* a process is configured?

E4.2: What happens *after* a process is configured?

E4.3: Discuss the role of process-based tools in adopting a process.

E4.4: Why is adoption or deployment of a process important for quality?

E4.5: What are the steps to be taken in a typical process adoption?

E4.6: What is a SEP based on?

E4.7: What are the advantages and limitations of a waterfall-based SDLC?

E4.8: Discuss in detail the benefits derived from the fountain model in SDLC.

E4.9: Discuss situations where you would consider the initial iteration to be more intense than the major iteration.

E4.10: What is the importance of a pilot project in adopting a UML-based process?

E4.11: Why do increments and iterations merge in practice? Answer with reference to Lucky Insurance's development plan, shown in Table 4.1.

E4.12: Compare Agile methodologies to a high-ceremony process such as the one described in this chapter.

4.8   References

Beck, K., *eXtreme Programming Explained: Embrace Change,* Boston: Addison-Wesley, 2000.

Boehm, B., *Software Engineering Economics,* 1981.

———, "A spiral model of software development and enhancement," *ACS Software Engineering Notes,* 1986, 11(4), pp. 14–24.

Fowler, M., and J. Highsmith, "The Agile Manifesto," *Information Age,* June/July 2002, pp. 20–25.

Graham, I., B. Henderson-Sellers, and H. Younessi, *The OPEN Process Specification,* Reading, Mass.: Addison-Wesley, 1997.

Henderson-Sellers, B., and J.M. Edwards, "The fountain model for object-oriented systems development," *Object Magazine,* 1993, 3(2), pp. 71–79.

———, and B. Unhelkar, *OPEN Modeling with the UML,* U.K.: Addison-Wesley, 2000.

Jacobson, I., G. Booch, J. Rumbaugh, *The Unified Software Development Process,* Reading, Mass.: Addison-Wesley, 1999.

Kruchten, P., *The Rational Unified Process: An Introduction,* Reading, Mass.: Addison-Wesley, 1999.

Serour, M.K., B. Henderson-Sellers, J. Hughes, D. Winder, and L. Chow, "Organizational Transition to Object Technology: Theory and Practice," 2002, presented at *www.lirmm.fr/OOIS2002.*

Sommerville, I., *Software Engineering,* Reading, Mass.: Addison-Wesley, 1989.

Unhelkar, B., and G. Mamdapur, "Practical aspects of using a methodology: A Road Map approach," *Report on Object Analysis and Design (ROAD),* 1995, 2(2), July–August, pp. 34–36, 54.

Yourdon, E., *The Rise and Resurrection of the American Programmer,* Yourdon Press Computing Series, Upper Saddle River, N.J.: Prentice-Hall, 1998.

5 chapter

Estimates and Metrics for UML-Based Projects

Most of us managers are prone to one failing: A tendency to manage
people as though they were modular components.
—DeMarco and Lister [1987]

We must, it is true, always proceed on the basis of probability,
but to have probability is to have something.
—Elton Trueblood

Putting This Chapter in Perspective

This chapter discusses the important issues of measurements and estimates in UML-based software projects. Starting with an argument for the need to make good estimates, and continuing on to discuss how good metrics make good estimates, this chapter delves into the importance of these measures and estimates in improving the quality of project models and processes. We also discuss the technical measures related to sizes and complexities of the UML artifacts and diagrams. Estimates for a typical example CRMS implementation project using the UML are shown, with a view to demonstrate the application and significance of metrics in a practical project.

The Prime Reader: Project Manager, Quality Manager

5.1 About Estimates and Measures in Software Projects

In discussing the elusive nature of quality in Chapter 1 we mentioned that the reasons for elusiveness of quality in software are exacerbated, because the nature of software itself is effusive and not concrete. As a result, estimations and measurements in software projects are always fraught with uncertainties. That, however, does not preclude us from making attempts to get the measures right. Here we discuss different types of measures and estimates that play valuable roles in improving the quality of work taking place in practical projects.

5.1.1 Relating Estimates to Quality

Measurements and estimates play an important role in quality assurance. As seen in our opening discussion in Chapter 1, quality gets pushed out if the project is under pressure due to the other three factors of time, budget, and functionality. If the estimates of these three factors are accurately ascertained, their negative influence on quality can be reduced. An accurate (or close to accurate) estimation of time and budget gives the project team sufficient breathing space to carry out the quality-related activities and tasks. It also gives the project team the opportunity to earn the confidence of the project sponsors and the users, facilitating easier extraction of requirements in subsequent project increments and iterations. Thus, overall, it is important for astute project and quality managers to correctly estimate the time and budgets in a given project.

5.1.2 Measurements and Estimates

Metrics are tools used to discern different degrees of probabilities. Metrics help the estimating process. Estimating is accomplished by setting up metrics to measure various factors within a project, including the size of the system, person-months required for development, data collected related to these metrics, and the results from such metrics used to estimate various aspects of new commercial projects. As Wohlin and Ahlgren [1995] state: "The objective must not only be to quantify product and process quality attributes, such as reliability, productivity, and time to market, but also to increase the predictability of these important attributes." For additional discussions on these important background considerations on applications of measures to practical projects, see Capers Jones [1991].

Since estimations require due consideration to soft factors (nontechnical factors or road factors), which in turn require experience and judgement, it is not surprising that IT literature is replete with stories of missed deadlines and budget overruns. Metrics and measurements go some way to mitigate the effect of these unpredictable factors on the estimation process. Measurements based on predetermined metrics should be stored, not only for use in the current project, but also for future projects. In fact, creating an organizationwide or perhaps an industrywide database of various project, model, and process metrics can play an important role toward improving the overall quality of estimation of time, budget, and resources.

Furthermore, in order to reduce estimating errors, the metrics function within the project must be well organized. What needs to be measured, why it should be measured, and how it helps to produce better estimates, should be understood in any metrics program. Consistency in the measurements and the way in which they are measured enables improved comparisons between measurement results and facilitates good estimations.

Usually, metrics fall into the three categories paralleling the three dimensions of a process. These three dimensions, as you will recall, are the technological dimension (where we measure the "what" that produces the software and the deliverables, including the software itself), the methodological dimension (the "how"), and the sociological dimension (where we measure the "who" aspects of the project).

5.1.3 Measuring the Technological Dimension

Examples of measurements in the technological dimension are the complexity of a class or a component. This measure deals with the design of a component, as well as its implementation language. These metrics vary to encompass the static aspect of the class diagram as well as its runtime object model. The technical metrics provide information to the programmers and the designers on the quality of the model they have built—which is usually in the solution space. Technical metrics also apply in the background space, when they provide information on the architectural and operational issues.

5.1.4   Measuring the Methodological Dimension

The methodological dimension of measurement deals with the number of
activities and tasks that need to be completed within a project. In its simplest
form the methodological measurement deals with a task list. A task list provides activities and tasks to be accomplished during software development.
One puts the time and budget estimates against such a task list. This is simplistic because it assumes that each of the tasks has an equal weight. While
this simple measure of activities and tasks within a process-component (PC)
might be acceptable in its configuration and deployment, the measure in the
methodological dimension must change as the process is enacted—because
a given activity and its corresponding tasks may be repeated more than
once, to satisfy the necessary and sufficiency criteria within a project.

5.1.5   Measuring the Sociological Dimension

The sociological dimension deals with the number of people needed for
the project, the length of time they are needed, and their skills and related
costs. Metrics are easy—until they are used in practice. They are still easy,
until they are used to measure a person's productivity. As DeMarco and
Lister [1987] correctly point out, it is difficult to measure people because
people are not modular components and they tend to behave in a nonlinear fashion. The sociological dimension of metrics deals with the challeng-
ing, vital, nonlinear people-productivity aspect of the project.

A simple measure of the sociological dimension is the number of
people needed for a project. That measure is further extended to state the
number of people needed in each of the project roles. For example, there
might be just two roles in a process-component—the project manager and
the system architect—but in practice, the number of people filling these
roles may be more than two. This usually happens when a process is
enacted in a large project and where more than one person is needed to fill
each of the given roles in the process-components.

The skills of the people filling the roles within the given process-
components are also important. For example, "Create a Use case diagram"
requires a different set of skills application and time than a task that says,
"Refactor use cases." While creating use cases and use case diagrams
requires extensive business knowledge and skills, refactoring use case diagrams needs even more experience than creating them and may require
more time. These are the kinds of things that we should consider when
creating metrics for measurements in the methodological dimension.

As discussed in Chapter 2, in addition to the fact that people have different skill sets, they also have different agendas and different commitments to the projects. For a detailed discussion on the personal objectives versus the corporate objectives and how they influence the commitment and the output from individuals, see Unhelkar [1999].

5.2   Project Metrics and Estimates

This section discusses the measurements and estimations that are relevant to the project as a whole. These metrics help a project manager to understand the type and size of the project and also to estimate the time and budget that will be expended in executing the project. An attempt is also made to spread the time, budgets, and people over the various modeling spaces for UML-based projects. Needless to say, project metrics, like all other metrics, continue to remain a combination of some good scientific theory and a lot of practical experience.

5.2.1   Project Size and Type

In Chapter 1 we discussed the various types and sizes of UML-based projects and the underlying reasoning for the classification. Here, we elaborate on that same discussion and look further into the reasons for the categorization.

First, we categorize the size of projects into small, medium, and large. This categorization is done with the intention of finding out how UML benefits these projects. Categorizing helps us to understand the intensity with which the UML quality checks are applied and the formality of applying the process. During enactment, more than one person fills a role described in a process-component. Also during enactment, one activity is repeated many times. Therefore, the categorization of projects in Chapter 1 is taken further here, in practice, to enable good measurements and good estimates.

Second, we consider the various types of projects, also discussed in Chapter 1. These project categories influence the way in which the project technology, methodology, and sociology are enacted. Readers will recall that the six types of projects are:

- Development projects
- Integration projects

- Package implementation projects
- Outsourcing projects
- Data warehousing and conversion projects
- Educational projects

Each project type is estimated differently. And the same process-components in different projects are estimated differently. This is because each of these projects has different needs for the UML diagrams, and therefore the time and effort spent on each of the UML diagrams varies depending on the type of project. Furthermore, the number of people fulfilling a particular role also differs based on the project type and the project size. A data warehousing project, for example, needs more than one person to fill the role of a database manager, whereas a CRMS implementation needs many business analysts but perhaps only one database manager (as the database doesn't need to be designed in a package implementation project—only fine-tuned).

5.2.2   Project Time, Budgets, and People

Let us consider some practical estimates in terms of distribution of time, budgets, and people over the various modeling spaces for projects of three different sizes. This is followed by brief comments on the variations to these estimates based on project types. It is worth mentioning at this point that process-components such as those of project management, process configuration, and quality management, which are executed in the background, are common across the modeling spaces. Therefore, estimates related to these process-components are shown in a separate column, whereas estimates related to the architectural work are shown in the MOBS column.

Small Projects

Table 5.1 *Sample distribution of budgets, time, and people in small projects*

	MOPS	MOSS	MOBS	Common	Total
Budgets	$300K	$400K	$200K	$100K	$1M
Time	2 months	3 months	1 month	all	6 months
People	2+1	4	1	1+1	10

Comments

In a small project a project manager should expect to spend around 30 percent of his budget and time in the problem space. The time assigned will be spent in understanding and modeling the requirements in the MOPS. Part of this work in MOPS includes discussion sessions on the whiteboard and later, optionally, in a UML CASE tool. The 2+1 people in the problem space include a user who may not be onboard full time for the project. Similarly, the common roles include the roles of the project manager and the quality manager. Small projects may not have budgets for both roles in a full-time capacity. Following the IIP lifecycle, the first iteration includes all aspects of modeling and management; therefore, the above distribution is also iterative. If it is an educational project, then of course the budgetary constraint may not apply. Furthermore, the time requirements will be limited to 14 weeks.

Medium Projects

Table 5.2   *Sample distribution of budgets, time, and people in medium projects*

	MOPS	MOSS	MOBS	Common	Total
Budgets	$2.5M	$3M	$3M	$1.5M	$10M
Time	4 months	6 months	3 months	all	1+ year
People	4+2	15+3	5+1	5	35

Comments

In the MOPS, one would envisage four business analysts, together with two users, conducting workshops and interviews to elicit detailed requirements. The people in the solution space involve approximately fifteen developers and three testers. The five people in the background space play the role of architect, process consultants, and senior designers. The one extra role shown here is filled by the vendor representative. This role is a combination of consulting support from component, database, and Web application vendors.

Large Projects

Table 5.3 *Sample distribution of budgets, time, and people in large projects*

	MOPS	MOSS	MOBS	Common	Total
Budgets	$5M	$10M	$15M	$5M	$35M
Time	1 year	1.5 years	6 months	all	3 years
People	20+10	100+20	20+10	20	200

Comments

Figures in Table 5.3, based on the description of large projects provided in Chapter 1, provide some interesting insights in the distribution of effort in the modeling spaces. Consider how, in this example, the amount likely to be spent in the background space is high—three times the amount spent in the problem space. The time, however, that the project spends in the background space is half the time spent in the problem space. This is attributed to the fact that the architectural work in the background space involves buying third-party components, application servers, and databases. If these infrastructural things are present in the project (unlikely in a large project), then the distribution provided here must be modified.

Furthermore, in a large project, one expects a large number of users involved in the problem space (shown by the +10 figure indicating 10 user representatives), working alongside the business analysts and requirements modelers in the problem space. Development teams in the solution space comprise the 100 developers, in addition to the 20 who focus on the quality control or testing part of the project. One would expect more than one project manager in this project, reporting to the senior project manager or equivalent role. Overall, in large-scoped projects, not only do all the roles of a process-component come into play, but also the number of people fulfilling the roles and the number of instances of deliverables produced multiply.

5.2.3   Caveats in Project Estimates

Project managers are surprised to find their estimates go awry despite having based them on as much logical information as was available. Furthermore, the exercise of estimation itself has an effect on the time and budget consumed by the project—as was shown by the Jeffery and Lawrence study at the University of New South Wales, reported by

DeMarco and Lister [1987]. Interestingly, this study reveals that productivity seems to increase where *no estimates* on the project are prepared.

Following the advice of this study verbatim is most likely impractical. Yet there is something of immense value in this reported study for those who make estimates: Extremely conservative or tight estimates may not always lead to a healthy working environment. Estimates that provide concessions for the road factors eventually turn out to be the most productive—or productivity-boosting—estimates. This also seems to ratify what most project managers already know intuitively, that compressing schedules beyond a certain point (for example, more than 30 percent of the original schedule) results in a recoil of a spring-type expansion of project timelines. Thus, considering road factors and the sociological impact of scheduling are essential to successful project estimates [Unhelkar 1995].

5.3   Measurement of Processes

The project estimates of time, budget, and people lend themselves to better interpretation if the process that is supporting the software development can also be measured. The size of a process-component in its configuration and enactment state provides valuable input in the project estimations conducted by a project manager. Process measurement can be used along with project estimates wherein the process metrics will provide support for the iterative and incremental aspect of software development. Alternatively, the process metrics may even replace the project metrics. The alternative of using process metrics exclusively may be considered only where the development processes within the organization are matured (for example, at least Level 3 on the CMM scale).

The necessary and sufficiency criteria, mentioned in detail underneath each of the process-components in Chapter 3, are also affected by the process measures. For example, an activity that has to satisfy the sufficiency criteria is executed with more intensity in the second iteration or, alternatively, executed only during the second iteration. During enactment of those process-components, the necessary and sufficient process criteria create the need of a certain number of people fulfilling a given role. This needs to be estimated and measured. Malleability of a process also plays an important role in enactment, as processes need to modify themselves to suit the changing requirements of the project without losing the discipline they bring to the project.

5.3.1   Why Measure Processes?

Any process measurement or metric is essential in providing a benchmark that can be used to make estimates and conduct comparisons of the three dimensions of a process, with additional focus on the "how" aspect of a process. In other words, essentially, we use the metric as a means of communicating the quantity of work. This measure can be used in conjunction with the time, budget, and people estimates made for the project. Some of the reasons why a process should also be measured are:

- To help us to understand the process better, by providing a benchmark for how we do things
- To help others to understand the process by facilitating communication of the effort needed in a process
- To provide a means to recognize the maturity and repeatability of the process
- To provide a set of historical data for future estimations of time and costs within the organization and, eventually, within the industry
- To provide a set of historical data for refining the efficiency of the process (ideally with a process tool)

5.3.2   Measuring Process-Components in Deployment

Since processes have the three dimensions of technology, methodology, and sociology, measurements of elements within these dimensions run the risk of being disjointed and uncoordinated. Although in practice, project managers are able to correlate the project measures with each other as they track and manage progress in a project, it still may be worthwhile to consider, optionally, a unified measure of elements in a project. This is achieved by measuring the three dimensions of a process together—and is made possible by measuring the process-components.

The three dimensions of a process-component, as you will recall, are the deliverables (technological), activities and associated tasks (methodological), and roles (sociological). What is proposed here, in terms of measuring a process, is a metric that converts the various elements of the process into a single unit to facilitate estimations and comparisons. Rather than providing conclusive numbers, this metric is meant to provide indicative numbers that can also be used in project estimations including timing, budgeting, and project-planning activities. Furthermore, it can also be used to refine the processes during enactment, when the malleability of a process becomes important.

In order to describe this process-components measure, let us consider our well-known example of baking a cake, shown as a process-component in Chapter 3. Figure 3.3 shows three roles (consumer, chef, and food inspector), one deliverable (baked cake), and four activities (environment creation, baking, food quality checking, and consumption). Assuming that each activity has an average of four tasks, a simple total of all these elements is shown in Table 5.4.

Table 5.4 *Total number of elements in the cake-baking process*

Description of the element	Number of elements in the process
Role	3
Deliverables	1
Activities	4
Tasks	12
Total Elements:	20

However, this is too simplistic a measure as it simply adds all elements in a process-component. Even if we were to use this measure simply to compare two process-components (for example, process-components of requirements modeling versus project management), the measurements would not provide a correct comparison. We need, in addition, to count two key pieces of information that are important in enactment. They are:

- Number of instances of each element (for example, how many chefs or how many food quality checks)
- Weighting factors for each element

These additional practical factors in measuring processes are discussed next.

5.3.3   Measuring Process-Components in Enactment

A process-component like the one that describes the cake-baking process will, during enactment, have more than one role in baking a cake, and perhaps many more deliverables than just one cake—depending on where it is enacted. Thus, that same process-component enacted at home, where mom is baking a cake, has one person playing the role of a chef, resulting in one deliverable (a cake), consumed by, say, four people. If, however, the same process-component is enacted for a wedding, the multiplier for each element of the process is much greater than for a cake made for home consumption. Thus, the number of multipliers of each element of a process-component provides one important piece of information in measuring a process in practice.

Another vital piece of information is a weighting factor applied to each element of a process. The roles, activities, tasks, and deliverables all have to be multiplied by a weighting factor in order to arrive at a common unit that can then be added to arrive at the total process-components of measure. For example, the roles may have a multiplier of ten, but a deliverable will be multiplied by fifty—reflecting the latent costs involved in creating and maintaining a deliverable as against the definition of a role.

These weighting factors for each element depend on the context of the project. While currently there are no benchmarks for these measures at the industrial level, they can still be applied successfully within an organization and, particularly, within a project. For the cake-baking example, the multipliers applied to the number of instances of each element for a cake baked and consumed at home are shown in Table 5.5.

Table 5.5   *Arriving at the measure of the baking process (total process-components)*

Description of the element	Number of instances of elements in enactment	Weighting factors or multipliers per element	Total strength: Process-components for the element
Role	5 (2 chefs, 2 tasters, 1 sponsor)	100	500
Deliverables	2 (two large cakes)	500	1000
Activities	4+2 (food quality checking and consumption repeated)	20	120
Tasks	40	50	200
Total Process-Components:			1820

Comments:

Note how the calculation of the total process-components for the baking could not be made in Chapter 3, where the baking process-component was simply described. In that baking description we did not know how many chefs and food inspectors would be required. It is only when a properly described process comes to enactment that we can assign the number of elements in enactment to the process-component. Furthermore, assigning the weighting factor is a job that should be done right at the beginning of a project, when the process is being deployed. This is because weighting factors enable comparison between various process-components, but they themselves need to be uniform at least during the comparisons (usually within a project and, preferably, within an organization).

Once an organization builds up a repository of process-components, as well as its estimates in enactment, it is possible to start making more accurate estimates in terms of time and budget required for its projects.

5.3.4   Refining the Project Estimations at the End of Each Iteration

In addition to making the estimates at the start of the project, it is also essential to continue to monitor and improve on the estimates as the project progresses. The IIP development lifecycle is helpful to the project managers when refining their estimates at the end of each iteration. Project managers can use the time, effort, and budget results from the first iteration to improve on their estimates for the second and subsequent iterations. This requires creating an IIP project plan, as discussed in Section 4.4.2.

As mentioned in Chapter 4 and reiterated here, the IIP project task plan is not a static document. It is essential to continue to update the plan at the end of each iteration. The update to the project task plan reflects three important things: time, budgets, and scope. Rescoping the project should also be considered, if necessary, at the end of each iteration. Figure 5.1 shows an example of such refinement, with hypothetical process-components.

Let's start our understanding of Figure 5.1 by assuming that the iterations in this plan follow the rule of thumb of three to four months per iteration. In the graphic representation of these project estimates shown in Figure 5.1, let's say that the development effort starts with 3,600 process-components for the initial three months. Measurements of the number of components in a process are based on the metrics discussed in the previous section. Applying those arguments, one can say that the actors, activities, tasks, and deliverables are

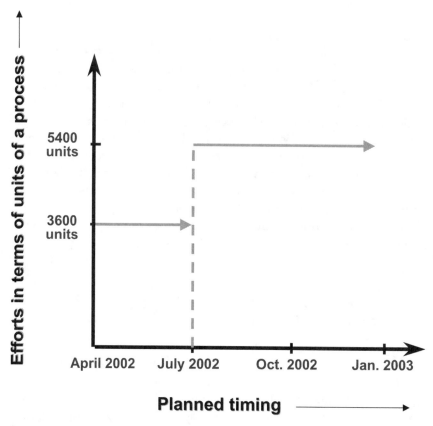

Figure 5.1 *Revising your estimates*

calculated based on their importance to the project and the past history of their performance within the organization (if such a history exists).

If the development starts in April 2002, then the first iteration is supposed to complete in July 2002. Now consider the fact that the effort required in the project, after the end of the first iteration in July 2002, is estimated at 5,400 components. This is a perfectly normal situation, wherein the effort in the first iteration is 3,600 components and the effort in the second iteration is 5,400 components. The increase in effort required is attributed to the fact that the second iteration is likely to be more intense and contain far more iterations of activities and tasks to satisfy the sufficiency criteria of a process-component.

The sociological dimension of the development process also comes into play in the second iteration in terms of games, interpersonal relationships, and so on—resulting in increased estimates of process-components in the second iteration. As a result of this estimation exercise of efforts planned for the two iterations, the product is expected to be ready by the end of 9 months (January 2003).

Having made these estimates, let's now consider what happens to these estimates in enactment. Let's assume that at the end of the first iteration the project manager discovers that the actual effort took four months instead of three months (May 2002, instead of April 2002). When this is discovered, the most commonly followed approach is to add the amount by which the project has slipped to the actual completion date. In our example, because the first iteration slipped by one month, the project manager is inclined to add one month to the completion date of January 2003, resulting in a new completion date of February 2003. *That would be naïve.*

It is important to consider the nonlinear aspect of this project estimation and project tracking. The process-component estimates need to be revised dynamically to reflect the slippage of time in the first iteration. This revision is achieved by considering a factor that reflects the measure of planned versus actual productivity of the development team resulting in an adjustment factor. The adjustment factor can be arrived at as follows:

Planned productivity = 3,600 components of process/3 months
= 1,200 components per month   (5.1)
Actual productivity (ascertained at the end of first iteration)
= 3,600 components of process/4 months
= 900 components per month   (5.2)

With normal productivity of 1,200 components per month, the development project was supposed to be completed by January 2003. However, at the end of first iteration, we have arrived at the revised productivity figure of 900 components per month. The adjustment factor for the rest of the effort and associated estimates for the process-components are given by:

Adjustment factor = Actual productivity/planned productivity
900/1,200 = 0.75   (5.3)

Equation 5.3 indicates that not only is the first iteration delayed by a month but even the effort of 5,400 components of process for the remaining six months (subsequent iteration) will have to be updated to one of the following options:

1. The effort of 5,400 components for six months will have to be refined to $5,400/0.75 = 5,860$ (approximately 5,900). This results in more resources added to the team, within certain limits.

2. The time of six months will have to be refined to $6/0.75 = 8$ months. This results in a new deliverable date of March 2003 (as against the naïve revised date of February 2003).

In both cases though, we have already lost a month in the initial iteration, which should be accounted for in all further calculations. Note, once again, that this example highlights the importance of revisiting the project plan and rescoping the use cases that may have been promised during the initial part of the first iteration. These measurements can and should be applied dynamically by astute project managers. Frequency of the checkpoint, shown at the end of the first iteration in this example, can be increased if more control and tracking is required for the project.

Process tools should also be able to facilitate this checkpointing, resulting in the continuous and dynamic tracking of the estimates versus the actuals in a project. Process tools must be able to help the project manager use the progress of the project to make fresh estimates for the rest of the project lifetime. These dynamic estimations ensure that we are not using metrics and measurements after the event is over, but rather, we are using the measurements to improve on our estimations as the project progresses.

An extremely small litmus-test iteration can also be used to arrive at process-component productivity figures before the project has started. This is either an actual iteration itself, or a special iteration used to create a prototype. Creating a prototype as a formal iteration not only serves the primary purpose of creating a prototype but also helps to estimate accurately the productivity of the project team (in terms of process-components).

5.4   Quality Metrics

Despite the previous discussion on dynamic estimation, the basic question still remains: How do you arrive at the PC-based estimates in the first place? Most project managers do not have the luxury of starting a project with estimates that can be substantially improved in subsequent iterations. A business sponsor, or the steering committee, has a certain budget and a certain business goal, in terms of timing, in mind. It is the job of the project manager to arrive at as accurate an estimate as possible to enable good decision making at the *beginning* of the project. For that purpose, the project manager can use many techniques. Some of these techniques are:

- Considering a group of senior managers in an estimation exercise. Each of the managers in the steering committee is asked to make an estimate, which is then collated to arrive at the project estimate.

- Estimating based on the expertise of the project manager, the quality manager, and the domain expert. This is the least objective, but perhaps the most practical measure of software projects. Past history of projects with similar technology, methodology, and sociology can provide many clues when estimating. Experts can factor in exceptional conditions, even in metrics and measurements, that ordinary estimators may not be aware of.

- Considering the road factors discussed in the previous chapter. These factors are also crucial in good estimation. All estimates are precisely that—estimates! They are bound to change. However, it is the extent to which they change that influences the way they serve their purpose.

- Planning for the unplanned. This is because unplanned changes are bound to occur in almost all projects.

- Ascertaining the correct metrics (what to measure, why to measure). This is important in making good use of the concept of metrics. For example, there is no point in measuring diagrams or process-components that are irrelevant to a particular project.

5.5   Measuring Size of Software

Project metrics provide time- and cost-related measurements. Process metrics provide the ability to measure and estimate units of effort needed in a project. Eventually, software projects produce software. How big is that software? And how does it relate to the estimates made earlier on in the project? This important correlation between what has been estimated in terms of projects and process, and what has been produced in terms of the software, can be ascertained if the size of the software can be measured.

There is a large number of metrics that deal with measurements of code, its complexity, and so forth.

5.5.1   Traditional Measures of Software

Measuring the lines of code (LOC) written in a system has been the traditional and, by far, the most popular way to measure software and has been used ever since the software community started writing programs. The question of how big is your system or program could be answered by counting the number of lines of code and documenting the results as 1,000, 10,000 or 50,000 LOC. While by no means adequate, in the days of COBOL and PASCAL, this was acceptable. This was because LOC was easy to measure: all we had to do was count the lines within a program, eliminate the comments, and we would have the answer to the question.

Even when fixes to the Y2K bug were attempted toward the end of the last decade, the first action was to count the LOC. This measure did not give enough credence to the nuances of individual programming languages. There was no reliable way to compare the estimate arrived at for software written in COBOL versus that written in FORTRAN. As Lorenz and Kidd [1994] describe it, there are a number of drawbacks to the LOC measure, including inconsistency across languages and applications, its inability to reflect complexity, and its inappropriateness as a measure of quality and progress. The issue gets further complicated in modern-day object-oriented languages, where reuse adds the complexity of measuring reused code.

5.5.2   Additional Measures of Software

In addition to the LOC measure of software, a number of additional estimation techniques exist, such as the Putnam model and Barry Boehm's COCOMO model. These are fairly objective and technical measures used in software projects. They provide the baseline in estimation and can be used on their own or combined with the standard LOC measure.

For example, the COCOMO model deals with the LOC metrics, as well. The estimated development time (and therefore the number of people required) is a function of the lines of code that are written in the software. Because of the relevance of LOC to this model and because of the limitations of the LOC measure in OO software discussed earlier, it is very difficult to apply the LOC metrics to the component-based software development approach that is used in most UML-based projects.

Function-point estimation has been very popular because it raises the measurement of software to a higher, more abstract, and more appropriate layer. Function points are measured based on the inputs, outputs, files, interfaces, and inquiries. Each of these factors is given an appropriate weighting, and the resultant total is used to estimate the size and complexity of the project. However, in the industry, a wide variation in measuring and interpreting function points exists. Furthermore, component-based development does not easily lend itself to this function-point measurement.

5.5.3   Object-Oriented Measures of Software

The above-mentioned measures not only have limitations, but these limitations are further compounded in object-oriented systems due to reusability through inheritance and aggregation/association. Jacobson et al. [1992] point out that LOC is not a good measure of productivity in object-oriented systems since the smaller the number of LOC written, the greater the likelihood that you have reused significant code chunks. This leads the project manager into a tricky situation wherein she has to reward a programmer for writing *less* code. Taken to an extreme, this leads to indexing the rewards to "no work" because, by reusing large classes and components, the programmer may not be doing anything at all related to actual programming in the project. However, reuse of large classes and components is at the heart of all modern software engineering approaches.

To circumvent these difficulties, Thomas and Jacobson [1989][1] have proposed a metric to measure the size of an object-oriented system. This is a much preferable way to measure an object-oriented system than the LOC, especially in an object-oriented development environment; I have used it myself (see Unhelkar and Henderson-Sellers, [1993]).

This metric states that for a system with N object classes, each of size s_i, the size of an OO system is provided by

$$S = \sum_{i=1}^{N} s_i = \sum_{i=1}^{N} (AW_A + MW_M)_i \qquad (1)$$

where A is the number of attributes in a class (weighting, W_A, less than W_M) and *M* is the number of methods in a class (weighting, W_M language dependent). Since the weighting factors are language dependent, the resultant size is different for projects using different languages. Work is still required to evaluate appropriate weights, W_A and W_M.

Without getting into the nuances of ascertaining the weighting factor itself, if the *same* weighting factors were to be used *across* multiple projects

---

[1] This metric has been further developed by Henderson-Sellers [1993].

using the *same* language and the *same* development environment, then we would be able to use the resultant figures to arrive at our productivity measure and thereby make estimations for the next project. This argument is similar to the one used for the "last in, first out" (LIFO) or "first in, first out" (FIFO) accounting practices. Either of these practices is right, as long as it's used consistently across the organization from year to year. Similarly, the number for the weighting factors selected is not in itself a major issue as long as it's kept consistent across projects.

The equation above can, therefore, be used to measure the size of object-oriented software much better than the LOC. It can also be used in design measures such as ascertaining the granularity of an OO system, as discussed in Chapter 5. We will see later how this measure can be applied in measuring the size of the system produced, and how it can be correlated to the project and process metrics discussed earlier.

5.6   Measures of UML Artifacts, Diagrams, and Models

5.6.1   Measuring Size and Complexity of Use Cases and Use Case Diagrams

One of the most important measures of models, especially in the problem space, is that of use cases and use case diagrams. While this measure is not standardized, it is still possible to arrive at the measure of a use case diagram by considering all the elements in the use case diagrams. These include the actors, the use cases, their relationships, and the documentation inside the use cases.

Use cases are usually classified as simple, medium, or complex. Simple use cases provide a set of interactions that can be described in a single sheet of paper. More than one page of use case documentation is a very rough yet practical measure of the increasing complexity of a use case—making it a medium use case. A use case with many alternatives and exception flows is a complex use case.

The flow within the use cases can be aptly described by the activity diagrams. Therefore, one measure of the size of the use case is the supporting activity diagrams. Scenarios based on use cases are shown visually by using the sequence diagrams. The sequence diagrams can also be used to measure of the complexity of use cases.

5.6.2   Measuring Size and Complexity of Classes

The size of a class depends on the number of attributes, the number of operations, and the possible weighting factor one assigns to the operations.

The complexity of a class depends on the relationships a class has with other classes, the visibility of its attributes, and operations. Dynamic complexity of classes depends on the number of objects instantiated off the class, and the relationship between these objects.

5.6.3   Measurement of a Component

A component should be measured in terms of its size and its execution. The size of a component invariably depends on the number of classes that are realized in the component. The size of a component also depends on the number of interfaces it has. The execution of a component is measured for its speed and ability to handle volume. Furthermore, the number of threads supported by a component adds to the execution capability of a component.

5.6.4   Testing Metrics

Testing metrics provide a measure of quality control. They deal with the defects found in a product as it is tested. The testing metrics also deal with the support for fixing and retesting the product after the errors found earlier are fixed. Furthermore, testing metrics can be used in estimating the potential for further defects in the system. These measures of the software are further discussed in Chapter 6.

5.7   Applying Metrics and Estimates to Lucky Insurance's Project

5.7.1   Considering Metrics and Estimates Specific to Lucky Insurance's Project

Let us consider applying some of the concepts discussed thus far to the example project at Lucky Insurance that is implementing a CRMS package (see the accompanying CD for Lucky Insurance's problem statement). Because the project deals with package implementation, it is important to consider the variations in the roles, deliverables, and the time and effort spent in each of the modeling spaces. For example, there will be more people playing the roles that deal with capturing the detailed requirements and creating the detailed business models than the roles of system designer and programmer. It is only later in the lifecycle that the technical roles become significant as the requirements are mapped to the solution.

Furthermore, most of the solution will come "out of the box" and be customized to fit the problem. Therefore the kinds of roles we need in larger numbers are the ones that exist in the problem space, not those in the solution space. In a new development project, however, this mix changes and the number of people playing the roles in the problem space are most likely the same as those in the solution space.

Returning to our CRMS project, we estimate between three and five business analysts working between three and six months going through the initial iteration of the process lifecycle, resulting in a first cut of the MOPS. This first cut reveals most use cases, a substantial number of business classes, and some technical classes. The first iteration also includes documentation of use cases and business classes as well as documentation of relevant UML diagrams in the MOPS.

In terms of the organizational roles of project manager and quality manager, the Lucky Insurance project should expect one project manager supported, in terms of organizing the quality function, by one quality manager. However, these two roles have independent reporting lines to the steering committee.

In all UML-based projects we recommend having real users onboard. This remains true for the Lucky Insurance project. One would expect that there will be at least two users representing the account executive role and the senior management role initially onboard during all requirements modeling workshops for between six and eight weeks, followed by availability for one week per month throughout the life of the project.

Domain experts may occasionally support user representatives. These are the people who in the case of the Lucky Insurance project have insurance domain expertise. Because of their high skill levels, demand, and costs, these domain experts may not be available on the project full time. However, the consulting expertise of these domain experts should be sought in the Lucky Insurance project and they should be booked for a given block of time, which can then be consumed and spread over the initial and major project iterations.

5.7.2   Project and Process Metrics in Enactment

Lucky Insurance's CRMS implementation project is becoming a medium to large project as discussed in Chapter 1. This is because the initial estimates of the project in terms of time, budgets, and people falls within the boundary of medium to large projects. However, as with all estimates, these figures are precisely that—estimates. They can go wrong, and our aim here is to consider the distribution of the process and project metrics over the life of the project to enable us to refine and adjust the estimates made earlier in the lifecycle.

5.7.3   Measuring Process-Components for Enactment

One way of making good, sensible estimates for Lucky Insurance's project is to consider how each process-component shapes up during enactment. It is worth keeping in mind the primary modeling space that each process-component supports, and also the fact that some process-components such as process configuration, project management, and quality management continue to remain in the background space and will influence all other process-components. These process-components, therefore, are difficult to estimate in a linear fashion. They will, instead, be spread out over the linear timelines of other process-components.

We consider only two example process-components for estimating their corresponding process-component requirements in enactment. This approach to calculating process-components is based on the example calculation for the baking process discussed earlier in this chapter. However, the numbers of instances of the elements in enactment as well as the weighting factors per element are different from those in the baking process. Your own practical projects may have their own weighting factors which may be different from the ones here. As long as these multipliers remain consistent across the entire project, they serve the purpose of estimation and comparison of PCs within the project. The rest of the process-components can be assumed to have followed this approach, when their PCs are listed.

Table 5.6 *Arriving at the measure of the business evaluation process-component in Lucky Insurance's project*

Description of the element	Number of instances of elements in enactment	Weighting factors or multipliers per element	Total strength: Process-component for the element
Role	2+1	100	300
Deliverables	2	100	200
Activities	4	20	80
Tasks	19	50	950
Total Units:	28		1530

Table 5.7 *Arriving at the measure of the requirements modeling process-component in Lucky Insurance's project*

Description of the element	Number of instances of elements in enactment	Weighting factors or multipliers per element	Total strength: Process-component for the element
Role	2+5+2	100	900
Deliverables	4	100	400
Activities	11	20	220
Tasks	34	50	1700
Total Units:	58		3220

5.7.4   Applying Process and Project Metrics to Lucky Insurance's Project

If the project starts in April 2002, the likely sequence and timings could be as follows.

The initial, major, and final iterations within a project will usually be spread as per the discussion in the previous chapter as 15 percent, 65 percent, and 20 percent time and effort. However, some process-components are more intense in the initial iteration and others are enacted with extra intensity in the major and final iterations. The following estimations demonstrate the method of estimation. Initial estimates, such as the ones

Table 5.8 *Applying process and project metrics to Lucky Insurance's project (weighting factors: Roles = 100, Deliverables = 100, Activities = 20, and Tasks = 50)*

Process-components in iteration 1 (initial)	Roles		Deliverables		Activities		Tasks		Process-components
Business evaluation	3	300	2	200	4	80	18	900	1,480
Requirements modeling	3	300	4	400	4	80	17	850	1,630
Project management	3	300	2	200	8	160	10	500	1,160
Process configuration	4	400	2	200	9	180	11	550	1,330
Quality management	4	400	2	200	4	80	17	850	1,530
Total effort in iteration 1									7,130
Process-components in iteration 2 (major)	**Roles**		**Deliverables**		**Activities**		**Tasks**		**Process-components**
System design	4	400	5	500	6	120	15	750	1,770
Implementation	3	300	2	200	7	140	23	1150	1,790
Requirements modeling	33	300	2	200	11	220	17	850	1,570
Project management	3	300	4	400	8	160	13	650	1,510
Quality assurance	4	400	4	400	8	160	33	1650	2,610
Quality management	4	400	4	400	9	180	27	1350	2,330
Total effort in iteration 2									11,580
Process-components in iteration 3 (final)	**Roles**		**Deliverables**		**Activities**		**Tasks**		**Process-components**
Deployment	3	300	3	300	5	100	13	650	1,350
Training	3	300	2	200	5	100	19	950	1,550
Total effort in iteration 3									**2,900**
Total Estimated Process Effort for Lucky Insurance									**21,610**

made below, should be further improved to bring the estimates closer to the aforementioned philosophy.

5.7.5   Arriving at the Productivity Factor for Lucky Insurance's Project

The aforementioned process metrics provide valuable information on calculating the effort needed and put in, in terms of the people, time, and budgets for the project. A correlation between the estimates of people, time, and budgets and the corresponding software produced is extremely valuable from a project-management perspective. In order to accomplish this correlation, though, it is necessary to measure the software-specific deliverables at the end of the initial iteration or at a checkpoint similar to the end of the initial iteration. While the time spent by people fulfilling the roles of a process can be calculated in terms of person-days, there is a need to calculate the size of the software produced using the class metrics described earlier.

In the case of the Lucky Insurance project, let us consider the classes produced at the end of the first iteration as a software deliverable. It is against this measure of the software deliverable (as against the LOC deliverable measure) that we correlate the process-component estimated in the previous section. Equation 1 in Section 5.5.3 proposed a metric to measure the size of a class. That metric gave due importance to the weighting factors. Therefore, consider the size of a class fully described in the MOPS for Lucky Insurance with the help of the following weighting factors:

$$W_A = 2; W_M = 10$$

Recall that the above values are picked empirically as there are no industry-level standards available for these weighting factors. It is, however, crucial that the same weighting factors are maintained in all other calculations within the project and, preferably, within the organization. Henderson-Sellers and Edwards [1994] suggest a weighting factor of $W_M = 5$–20 and $W_A = 1$. We have modified that suggestion for the Lucky Insurance project.

The total size of the software produced so far is based on the sum of the sizes of individual classes. The size (S) of each of these classes is measured based on the actual number of attributes (A) and methods (M), using the corresponding weighting factors as shown in Equation 2 below:

$$S = AW_A + MW_M \qquad (2)$$

Thus, by adding the actual sizes of each class we are able to arrive at the total size of the system, the average size of each class, and the average number of attributes and methods per class. These example calculations are as follows:

Total size S of the system = 20,000   (3)

(as can be actually measured using the spreadsheet)

Total number of classes N in the first iteration = 100   (4)
Average size of a class in the system = 200   (5)
Average number of attributes A per class = 10   (6)
Average number of methods M per class = 18   (7)

Dividing the size (S) by 100 for the sake of convenience, we arrive at the size units of classes fully modeled for the Lucky Insurance project in the initial iteration as follows:

Size of Lucky Insurance (first iteration) = 200 units   (8)

The next metric needed to arrive at the productivity figure is the average person-months spent on the project, derived from Lorenz and Kidd [1994]. Let us assume that the Lucky Insurance project has been lucky enough to organize its project team around the "I + You +" life position discussed in Chapter 2. In such a project, the teams function without the enforcing of detailed timesheets; therefore, measuring the time spent by project members has to be done with utmost sensitivity. Asking the programmers to fill out timesheets is a sensitive issue and should be handled in a sociologically careful way. Hence, a simple spreadsheet can be used by the project manager to log the number of working days each team member works on the project (excluding holidays and weekends). Let us say this gives a total person-month figure for the first iteration as described in Equation 9 below:

Person-months = 55   (9)

Using Equations 8 and 9 gave the following productivity figure:

Average S-Units per person-month = 3.63   (10)

There are a number of variables to this metric including the skills of the people, holiday breaks,[2] process maturity, and time required to fix the errors found and doing the rework.

---

[2] This is especially true if it is an outsourced project. A development project from a company in San Francisco outsourced to a software company in Bangalore will have to prepare for two large breaks toward the end of the year—the well-known Christmas break in December and the big break for Diwali, the Indian festival of lights in October and November.

It is hoped that the project manager of this CRMS project is aware that she is not collecting the metrics as an end in themselves, but rather as a tool to come as close as possible to estimating *probabilities,* in managing the project. This approach is in tune with the street directory approach discussed in Chapter 4. The productivity figure arrived at in Equation 10 can be used to keep the caveats of the road factors in mind.

5.7.6   Refining Estimates Based on the Productivity Factor for Subsequent Iterations

Once we have the productivity figures for the team toward the close of the first iteration, time and budgets for subsequent iterations can be *estimated* based on this figure because the development environment and other road factors can be expected to remain more or less the same. If, on the other hand, the language of implementation changes from one iteration to another, it will be necessary to consider that factor in calculating subsequent time and cost estimates.

Furthermore, just as we arrive at the productivity of the team based on the classes, we can similarly correlate the classes to the use cases in the project. If, for example, the use cases documented and analyzed in the first iteration can be mapped against the business classes produced, then a reasonable estimate of the number of classes in the subsequent iteration can be produced. An estimate of three times the number of classes discovered and documented in the first iteration provides a reasonably good estimate of the total number of classes in the system. Thus an *estimate* of 550 classes can be made for the Lucky Insurance project.

$$\text{The Lucky Insurance estimated size based on class metrics} = 50 \quad (11)$$

Note that this estimate is based on the assumption that the average size of the new classes is the same as that of the first iteration (Equation 5). Furthermore, while this estimate is derived from the use cases, similar mappings can be estimated from other things in the initial iteration such as activity diagrams.

Furthermore, if the process-component of reuse is followed, then it should be possible to identify some classes in the initial iteration that can be reused in subsequent iterations. For example, the `Policy` and `Client` classes discovered in the first iteration can be reused for specific new policy products such as Health Insurance or Travel Insurance discovered and documented in the second iteration. Similarly, there are GUI and utility classes (for example, date and time parsing, charting, and printing) that will find substantial reuse in the second iteration. Let us say that the Lucky Insurance project is able to identify approximately 100 classes that belong to the various subsystems (packages) discovered and documented in the first iteration. These classes would lend themselves to reuse in the second iteration as shown in Equation 12.

Number of classes reused from iteration 1 = 50 $\qquad$ (12)

This leaves the number of new classes required to be discovered and implemented as:

Number of new classes for second and third iteration = 500 (13)

The next step, in arriving at the size of the system, is to determine the average values for attributes and methods. For a totally different application domain, these values are not likely to be the same. However, that not being the case here, we proceed with the values we get from the first iteration, as shown in Equations 6 and 7. Keeping the weighting factors the same as for the first iteration, that is:

$$W_A = 2; W_M = 10$$

We arrive at the size of the effort in the remaining iterations of the system as follows:

$$S = \sum_{i=1}^{N(=500)} (AW_A + MW_M)_i = (10 \times 2 + 18 \times 10) \times 500 = 100,000 \quad (14)$$

Dividing the total S-Units required for the subsequent iteration (Equation 14) by the productivity figure of the team in the first iteration (Equation 10) gives the total person-months required for the remaining part of the project as 275.5, or 22.9 person-years. This translates to a requirement of approximately 22 people for 1 year.

Estimates similar to these can also be made based on use cases themselves, without going into classes and class diagrams. If projects are not using the UML they may base the estimates on function points. However, my experience with most UML-based projects has been that better estimates are possible from classes and class diagrams than any other element of the UML.

5.8   Prophetic Statements on Estimates and Metrics

All previous discussions in this chapter are supported by some direct statements that I have arrived at in practice. These are not logically derived statements but, instead, statements of my experience and that of some of my colleagues. Since they can go wrong, it is safer to call them prophetic statements. By considering these prophetic statements in UML-based projects you will arrive at one of two conclusions: (a) these statements are wrong, in which case you have arrived at the right estimates for your project, or (b) your estimates are wrong and can be improved upon. In both cases, these prophetic statements will have served their purpose of providing you with a boundary. With such a boundary, you can always ascertain whether you are inside or outside of it and, more importantly, whether you *want* to be inside the boundary or outside of it.

Prophetic Statements in UML-Based Projects:

- A walkthrough lasts for approximately two hours and may involve five to ten people.

- An inspection lasts for 30 minutes and may involve two people.

- A review may last from half to one day, and may involve five to ten people.

- An audit may last from a day to a week or more, and will involve all members of the project team and the auditors.

- A simple use case, and its associated activity and class diagrams, may take one person-week to be fully modeled in the MOPS. A complex use case will take between two and four weeks to complete the modeling.

- One business class (or business-level entity) will usually have two more associated classes in the solution space MOSS.

- Ensure that estimates for development of a use case, a class, and a component do not overlap each other.

- A package, or a subsystem, will contain all diagrams and documentations in it. A package may take approximately six person-months for modeling and development.

- Total modeling time in a project is approximately 40 percent of the overall time allocated for the project.

- Total modeling effort (as measured by process-components related to modeling) is also approximately 40 percent of the overall effort estimated in the project.

- Good quality modeling and processes save the time and effort spent on them—40 percent. Therefore, the advantage of using modeling and processes will accrue only after the second project.

5.9   Bibliographic Notes

Measurements and estimates continue to improve as we use them; the more we use them, the better we become at it. That is the way I differentiate a guess versus a gamble. While both are based on probabilities, in the case of an educated guess you have an opportunity to practice and improve your estimates as you build experience. This can ultimately benefit you by reducing the risks in your projects. In the case of gambling, the more experienced you are, the more you are at risk!!

For practical project reports on measurements and estimates on various projects I have been involved with, please visit *www.MethodScience.com*.

5.10   Frequently Asked Questions (FAQs)

Q1: Which element of the UML is the most reliable measure in UML-based projects?

A1: Class and class diagrams. This is because they are far more concrete than use cases and other elements in the problem space.

Q2: What is the most important measure in UML-based projects?

A2: If, somehow, the project can map use cases to productivity, it will result in the most important measure. This is because it is use cases that get discovered first in the project. A measure of use cases to productivity will therefore provide an excellent means to estimate projects at an early stage of the lifecycle.

5.11   Exercises

E5.1: What are the important metrics in the three dimensions of a process?

E5.2: How do you differentiate between metrics, measurements, and estimates?

E5.3: Why are good estimates important in enhancing the quality within a project?

E5.4: What are the three important project metrics?

E5.5: How does a process metric differ from a project metric?

E5.6: Compare and criticize the project metrics in the MOPS for the three different sized projects.

E5.7: Repeat the above comparison for MOSS and MOBS metrics.

E5.8: Describe how you arrive at the process effort needed in measuring the process of baking a cake.

E5.9: Why is refinement of estimates dynamically important?

E5.10: What are the risks associated with dynamic revisions to estimates (reports to steering committee)?

E5.11: How would you measure the size of a use case?

E5.12: How would you measure the size of a class? (Describe the Thomas and Jacobson measure.)

E5.13: Why is the Lines of Code measure inappropriate for a class?

E5.14: What are the advantages and limitations of the measurements described for the Lucky Insurance project?

5.12   References

DeMarco, T., and T. Lister, *Peopleware: Productive Projects and Teams,* New York: Dorset House Publishing Company, 1987, pp. 26–29.

Henderson-Sellers, B., "The Economics of Reusing Library Classes," *Journal of Object-Oriented Programming,* 1993, 6(4), pp. 43–50.

———, and J. Edwards, *Book Two of Object-Oriented Knowledge, The Working Object,* Upper Saddle River, N.J.: Prentice-Hall, 1994, p. 485.

Jacobson, I., M. Christerson, P. Jonsson, and G. Overgaard, *Object-Oriented Software Engineering: A Use Case Driven Approach*, Reading, Mass.: Addison-Wesley, 1992, p. 460.

Jones, C., *Applied Software Measurement: Assuring Productivity and Quality*, New York: McGraw-Hill, 1991.

Lorenz, M., and J. Kidd, *Object-Oriented Software Metrics*, Upper Saddle River N.J.: Prentice-Hall, 1994, pp. 4–5.

Thomas, D., and I. Jacobson, "Managing object-oriented software engineering tutorial," *TOOLS '89*, Paris, 13–15 Nov. 1989, p. 52

Unhelkar, B., and Henderson-Sellers, B., "The Role of Granularity in the Reuse of Object-oriented Systems," *Proceedings of ACOSM'93 First Australian Conference on Software Metrics*, Sydney, Australia, June Verner (ed.), Australian Software Metrics Association, November 18–19 1993, pp 51–66.

Unhelkar, B., "The MOSES experience," *Object Magazine*, June 1995, p. 51.

———, *After the Y2K Fireworks: Business and Technology Strategies*, CRC Press, 1999; further work by this author is in the offing, titled *Games IT People Play*.

Wohlin, C., and M. Ahlgren, "Soft factors and their impact on time to market," *Software Quality Journal*, September 1995, 4(3), pp. 189–205.

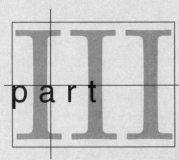

part III

Testing the Product: Quality Control

Part III contains only one chapter, that on testing. The reason this chapter is treated as a separate part is because it deals with an almost independent activity that occurs toward the end of a software development lifecycle. So far we have discussed creating and enacting a process. Quality control (testing) is a major process dedicated to verifying and validating the results of our efforts of creating models and following a process. Good quality control is inherent as it aims to break everything in a system—its logic, its execution, and its performance. Thus, although quality control is an integral part of quality assurance, it is not synonymous with it. This separation is given its due importance in Chapter 6.

Quality Control of Software Products

There is no need to agonize over what might have been forgotten,
because quality assurance (Control) keeps track of everything. There is no
need to worry about what surprises may come from a user's acceptance test, or
from the first few months in the field, because quality assurance (Control) has
savaged the system more than any user ever could, and done it in privacy,
where the consequences are merely extra work rather than litigation.
—Boris Beizer [1984]

Putting This Chapter in Perspective

One of the crucial aspects of quality assurance is testing, or quality control. Software testing has always been a challenge because the product being tested is not a physical product built on an assembly line. In the engineering domain, quality control results in accepting or rejecting a manufactured product—in software it's more often the case of correcting than rejecting. While the process aspect of testing was put together in the quality-control process-component in Chapter 3, here we cover the theory and practice of testing in far greater detail. The topics discussed in this chapter include various types of testing approaches (for example, black versus white box, and automated versus manual), testing architecture (encompassing unit, component, system, acceptance, and regression tests), test planning, test scripts, test execution, and test results collation.

The Prime Reader: Quality Manager, Test Manager, Developer, Tester

6.1   Testing in Context

Quality control deals with ensuring that the quality of the end product meets a given specification. In the manufacturing domain, quality control deals with checking the nuts and bolts on goods produced for their adherence to given standards. In the case of software, quality control deals with whether the software product functions correctly, according to specifications, and in conjunction with other software products and databases. The ultimate aim of software quality control (or testing, as it is routinely known), is to "break" the system long before it reaches the user in real life.

Ideally, therefore, if a tester manages to pass an illegal transaction through the system being tested, or is somehow able to crash the system, then that test is hailed as a pass or success. This is because the tester has successfully managed to discover an error under controlled test conditions, which if gone undetected, may have the potential to bring a real system (and probably a real business) to a halt.

However, testing is an operational and tactical effort. A tester is bent on finding as many errors as possible. This is different from the role of a quality analyst, who is interested in reducing the occurrences of errors in the first place—primarily by ensuring compliance with a process discipline and modeling. A quality manager is responsible for creating the right environment—with the right technology, methodology, and sociology conducive to the quality software development. Figure 6.1 shows the three major areas of work related to quality and their strategic versus tactical nature. Quality management is shown to influence quality assurance, which in turn influences quality control or testing. The responsibilities of the three major areas of work shown in Figure 6.1 are summarized as follows:

- Quality management, together with project management, deals with the overall approach to project quality. Creating a quality environment with a good environmental factor, creating and managing teams, and handling the overall sociology within the project are some of the responsibilities of quality management.

- Quality assurance ensures that the models and processes within software development are followed in a manner that results in good software. By following a quality process, one expects to find fewer errors and bugs and more satisfactory acceptance tests, resulting from the fact that the software development has taken place in response to a well-defined problem. Quality assurance provides all the necessary

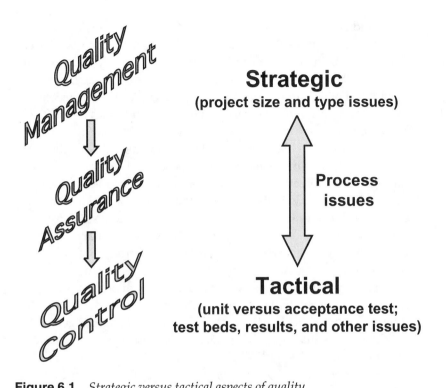

Strategic
(project size and type issues)

Process
issues

Tactical
(unit versus acceptance test;
test beds, results, and other issues)

Figure 6.1   *Strategic versus tactical aspects of quality*

techniques (such as the detailed syntax, semantics, and aesthetic checks in the three modeling spaces) and the process (as described in Chapter 3). It provides the templates for deliverables and verifies the compliance of the deliverables to the standards within the project. This results in the overall quality of models and processes, which is reassuring to the stakeholders in terms of the expected and accepted level of system quality.

• Quality control or testing does the policing work on the software system. The following sections discuss the best way to approach this testing work so that maximum errors are found during the last stage before the system is released into the real world. Testing is mentioned as operational in nature in the context of the overall project. On its own, however, testing requires careful planning and an approach that suits the system being tested. The type of project, as discussed in Chapter 1, influences the creation of the test plan. For example, in integration projects, testing of new interfaces to the existing legacy application requires extensive testing, whereas the testing needs of a data warehousing project simply focus on the accuracy and relevance of the data being used. The project size also influences the testing approach. For example, large projects need a much bigger system-testing lifecycle and have to factor in the costs and times for the necessary rework resulting from testing. Small projects, on the other hand, may focus on black box acceptance tests (described in the next section) right from the beginning, as opposed to the detailed walk-throughs and inspections needed on large projects. Project criticality is also important in quality control. Although one would like to test every possible alternative, in practice, after the basic system testing has been accomplished, the scope of testing should be narrowed to focus on the critical needs of the system. For example, preferably, a submarine project should undergo extensive zero-tolerance testing, but a name and address system for an insurance mail list may be released in production if it is "good enough." It is not always possible to get this balancing act right. The quality manager, together with the project manager, should ensure that testing is not reduced under the guise of less criticality, but is also not "done to death" at the cost of missing business opportunities. Experience helps in getting this balance right.

6.2   Testing Approaches in UML-Based Projects

Testing approaches provide a background understanding of the various ways in which software is tested. This understanding helps to produce a comprehensive testing strategy for UML-based projects. Figure 6.2 describes the testing approaches that can be used to create testing strategies for any of the various types of projects of differing sizes. It should be noted that these testing approaches are *not* exclusive; it is not a question of choosing one approach over the other. These testing approaches are discussed here to help us to use the right combination of testing approaches during the testing process-component. The testing approaches are described here:

- Black box/white box testing deals with the openness or closedness of the code.
- Manual/automated testing indicates the type of people and tools used in testing.

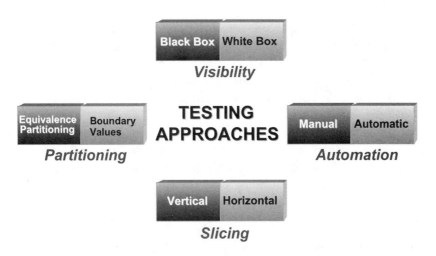

Figure 6.2 *Testing approaches in a good testing architecture*

- Vertical/horizontal testing indicates behavioral versus technical slicing of the system for testing.
- Equivalence partitioning/boundary values indicates how the test data is to be sampled for testing.

Test plans and real-life tests are a combination of the above approaches. The following section discusses these approaches in further detail.

6.2.1 Black Box

When testing concentrates only on the input and the output, without worrying about the internals of the system, the testing approach is called black box testing. This is also closed testing, wherein the system is closed in a box and not open for inspection. The aim of black box testing is to analyze the behavior of the software with respect to the functionality specified in the requirements. This type of testing is particularly interested in the interfaces (GUI and others) and the end results coming out of the system interfaces. There is no desire to explore the internal structure and behavior of the system. This type of testing approach is also ideally suited for verification of business processes in the system, as the gory details of implementation of such business processes in the system are hidden inside the black box.

Typically, black box testing is conducted by the system users and forms a major part of the system acceptance. These user testers are likely to be the ones who helped to specify the system in the first place—primarily through use cases and activity diagrams. Since the user community is not concerned with the architecture of the system, they treat the system as a black box and test it as such.

Use case documentation provides the starting point for black box testing. The flow within the use cases can be executed, one step at a time, and verified against the expected results. Black box testing can also be related to other UML diagrams in MOPS. For example, activities within the activity diagrams and messages within a sequence diagram can be verified from outside the system in terms of accuracy of their results. Black box testing in MOBS, or background space, can be used during the testing of infrastructure products (a Web application server, for example) for their performance and accuracy.

6.2.2 White Box

The white box approach to testing is the opposite of the black box approach, and requires a detailed and open examination of the models, programs, and business processes. The quality techniques of inspections and reviews, either as a checklist or in a workshop, are most helpful in conducting the white box testing. White box test design focuses specifically on the internals of the software—seeking to open the software and peeping inside to figure out how a particular program or class is structured, how the algorithms can be improved and made efficient, and whether there are opportunities to improve the way, say, a controller class manages message sequencing.

The white box approach is not restricted to code. Since models themselves are not executables, the best way to test the validity of the models is by inspecting their internals many times over and from different angles. Furthermore, during the early phases of development, specifications and documents can also be subjected to white box testing. This results in detecting problems long before the development has reached the coding state. Therefore, white box testing can result in considerable time savings and less physical testing effort during later phases of the project.

As mentioned here, two of the common ways to perform white box testing are walkthrough and inspection. During walkthrough, the person who has produced the deliverable (for example, a programmer if it is a class or a package, or a technical writer if it is a document) is asked to present their work to the quality assurance (in this case, testing) person or team.

Thus, in the walkthrough of a technical document, the technical writer describes the document to the test team and provides sample test cases, which are positive in nature. These positive tests mean that we do not try to break the flow within the document but try to understand its flow and pass comments on it.

In the case of inspection, however, the program or document is divided into its individual modules and carefully inspected in small steps to ensure that it does not have any logical bugs. Inspection of these modules is assigned to team members who have expertise in their particular area. The experience of the inspector helps not only in finding bugs, but also in ensuring that unnecessary bugs are not introduced when the producer of the artifact tries to fix the errors.

The best tools for white box testing are pencil and paper or whiteboard. By using these simple tools to highlight and correct erroneous models or buggy classes, the artifacts can be discussed, corrected, and subjected to various scenarios without being executed. Transparencies can be used to display a common image of the artifact being tested, as discussed in the quality techniques in Section 2.6. The result of these tests, however, differs in nature from those of the black box testing. This is because if problems are found they are usually related to the semantics or logic of the module rather than its syntax.

Since these tests are conducted in a workshop format, wherein errors in the artifact being inspected are publicly displayed, they have a sociological angle (as discussed in Chapter 2). For example, people may not always take criticism positively, and may want to continue to justify their designs or code even in the face of facts proving their inadequacy. This can lead to nonproductive games, causing teams to lose their harmony and synchronicity.

If testing has started with the black box approach, then it will localize an error-prone module or program. It is then necessary to go inside the artifact in order to identify the problem. Errors related to business logic as well as technical errors can be identified by testing them using the white box approach. However, because of the semantic nature of this testing, the white box testing approach may not be very convenient in data warehousing or conversion projects, where a large amount of data needs to be tested for its physical accuracy.

6.2.3   Manual Testing

Manual testing is based on human intervention with the application under test. In this approach to testing, the software programs are executed manually by the tester, usually by pressing buttons on the user interfaces that drive the system. The results are manually checked for their accuracy.

Furthermore, system designs and internal class or program structures can also be checked manually, as against attempting to check their complexities and correctness through automated tools for testing designs. Some testing situations demand writing special programs to test sections of data or to replicate code with small variations to its logic. This requires manually writing detailed test programs. Writing of test harnesses inside of classes, or as associated skeletal programs that drive larger programs being tested, can also be categorized as a manual-testing approach.

Test teams comprising the user and the tester can manually step through the use cases and classes, as well as through existing legacy programs and their interfaces. Test programmers can also write test harnesses and users can help to create the selective variation in the input test data needed for these kinds of tests.

6.2.4   Automated Testing

Automated testing of any kind necessarily employs a testing tool to achieve the purpose of testing the artifact. When a large number of repetitive transactions needs to be passed through a fully functional system under test, and if a tool can be made to do this repetitive task with relevant variations to the input data, it becomes automated testing. Testing, when conducted with a testing tool, requires the capture of scripts by executing the system being tested. Scripts can also be directly written by testers who understand the testing tool's syntax for writing scripts. This reduces the time required in regression testing, as entire tests can be left running overnight without manual intervention from the testers.

While manual testing provides depth in testing the systems, automated testing is able to provide the breadth or coverage of a large amount of input, which can be passed through the system. This is the most efficient way to conduct regression testing, ensuring that although a small part of the system has changed, the rest of the system has been tested thoroughly by conducting the automated tests as a part of the routine.

Some of the other advantages of automated testing include:

- The ability to reproduce bugs at any time in order to demonstrate them to the programmer responsible for the module
- The ability to record the results automatically
- The ability to compare results with a predefined standard set of results and to record the differences and report them without manual intervention

- The ability to reduce the time to conduct regression tests because the tools are able to replay the sequence of events much faster than when they were manually keyed in

6.2.5   Vertical Testing

When a testing approach slices the system vertically, it essentially divides the system into subsystems from the application viewpoint. For example, an insurance application, divided into the packages of Client and Policy, can be tested for each of these packages only. When the testing focuses on all aspects of implementing one package only, it is vertical testing. During this testing, the dependencies of, say, the Client package on other packages and subsystems are not the main focus of testing. Instead, the database tables related to Client, the business objects, and the GUI (all related to Client) are tested.

Vertical testing follows on from vertical slicing of the system during architectural work in creating the MOBS. This approach is put to good use when specialist users and domain experts are involved in testing the system. Each subsystem forms part of an individual's expertise. Therefore, dividing the testing into vertical slices can lead to thorough testing by the people who are experts in a narrow module of the system.

6.2.6   Horizontal Testing

Horizontal testing occurs when the approach to testing a system is based around its infrastructure rather than its functionality. For example, in the insurance system, if the entire system is tested first for its data only, followed by the testing of its business objects and its GUI—cutting across all packages and programs—then we have horizontally sliced the system for testing. Thus for the purpose of testing, if the system is divided into data and logic and operating system and network, then technical testers who have expertise in these relevant technical areas will be able to conduct a far more thorough testing of the respective areas. For example, a networking expert will focus on the bandwidth and security aspects related to the network for all packages within an insurance application. Because of the technical nature of the tests, one does not expect a large amount of user involvement in the horizontally sliced tests—as the infrastructure is essentially a black box for the users.

6.2.7 Equivalence Partitioning

Creating a succinct set of test data is crucial to any successful testing approach. This is because a good suite of data helps in the balancing act between testing ad infinitum (a game in the sociological sense) and testing to arrive at a suitable level of confidence before the system release.

Equivalence partitioning is the partitioning of the target test application and its data in such a way that each of the partitions provides homogeneous test targets. Usually, it is the data that is divided into equivalent partitions, and test targets are selected from within the partitions. For example, an insurance application may be made up of 10,000 policies, which may be divided among four different types of policies as shown below.

Policy types	Number of policies
Home coverage policies	2,000
Life coverage policies	4,000
Travel insurance policies	3,000
Vehicle coverage policies	1,000

If the aforementioned sets of policies are tested, then their equivalence partitioning results in four partitions. Each of these policy types is made up of its respective number (different) of policies. In equivalence partitioning we sample the test data that suitably represents the collection of original data in terms of numbers. For example, if we were to create ten test case data per 1,000 policies, then we would be sampling 20 home cover policies, 40 life cover policies, and so on, in creating a test bed.

Equivalence partitioning is applicable to the data, time, or any other variable that makes up the data entity. For example, the above policies are divided according to their numbers so those samples from each of the policy partitions can be selected for testing. However, when we divide these policies by dates (in this case, the date of opening the policy), then the equivalence partitions will be as shown as in Figure 6.3. Although the difference in time from January 1, 1981, to February 29, 1984 (2 years and 2 months), and from December 31, 1990, to September 9, 1999 (9 years and 9 months), is not equal, if nothing significant happens during this time span then the partitions will still hold true. We will select randomly from within these dates in order to conduct testing.

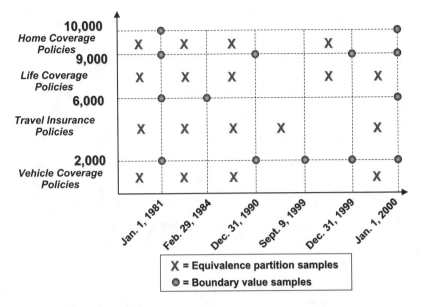

Figure 6.3 *Applying equivalence partitioning and boundary values to test data*

6.2.8 Boundary Value

The edges of the equivalence partitions, as shown in Figure 6.3, are the boundary values. Thus, in the case of numbers it will be a few policies from each of the partitions that have boundary values of very high or very low, high or low transactions, and so on. In the case of dates, it will be the dates at the edges of the partitions (for example, February 28, 29, and March 1, 1984; December 31, 1990 and January 1, 1991). The boundary values provide the opportunity to test the extreme cases within an equivalence partition. This leads to a concentration of the testing effort in the areas where the system is the most vulnerable. It also helps to avoid unnecessary and repetitive data in creating test beds.

6.3 Testing Architecture

The testing approaches feed into the testing architecture. The architecture, as shown in Figure 6.4, depicts the various types of tests and how they combine to provide a comprehensive testing strategy for any software system being tested. The testing architecture decides the level at which tests are

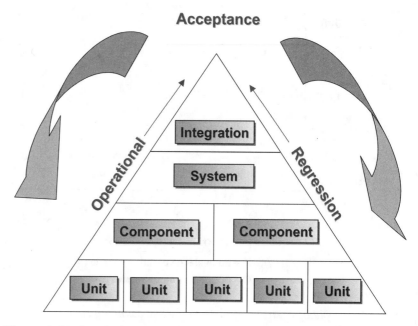

Figure 6.4   *A typical testing architecture*

conducted (for example, unit versus system), and the frequency, intensity, and repetition of tests. The influence of the previous discussion on testing approaches affects all elements of good test architecture.

6.3.1   Unit Test

The unit test is the most immediate testing of the class or program and is usually conducted by the programmer herself. It deals with an individual class or program and is more focused on the correctness or accuracy of execution of a program, rather than its meaning within the overall system. Unit tests benefit by manually creating test harnesses (writing a small piece of code and attaching it to the class) and a very basic set of data. It is always a good idea to store test harnesses and/or test scripts together with the source code being tested. Alternatively, a complete test environment can be created and classes tested under this environment every time the programmer makes a change to the classes. In either case, it is important to modify the test script/harness together with the modification to the actual source code.

Unit testing continues until the developer is satisfied that the results from the test match the expected results and that all the functionality that the class is supposed to satisfy is indeed satisfied. During unit testing the programmer may also check the implemented structure of the class against its intended design structure. From this description it is obvious that unit testing is restricted to the performance of an individual class or program and, therefore, the detailed functionality of the rest of the system may not make much sense at this stage. Recording the results and retesting the code may also be informal at this stage. This is because at the end of a test the programmer may realize the error, correct it, and retest—without ever recording the error. However, depending on the importance of the class, formal recording of errors and fixes at unit test level may be carried out.

The testing approaches discussed in the previous section have a bearing on the unit tests. For example, white box testing is very common when unit tests are conducted. The programmer may step through the code herself and inspect it for statement syntax, branching logic, and adequate coverage of all alternatives. While statement coverage only inspects the statements that are executed, the inspection of branching logic involves each of the conditional statements within the program and the results appearing as true or false at the end of each test. Black box tests occur when the GUI classes are tested. In these unit tests the programmer wants to ensure that the data content and the display from the class she has written satisfies the requirements of the class.

6.3.2   Component Test

A component test is conducted when a few classes are ready to be tested together. Thus, this test not only concentrates on the output from the given classes, but also on how the classes behave in relation with each other. For example, a Client component that is made up of ten classes related to various types of clients will have to be tested for their implementation together, in a component. The concept of coupling between the component under test and other components, as well as the concept of cohesion for classes within the component, comes into play during the component test. Once again, a component test can be a white box manual test wherein we are stepping through the designs of the component, or a black box test wherein we are writing test harnesses, which run a large amount of data through the component in order to test every possible variation to the input.

6.3.3   System Test

The system test is still within the technical domain and is involved with detailed testing of the system not only with respect to its functionality, but also with respect to its performance, installation, backup and recovery, security, and stability. System testing involves end-to-end testing of all components within the system in an integrated fashion. System testing involves both black and white box testing approaches, and the test suites comprise test harnesses to pass a large amount of data through the system.

The functionality of the system is tested by using the test designs and the test cases within the test designs. These test designs are created by using the use cases and scenarios in the requirements-modeling activity. The performance is tested by simulating the real environment in which the system has to operate. This involves creating a large amount of test data and loading the system with a large number of transactions by using an automated test simulator. Installing the application (if physically deployed) on a new machine tests out the installation and deployment of the new application. Sociological aspects (like graceful recovery of software from a crash) are also tested within the system test. Saving these test scripts and their results is of immense value when future modifications are made to the system throughout its lifecycle.

Garbage collection should be tested by running the systems many times over, and over a long time. Memory leaks and related garbage can be tested not only by using memory testers, but also by physically running the system over substantial periods. Dangling pointers left in the memory by unsuspecting programmers should be detected during testing—better still, should be prevented from occurring by good quality modeling in the MOSS.

Exception handling can be a project or an organizational level issue. It can be an internal standard.

6.3.4   Acceptance Test

During acceptance testing the system moves from the technical domain into the user domain. It is up to the users to accept (or reject) the system by testing its functionality against the specified requirements. This test decides whether the system is ready for deployment or not. Therefore, it is important that the users of the system test out the system using all relevant approaches to testing. Testing and verification of the specified help system, the accompanying user guides, and so forth are also carried out in this test.

Users may need technical support at this stage. This support involves creating databases, installing the application, and providing help in using test harnesses and/or automated testing tools, if relevant.

The acceptance criteria for this testing (acceptance testing) have some influence on the way the test cases are designed. For example, if one of the important acceptance criteria is system performance (3-second response times under all conditions) then the acceptance test cases must not be limited to testing the functionality of the system only. They should also test the system operationally. In those situations, it is also important to note the differences in the capabilities of the testing hardware and the production hardware.

6.3.5   Regression Test

Regression tests are conducted in the later iterations of a development project. After the system has undergone all the formal testing processes and the errors are recorded *and* fixed, it is essential to ensure that not only are the fixes sufficiently working, but also that by fixing the errors we have not introduced additional errors in other parts of the system. This flow-on effect of errors is minimized by the object-oriented designs—wherein it is easier to locate the errors because of encapsulation of classes. However, regression tests are still essential after the errors have been fixed.

They can be performed by means of the automated tools and may be black box tests—unless a design or code inspection is deemed necessary, in which case they should be white box manual tests. Regression tests are facilitated by the cyclic approach to testing, as the experience and the results from the first cycle of testing can be reused in the next cycle. If the results from the initial cycle of the overall tests are minor errors, then a smaller number of samples may be selected from within the equivalence partitions. However, it is recommended that all boundary values should be selected in all passes of the regression tests.

6.3.6   Operational Testing

Operational tests can be applied to system, integration, and acceptance testing, as shown in Figure 6.4. Since they are tests of the system in operation they make more sense later in the lifecycle. Some of these tests include performance, security, and scalability as discussed in the subsequent subsections.

6.3.7 Performance (Stress and Volume) Testing

The performance test deals with the capacity of the database as well as its speed of response. It is important to test out the ability of the database to respond to the transaction hits when the system goes into production. In order to test this it is necessary to load the database with dummy records. Tests can then be carried out on the speed of searches on the database and the corresponding response times. The capacity of the database to store records is its volume. The performance test ensures the adequacy of the database's speed of response and its capacity to hold data.

6.3.8 Security Testing

This test ensures that there is no unauthorized access to the system or any of its components. Security-related technologies (for example, 128-bit encryption) are investigated, incorporated, and tested in this exercise. It should be noted that software security is important but so is the physical security of the system. Most modern hardware is sophisticated enough to continue to support the system even if the permanent storage is removed. Therefore, in addition to software security, the physical security of the hardware must be considered in this testing. Finally, the system should be secured from various virus attacks by using the latest anti-virus software together with the latest anti-virus file definitions.

6.3.9 Scalability Testing

This test deals with the potential of the system to grow as the demands increase. This is an important test that ensures that once the system is in operation and the demands on the system resources start growing, the system is geared to handle the necessary upgrades to both the hardware and the software. The potential increase in demand and the corresponding support by hardware and software should be tested *before* the system is released.

6.4   Test Planning

Test planning is a part of quality-assurance planning or project planning within the quality process. The test-planning discussion here focuses on the strategy for testing, the resources required for the tests, the risks associated with testing, scheduling the test cases, and creating and maintaining the test environment that is required to conduct the testing. This test plan provides the necessary background for the overall testing activity as described by the testing process-component.

6.4.1   A Good Test Plan

A good test plan involves the objectives, the acceptance criteria, the system and integration test plans, the testing approaches and methods, and the responsibilities and schedule for testing. A good test plan also specifies the modules to be tested and the resources available to do so. The test plan further decides the order in which the modules are to be tested.

A good test plan should ensure that the testing activity starts as soon as the first class is implemented. This requires that the test plan is developed during the initial iteration of the process. The focus of the test plan should be toward the higher, strategic aspect of testing where the scope of testing, the time and cost of the required resources, and other such complexities are sorted out.

The test plan schedule (perhaps within the quality or project plan) should also have a schedule of specific dates when individual tests are to be administered and completed by the responsible team member. A good test plan includes creating a database in order to record and report software incident reports. Such a database enables analyzing the test results and making educated guesses on the risks associated with testing.

6.4.2   Analyzing Risks in Testing

As mentioned in the beginning of this chapter, test management is a balancing act. No system can be left forever in testing, and no system should be released until it has been sufficiently tested. This leads us to the discussion on analyzing the risks associated with what has been tested and what has been left out. In addition to the risks associated with choosing the scope of testing, there are also risks associated with the actual testing cycle. This risk includes situations that can hamper the testing effort (like resources, system, or network availability). Hence, proper test planning is required to identify and prioritize these risks. Analyzing testing risks during the initial iteration of the development process helps to avoid many problems—both organizational and operational—at the later testing stage. Early identification of testing risks is essential to keep testing schedules on time and within budget.

Some of the common examples of testing risks are:

- Limited experience of staff in testing object-oriented solutions. Object-oriented systems require a special focus on encapsulation of components and inheritance of objects. Without this special focus, the benefits of object-orientation may not be fully realized, and may not be pointed out during the testing phase. This risk can be mitigated by proper training in the OO concepts.

- Lack of UML experience. This is slightly different from just OO experience. Testers should be able to understand the UML diagrams—especially the class, sequence, and component diagrams—that give them an idea of how the system is organized from a testing viewpoint. This is possible when the testers are UML literate. Lack of UML skills can lead to inappropriate testing.

- Unavailability of suitable test environment. It is essential to test the system under a separate, dedicated test environment during both system and acceptance tests. This includes not only the physical test environment, in which the testers sit and execute the tests, but also the software environment, including the separate operating system, test database, and latest software release. Creating and maintaining this environment is a testing overhead that needs to be considered during test planning. If a suitable test environment is not created early in the testing cycle, then it poses a significant risk to the project.

- Discovery of major errors in the later cycles of testing. We plan for regression tests to ensure that the errors detected in the earlier cycle are fixed, and that those fixes have not created problems elsewhere. Significant risks are associated with the assumption that no major problems will be discovered during the later cycles of testing. Provision must be made for fixes and regression tests if errors are found.

- Unavailability of test data. If suitable test data is not available for creating the test database, then we cannot guarantee sufficient and thorough testing. Design and creation of data is a vital element of test planning, without which the testing of the system is at a considerable risk.

- Distributed applications must be tested over a real-life network. Unavailability of such networks or their inability to simulate real-life situations leads to inaccurate performance tests.

- Sufficient hardware. Machines, memory, and communications should be available for testing.

Depending on the criticality of the risks described in the previous section, it is essential to prioritize these risks so that the test manager can assign sufficient resources to mitigate them. Prioritizing the risks involves understanding them in the context of the project—the type, size, and critical-ity of the project influence the process of prioritizing the risks. For example, a CRMS project (as described in the Lucky Insurance example provided on the CD) has a high priority on testing the MOPS—in other words, the functionality specified must be met. This requires extensive black box test-ing techniques in the test cases. A project that integrates the new develop-ment or package with an existing legacy application needs extra testing focus in the background space. A data warehousing project needs to miti-gate the risks associated with data testing and data conversion.

6.4.3 Test Environment

The test environment includes the hardware, software, operating systems, databases, people, tools, and the overall physical environment in which testing will take place. A good test plan specifies how this environment is created and maintained during the testing period.

6.4.4 Test Resources

People are the primary test resource—the testers who coordinate with the developers as they plan, organize, and execute tests. Because testers need similar skills to the developers of the artifacts being tested, it may be nec-essary to swap the roles of developers and testers as the testing pro-gresses. Some of the testing roles specific to UML-based projects are:

- Test manager. This person is responsible overall for planning and exe-cuting the quality-control process-component. In a small project, this role may be played by the person playing the role of quality manager.

- Tester. This person writes test cases and carries out the actual tests. Writing and carrying out the tests involves testing classes (program), data, operational tests, and usability, to name but a few. The program-mer, data modeler, and the technical roles closely associated with the tester occasionally swap roles.

- Quality analyst. This person facilitates the overall testing process itself.

- Database manager. This person is involved not only in the testing, but also in creating test beds in test databases. Thus, the database man-ager helps to sample data and load it in the database for testing.

- User (end user). This person is involved particularly in acceptance testing and usability testing.

6.4.5   Development Environment

The development environment is where the software development takes place. However, there are many testing-related activities that take place in the development environment. For example, unit tests of each of the classes, as they are developed by the programmers, are tested in the development environment. Furthermore, component tests and system tests also take place in the development environment. The development environment needs a good set of test data loaded in the test beds, based on which unit, component, and system tests are carried out.

6.4.6   Test Environment

Testing of any application should be done in an environment that matches the environment of the application's end user. This environment includes the acceptance test environment. To create such an environment, first identify the equipment, software, and sites where the software will operate. Establishing an effective test environment takes major planning and implementation efforts. It is easier to analyze the test environment by considering acceptance test cases and test data. Determine the tools and mechanisms required for creating, running, and storing test results. Requirements may include various software and hardware products. The common requirements are:

- Separate testing area (physical location)
- Physical movement of testing staff (environment factor for testing)
- Configuration for testing
- Similarity to production environment
- Creation of test beds in test databases
- Management of test databases (backups, consistency)
- Tools for recording and analyzing results
- Network administration

6.4.7   Test Schedules

Test schedules are part of test planning. Here we try to answer the questions "How long do I need to test the system?" and "In which sequence?" For software developed following a process and based on extensive UML-based modeling, I tend to budget 20 percent of the development time for testing.

Working on a three-month development iteration, I budget for two to three weeks toward the end of the project for intense and dedicated testing.

Another question to be answered here is "When do I start testing?" For an iterative development process, system and integration testing should be conducted at the end of each iteration. Testing at unit and component levels can follow the development effort. Ideally, testing should follow the development of the class or component by three to five days—allowing time to fix the errors discovered during dedicated testing and to retest the fixes.

Test schedules and timelines are not restricted to creating and executing test cases. Timelines for testing should also include the considerable time required to create the test environment, load test data, design test cases, and staff and manage the test resources. All these aspects of testing are outside the time *per test case* and should be included in the overall planning for test time.

"When do I stop testing?" is an equally important question, if not more so. This is because the nature of testing is to discover errors that we do not know exist. It is not possible to state with total confidence that all errors have been found. In practice, I trust the experience of a tester and a test manager, together with some dependence on past testing trends within the organization. (This is discussed separately in Section 6.8.3 on analyzing the test results.)

Regression testing becomes more time consuming toward the end, as more tests need retesting as the test lifecycle progresses. The time allocated to bug fixing and retesting needs to be carefully monitored.

6.4.8   Test Cycles

The need for test cycles (passes or iterations) arises because it is neither possible nor worthwhile to test an entire system in a single attempt. Testing (especially a component-based system) requires a cyclic approach, which ensures that the testing is carried out in the most efficient and effective manner. The test cycles achieve the following two main purposes:

- They accumulate the experience as well as the data resulting from the execution of the earlier test cycles, thereby ensuring that the first broad-brush cycle provides input into the next detailed cycle.

- They handle dependencies in testing by scheduling tests in an appropriate manner, so that the results of testing a particular module can be used in testing (or postponing the tests) of another module.

The number of testing cycles depends on the type of testing being conducted. For example, unit tests conducted by an individual programmer may have as many informal cycles as he wishes. However, an integration test of a large package implementation requires at least three test cycles. In our example case, the first cycle deals with testing the overall function of the insurance package and testing the client package. The second cycle depends on the results of the first cycle and therefore has all client test details available, which can be used for the testing policy. The third cycle tests claims and settlements. Without test cycles we may end up trying to test functionality that has not yet been implemented, or the package/component it depends on has itself not been tested.

6.4.9   Reusability in Testing

Following are the reusability aspects of testing that should be reflected in a good test plan:

- Reusing the large suite of test cases that an organization has created for its earlier prevention effort. These test cases require careful study and modifications in order to ensure that they test the system for the various formats to date.

- Reusing the test harnesses and test cases used in the initial iteration of testing components in the later iterations.

- Reusing the test data from the testing effort in the development environment when the acceptance and usability tests are carried out.

- Reusing the designed test harnesses by following object-oriented principles. This is achieved by inheriting from the existing harnesses in order to test new functionality.

Test patterns can capture recurring situations in testing. They may be organization specific, or even project specific. They can help in saving time and improving the quality of testing itself. As Brian Marick states on his Web site (www.testing.com):

> We believe that testers lack a useful vocabulary, are hampered by rigid "one-size-fits-all" methodologies, and face many problems whose solutions are under described in the literature. Patterns can help with all of those things. Moreover, the community of pattern writers is a healthy one that regularly spawns new and useful ideas. We testers should link up with it, and we might find its style of work useful as we look for new ideas.

6.5   Test Design

Test design follows test planning. This is where the quality analyst, the tester, and the programmer sit together to figure out a combination of test approaches needed for a particular class, component, or package. For example, GUI classes require a test design with more black box tests, whereas a component that deals with calculating insurance premiums needs many test harnesses and open white box testing. The various test architectures and testing approaches discussed earlier come together in a package test design. While only one test plan is expected in a project, there will be several test designs. Test designs are typically prepared for a subsystem or a component. The test designs are made up of a group of test cases.

6.5.1   Description of Test Designs

Test designs ensure that a group of cohesive test cases is created for a package or subsystem. Test designs also ensure that the right environment, including software and people, is available for a suite of test cases. For example, a test design for security testing requires a security expert and a tester to be available for testing, whereas a test design for an insurance package calls for a vertical test by an insurance expert. Thus, organizing the immediate needs for testing a subsystem or package, and putting together the right number and type of test cases, is part of test design. Test designs are created within the overall framework of the test plans.

Test-design subject areas are derived from the vertical and horizontal slicing of the system for testing. The vertical slicing provides the subsystems. If these subsystems are smaller in size, then each of the subsystems results in a test design. If the subsystems are larger in size, then we will have two or three test designs handling each of the subsystems. Each test design incorporates a series of test cases handling all aspects of testing the system from the application perspective. Note that as shown in Figure 6.5, test designs are created within the overall framework of the test plan. However, they are not test cases themselves. Instead, the test designs encompass the test cases.

6.5.2   Sources for Test Designs

Test designs can be created based on understanding the system at the subsystem or component level. Documenting use cases in the MOPS also provides an excellent starting point for the test designs. These test designs

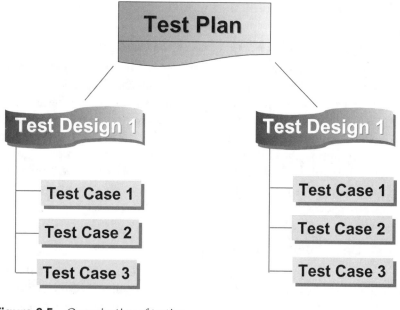

Figure 6.5 *Organization of testing*

give a broad coverage of the required functionality rather than the specific lower level tests for each class or component of the system. The test designs resulting from the use case documentations and package diagrams in MOPS ensure that the division of system testing is ideal—the test designs reflect the need to test the system in a modular fashion. The user can also contribute to these test designs and later use them to conduct acceptance tests. The test designer incorporates the requirements, their variations, and their extensions within the test designs.

Test designs also consider the number of classes to be tested and their corresponding complexity. For each class there are a number of test cases that test different functionality of the same classes. Test designs also incorporate extra test cases that deal with testing the entire component—as opposed to individual classes. For example, a set of test cases within a test design may test the date class and another set of test cases may test the account class. However, a good test design ensures that there is a third group of test cases that test the working of the two classes together.

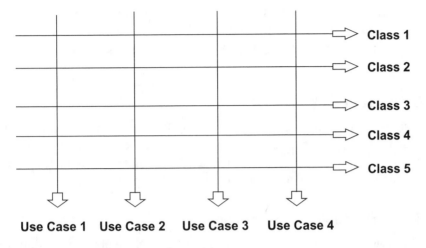

Figure 6.6 *Use case versus class testing*

6.5.3   Format for Test Designs

A typical test design contains the following:

- Name. This identifies the test design, which may be stored as a document. The name should ideally reflect the nature of the test design. It may be the name of a package prefixed by "Test," as in TestClient.

- Module. This indicates details of the subsystem, package, or any other module within the target system that is targeted by the test design. It contains a brief description of the type of package being tested, the preparation required for the package (creating test data or procuring a domain expert's services, for example), and the various categories of test cases needed.

- Dependency. This indicates the other test designs on which this design depends. This is helpful when creating test cycles, or may itself be created based on the test cycles. For example, the dependency of the TestClient design is TestSecurity—one should ideally be testing the creation and maintenance of clients after the user codes and passwords for the overall system have been tested.

- List of test cases. This is the list of test cases that make up the test design. All test cases belonging to this design are listed together with a brief one-line description. Test cases may have been numbered and may be grouped according to the needs of the design (for example, all interface test cases may be grouped together in a test-design document, separately from all database-access test cases).

6.6   Test Cases

Test cases are the atomic or smallest units of testing. They form part of test designs. They are created based on test approaches (automated versus manual), are part of test architecture (some are unit tests, others deal with the component), and contain inputs, steps, and expected output.

6.6.1   Description of Test Cases

The basic purpose of a test case is to test a single element within a component. This single element can be a class or it can be a function within a class. In order to accomplish this, a test case has to provide a set of input data and parameters, the steps that are needed in order to execute the tests, and the expected results.

In large or complex projects, test cases may also be generated automatically. They keep track of configurations and automatically retest changed components. The purpose of generating a large number of test cases automatically is that it ensures that sufficient numbers of test cases are available to test every aspect of the software. Auto-generation of test cases is also associated with auto-generation of test data—otherwise it takes a long time to generate manually.

Test cases may also be made up of test harnesses—which are test classes that execute a large number of variations of logic within the target class. These harnesses may be part of a class, in which case they serve the purpose of instantaneous testing of code as it is written.

Although test cases are usually executable, manual testing also includes the inspection and verification of classes. Thus, sometimes a test case may not always include execution of the program.

6.6.2   Designing the Test Cases

Designing the test cases follows the component test designs. Each test case should be at an atomic level and should thoroughly test a single element of the system. This allows good management of the test execution and recording and analyzing the results from the test cases. However, within the element being tested, the test cases should ensure that maximum variations of the input are passed through the class and that all possible outputs are verified. A good test case covers a wide spectrum of usage of a class or component, under different conditions, and with a wide variety of inputs.

Test cases should be properly documented and their repository should be kept current at all times. This is because with small changes in functionality, it should not be necessary to recreate a new suite of test cases. Existing test cases should be modifiable and reusable. Proper documentation of test cases allows this to happen.

Test cases may also be generated from the requirements, if those requirements are documented in a proper format. This considerably reduces the cost of creating test cases. For example, steps within a use case documentation and activities within an activity diagram are candidates for test cases—all they need is an additional set of inputs and expected results.

6.6.3 Format for Test Cases

In general, a test case format consists of the following parts (see the accompanying CD for a template):

- Identification. This is a name and number to identify a test case.
- Purpose. This is the reason for the test (for example, verifying business logic or checking the validity of the date field on a screen).
- Prerequisites. Whatever is necessary before the test is carried out. These prerequisites relate to a particular test case. The prerequisite for the entire test design for the module is documented separately.
- Input. This is the data to be inputted in the system.
- Actions. These are the actions or steps required on the part of the tester in order to carry out the test.
- Expected output. This determines whether the test was a success or a failure.
- Actual output. This is a placeholder for recording the actual output as the test case gets executed.
- Administrative details. These include the tester carrying out the tests, for example.

It is essential to ensure that the input covers a broad range of data and the expected output matches the corresponding input for the test case. The input may be comprised of an input file containing a large number of records; the corresponding output can also be a file. The file can be matched against a predetermined set of records to ensure verification of test results. Input can also be provided by automated test tools.

6.6.4 Example Test Case

Here are some examples of test cases within the Lucky Insurance project, for a test design related to claims. These should be treated as suggested examples and readers should add their own field as needed, in their test cases.

Table 6.1 *Enter Claim Details*

Test identification	101 enter claim details
Purpose of test:	To test the ability to record claims details in Lucky Insurance's claim module, together with basic date and status code table checks
Description:	Client reports an event on a risk for which she has a policy cover. The account exec (or user of the system) creates a claim and records the incident details using the mandatory fields and the codes
Prerequisites:	The client is a valid client, and she has a `policy`.

Date	Performed By	Result	Comments

Step Number	Action	Expected Results	Actual Results	Software Incident Report No.
1	Enter all details of the client on the inquiry screen. Account exec has to confirm system has populated the	Client details are successfully entered by the account exec on the claims inquiry screen		

Step Number	Action	Expected Results	Actual Results	Software Incident Report No.
	necessary client information			
2	Account exec to capture details about the claim. These details are further checked for their correctness, particularly as regards the following fields: Date of event Date of reporting Status of the claim Description of event Relation to policy	System to make sure all mandatory fields are filled in by the user Date of event (can't be greater than the date of reporting) Date of reporting (today's date is default) Status of the claim (check claim state chart diagram for valid statuses) Description of event Relation to policy (policy number)		
3	Test that claim status codes are available on the screen as a drop-down table	A drop-down list of status codes is available		
4	Test in further detail the renewal date on the policy (renewal date of policy must be greater than the date of loss, as that proves the policy is current)	If renewal date is in the past, and the policy is not renewed, the system should display a warning message with OK and cancel buttons		
5	If account exec (user of the system) clicks on OK, the system should let the user proceed with the claim inquiry	User is able to continue with the inquiry after clicking on OK		

(continued)

Table 6.1 *Enter Claim Details (continued)*

Step Number	Action	Expected Results	Actual Results	Software Incident Report No.
6	If account exec clicks on cancel	System to put the cursor back into the date of event field		
7	Account exec to confirm that correct client and insurer information is entered on the inquiry screen	Correct information is populated		

Table 6.2 *Claims Payment*

Test identification	250 Make Claims Payment
Purpose of test:	To test the ability to make payments against claims in Lucky Insurance's claim module
Description:	The user needs to Record payment details in claims module Generate the client claims advice Set follow-up for upcoming part payments
Prerequisites:	The `client` has registered a valid `claim` that has been processed.

Date	Performed By	Result	Comments

Step Number	Action	Expected Results	Actual Results	Software Incident Report No.
1	User to locate the client and claim—by searching for the client record by entering the claim number	System to take the user to the 360 degree view for the client and display the existing claim inquiry		
2	User to select the internal contact and select the correct claim inquiry	System to display the claim inquiry detail screen to the user		
3	User to update the notes on the inquiry—client accepts	The details are updated		
4	User to record the payment details on the payment tab	Ability to record part payments and multiple check details and insurer names on the payment tab		
5	User to save the inquiry	All changes made on the payment tab are saved Changes to notes saved		
6	User to generate the client claim advice to send the payment	Ability to create a client claims advice		
7	User to create a follow-up for themselves for the remaining part payments	Generate the follow-up to the user's worklist		
8	User to check that the follow-up item appears in the worklist			

6.6.5   Verifying the Test Cases

Once the test cases are designed and created in the specified format, it is essential to verify that the test cases are themselves correct. They can be cross checked against the results from the existing system. For example, if an insurance application is getting replaced, at least the core insurance calculations can be verified against the existing legacy insurance application. Test cases can also be verified against sample manual calculations performed by expert users of the system.

6.6.6   Modifying the Test Cases

Once the test cases are verified and accepted within a suite of test repositories residing within a test design, they should be placed under a formal change-control mechanism. There will be a number of reasons to modify the test cases that have been accepted within the suite. The modules being tested are undergoing change and so are the data being input to the classes. Also, as the testing progresses, new needs for additional testing will be discovered. Therefore, test cases will need modifications and upgrades during the test cycles.

6.7   Test Execution

We have planned for testing and have created test classes thus far. Test execution is the actual execution of test cases against the given software. This requires the implementation of all planning done so far. Herein we describe the general approach to test execution.

6.7.1   Getting Ready

Preparation is the initial part of executing tests. All test cases need some preliminary preparations before they can be successfully executed. This includes the preparedness of the modules that are to be tested, the availability of test data, and the availability of sample test results against which the results of the test execution can be measured.

Getting ready for test execution also includes familiarization of the tester with the test cases and the input and output of the test cases. While test data is prepared when the test designs are finalized and the test cases are written, it is not unusual for the test data to be incomplete during the initial cycles of testing. In preparing for the test execution, this data may have to be augmented by the results of the previous cycle, or from any other relevant source. In preparing for the tests, it is necessary for the tester to familiarize himself with the associated test cases.

Test cases that test the remaining functions within a class, or other classes within the component, will have some bearing on the current test case. An overall idea of the test designs is essential for all testers before the formal tests are executed. Finally, administrative procedures like backing up and re-creating test data and test cases also need to be put in place before the test execution begins. It is a part of the getting-ready procedure.

6.7.2   Acceptance Criteria

It is important to understand the criteria that will decide whether the test is a success or not. These criteria may range from the single criterion for a unit test to a broad description of acceptance of the system at the integrated-test level. Although the expected results are a part of the acceptance criteria, the acceptance criteria are more than just the results. A user may accept the results as valid, but may point out a change in input data in practical usage of the system. The user may also accept some results as valid but with additional conditions. Also, the acceptance of a test as a pass in the initial cycle of testing may not hold in the subsequent cycles of testing. Therefore, it is essential to understand what constitutes a pass for a test from the user's perspective.

Acceptance criteria determine the success or failure of a test case. If the results of the test case satisfy the acceptance criteria, then the test case is successful. The criteria itself need not be positive. The criteria may specify the requirement of a failure (negative), and accordingly the test case should produce a negative result. For example, if invalid logon is supposed to reject the logon attempt, then a failure to logon is a success as far as the test criteria are concerned. Acceptance criteria also specify more than the simple pass or fail. They specify the understanding of the user of the test case. Thus, acceptance criteria can be specified at the unit-test level to indicate a unit level pass or fail. More importantly, they can also be specified at the system or integration test level, wherein the user or business sponsor may formally state what would be an acceptance of the system.

Some of the test criteria that can determine the acceptance of the system follow:

- Results validation. All actual results match up with the expected results. However, specifying correct expected results is the responsibility of the user.

- Logic validation. In addition to verifying the results, users may also want a proof of the logic, by doing a white box test for the same. Users may state that they will accept the system only after its logic has been validated.

- Error handling. A system may be accepted only after it proves proper error handling. Users may decide not to accept a system that performs all calculations correctly when correct input data is provided, but crashes if the user enters invalid data. Informative error messages and graceful error handling may be valid acceptance criteria. This assures that the system is able to recover from a crash— an important acceptance criterion even for routine transaction-based banking and financial applications.

- Operational requirements. Performance, scalability, and security are vital criteria for user acceptance of the system. For example, various attempts at logins, physical access to the system, software aided attempts to get in the system, and so on form part of the security criteria. Furthermore, the ability of the system to operate under different configurations and versions of the environment (such as operating systems and databases) is also part of the operational acceptance criteria of the system.

- Help, CBT, and user documentation. Context-sensitive help, associated computer-based training (CBT), and supporting documentation on how to install and operate a system are, more often than not, necessary for a system's acceptance.

6.7.3   Execute Test Suites

Once the test cases are designed and understood, and their dependencies worked out, it is time to conduct the actual testing. This requires executing the set of test cases and comparing the results in order to record the success or failure of the test cases. The testing follows the test plans and uses the test cases within the test designs to test the executable components of the system. Depending on the architecture of testing, some test cases are executed by actual execution of components; others can be white box walkthroughs. Also, depending on the testing cycle, some test cases will be broad-brush runs, whereas the same test cases during the major iteration of testing will be thorough and will provide a wide coverage of data and functionality.

6.7.4   Record Incident Reports

The results of the test cases are normally categorized as pass or fail. However, it is essential to categorize the results in further detail. This facilitates the analysis and understanding of not only the system being tested, but also the testing process itself. The results of the test execution are called incidences within the resurrection process. Recording and analyzing these results is described in the next section.

6.8   Recording and Analyzing Test Results

Test results provide valuable information on the system being tested. They are produced as a result of test execution. It is important to categorize and analyze the results formally in order to take advantage of the test execution events. The test environment or test project plan can be modified and updated based on understanding the testing results during each cycle of testing. Hence, it is important to collate all test results generated during all testing phases in a manner which is intuitive and useful.

6.8.1   Software Incidents

As the execution of a test suite progresses, results are produced. Although we normally expect the results of the test case to be a pass or fail, in many situations the results are not that clear-cut. Therefore, it is not appropriate to call every recording of a problem a "bug." There are three categories of events that result from testing:

- Problems. What we normally call bugs. These are errors in the system and they need to be fixed.
- Enhancements. These are not errors. However, they have to be handled in the system upgrade.
- Informative. These are only statements of events that are recorded within the incident database. No action is required on them, but they provide help in future testing and development.

This categorization of test results makes it convenient to record them and group them for appropriate action. For example, informative incidences may not need a corrective action, but may have to be published to the rest of the testers and perhaps included in the user guides.

6.8.2   Recording Test Results

Test results should be formally recorded, preferably in a database. They should be viewed by the testers, programmer, user, and quality manager. The quality managers, together with the project managers, may prioritize the test results, especially the ones requiring further action. All test results must be categorized, in addition to the type of incidents, into their priority (high, medium, low) and severity.

Timely reporting of test results provides valuable feedback to the quality manager and the project manager on the status of the project. Test results must be formally reported at least once a week. Test incidences should be sorted according to their criticality and date/time of generation. Also they should be located (stored) at a central place, so that project manager and each team member have easy access to them.

The best way to facilitate reporting is by storing the results in a separate database for storage of test results. The database must hold sufficient details such as date, trial version, problem, its urgency, output results, and remarks of quality and product managers. Once a particular record is sent to the development team for implementation, the database should be immediately updated with the rest of the details such as developer's remark, date of modification, date of fix, fix version, and so forth. Once a bug is fixed, it may appear again in a future release because of changes made in related or other areas. Hence, it is advisable to keep such reports in a database for future reference.

Comprehensive reporting ensures maximum productivity and utilization of available IT assets. Up-to-date maintenance of results leads to improved quality of the application under test. By using these results, project managers can constantly improve the development process, as well as make proper estimates on the time remaining for the completion of the project.

6.8.3   Analyzing Results

Once the testing is under way and we have started to record the results of the tests as described in the previous section, it is important to analyze the results as the testing progresses. Understanding the test results is based on a number of metrics, such as the number of incidents found per module (application based), or the number of incidents per week (time based). Whatever criteria

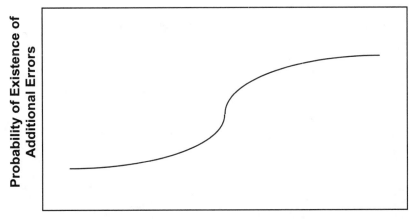

Number of Errors Found Already

The probability of the existence of more errors in a section of a program is proportional to the number of errors already found in that section

Figure 6.7   *Error probabilities based on errors found (from Meyers 1979)*

are used to analyze the results, the results should be able to provide some confidence in the state of the software solution—whether the developed software is able to meet the stated requirements in the requirements model.

It is important to continue to monitor the state of the test results as the testing progresses, rather than waiting for the testing phase to be completed. This is because data from the initial testing not only provides information on the state of the software that has been tested, but also indicates the areas in which there is higher probability of finding bugs. Glenford J. Meyers [1979] has described how the probabilities of finding software bugs change as the testing progresses. He states that within a given limit, the probability of finding more bugs *increases* if comparatively more bugs are found in a module. This can be correlated to the skills of a programmer or the manner in which a business analyst had specified the requirements in the problem space. Meyers's understanding has been further extended by me, as shown in Figure 6.8.

In this figure, the logic-related incidents follow the Meyers curve. With logic-related errors, the chances of finding problems increase slowly (as compared with the data-related problems) as more bugs are found in

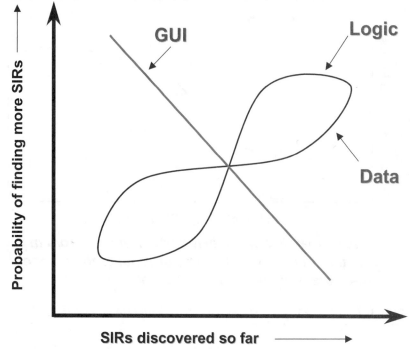

Figure 6.8   *Probabilities of finding SIRs based on SIRs found so far*

the logic of the software. However, after a certain break-even point, the probability of finding more bugs grows exponentially. This is because if the software is written in haste, without following a process, or by an inexperienced person, then those characteristics percolate throughout the entire module for which the person was responsible.

The data errors follow the reverse trend of logic errors. The probability of data errors grows later, indicating a bad conversion of data. This is because if, say, a policy-creation date in a particular table is corrupted, then the chances of other dates in the same table being corrupt are high. Thus, the data problems can multiply quickly, based on their existence in the data tables in the first place.

Compared with data and logic errors, the GUI-related errors continue to drop as testing progresses—because the more errors are found, the fewer errors remain in a GUI where business logic is not present.

6.8.4 Reporting

Finally, after the results from the testing cycle are collated, it is essential to report them to the person who can make decisions based on them. The test manager usually performs the reporting function. The results of the initial cycles need not be reported to the senior management of the company, as these initial results may not be a true reflection of the state of the software. The test environment and the testing experience of the tester may skew the initial results. However, once the major testing iterations are performed, it is necessary to let the business sponsor and the steering committee know the status of the testing. If testing indicates major problems with the system, they should be immediately investigated in further detail. If the architecture, requirements, and designs of the system have been created following the quality processes outlined in this book, then the test results should not show major errors in the system.

However, if the requirements have changed since they were first specified, the test results will indicate that the system does not satisfy the new functionality. In such cases, the tests themselves should not be called a failure. Informing all the developers and testers of the results is also helpful in providing them with an overall idea of the software status.

6.9 Bibliographic Notes

For additional excellent work on testing, specifically focused on UML-based projects, see McGregor and Sykes [2001].

Some of the thoughts in these chapters are based on my work in Y2K testing [Unhelkar 1999]. This is because Y2K was massive and unsurpassed testing work undertaken by the IT community, and many concepts applied during that work still hold true.

6.10 Frequently Asked Questions (FAQs)

Q1: How important is QA in the context of testing?

A1: Quality Assurance (QA) is separate from Quality Control (QC). Testing is QC and is always different from QA.

Q2: Do I need a testing approach?

A2: Yes, testing approaches help to create a good strategy for testing. Testing approaches will appear prominently in test plans.

Q3: How is a test plan different from a test design?

A3: Test planning is organizational in nature, whereas test design is tactical. Test design corresponds to subsystems or packages of the UML.

Q4: Where does usability testing occur?

A4: Usability testing can be a part of both integration testing and acceptance testing.

Q5: How often do we need to test and what are the circumstances involved?

A5: Testing should follow the testing architecture outlined in Figure 6.4.

Q6: When do I stop testing?

A6: After undertaking all tests when the system moves into acceptance testing, and if additional tests stop revealing additional errors, the testing effort can be formally concluded. This is, of course, subjective and benefits by experience.

6.11 Exercises

E6.1: List some of the risks associated with testing.

E6.2: What are the important phases of testing?

E6.3: What is meant by vertical and horizontal testing?

E6.4: Discuss the importance of recording test results.

E6.5: What are the differences between black and white box testing?

E6.6: Analyze various test results and record them as per instructions in the book.

E6.7: What are the various steps involved in executing tests? Give a brief explanation of each.

E6.8: How will you go about putting together a test case?

E6.9: What are the do's and don'ts of testing?

E6.10: How important is testing in the software development lifecycle?

6.12 References

Beizer, B., *System Testing and Quality Assurance,* New York: Van Nostrand Reinhold, 1984.

Marick, B., www.testing.com.

McGregor, J., and D. Sykes, *A Practical Guide to Testing Object-Oriented Software,* Boston: Addison-Wesley, 2001.

Meyers, G., *The Art of Software Testing.* John Wiley and Sons, 1979.

Unhelkar, B., *After the Y2K Fireworks: Business and Technology Strategies,* CRC Press, 1999.

Glossary of
Acronyms and
Important Terms

BA	Business Analyst
CBT	Computer-Based Training
CMM	Capability Maturity Model—provides the basis for measuring and comparing the process maturities of various organizations and projects. Initiative of the Software Engineering Institute of the Carnegie Mellon University
CMS	Content Management System—dealing primarily with the contents of a Web site
COBOL	COmmercial Business-Oriented Language
COTS	Commercial Off The Shelf—software products
CRC	Class Responsibility Collaborators—a simple technique proposed by Cunningham and Beck in 1989 to help identify classes and their responsibilities
CRMS	Customer Relationship Management System
CWM	Common Warehousing Metamodel
DE	Domain Expert
DM	Data Modeler
ERP	Enterprise Resource Planning

ICT	Information and Communication Technology
ID	Interface Designer
IIP	Iterative, Incremental, Parallel—software development lifecycle ideally suited for OO development
ISAM	Index Sequential Access Management—file access
IT	Information Technology—increasingly being referred to as ICT due to the closeness of information and communication in today's software world
LOC	Lines Of Code
MDA	Model Driven Architecture (OMG's initiative)
MetaModel	Model of a model that dictates the rules for creation of modeling mechanisms like the UML
MOBS	Model Of Background Space—created primarily by the System Architect in the background space using UML notations and diagrams
MOF	Meta Object Facility
MOPS	Model Of Problem Space—created primarily by the Business Analyst in the problem space using UML notations and diagrams
MOSES	Methodology of Object-oriented Software Engineering of System—a second-generation object-oriented methodology outlined by Henderson-Sellers and Edwards
MOSS	Model Of Solution Space—created primarily by the System Designer in the solution space using UML notations and diagrams
OMG	Object Management Group—responsible for unification of modeling notations resulting in the UML
OO	Object Oriented—earlier considered only as a programming technique, OO now permeates all aspects of the software-development lifecycle
PC	Process Component

PE	Process Engineer
PM	Project Manager
QA	Quality Assurance
QM	Quality Management
QSP	Quality Software Process
RM	Requirements Modeler
SA	System Architect
SD	System Designer
SDLC	Software Development Life Cycle
SEP	Software Engineering Process (also Software Process)
TA	Transactional Analysis—a practical human-relations approach outlined by Eric Berne in the 1970s that has also been applied in management practice
UML	Unified Modeling Language—result of the effort of a number of well-known methodologists, notably Jacobson, Booch, and Rumbaugh; stamped by the OMG as a de facto software modeling standard

Bibliography

Ahmed, Z.K., and C. Umrish, *Developing Enterprise Java Applications with J2EE and UML*, Boston: Addison-Wesley, 2001.

Alexander, C. et al., *A Pattern Language*, New York: Oxford University Press, 1977.

Armour, F., and G. Miller, *Advanced Use Case Modeling*, Boston: Addison-Wesley, 2001.

Beck, K., *eXtremeProgramming Explained: Embrace Change*, Boston: Addison-Wesley, 2000.

Binder, J., *Testing Object-Oriented Software*, Reading, Mass.: Addison-Wesley, 1999.

Boehm, B.W., "A Spiral Model of Software Development and Enhancement," *ACS Software Engineering Notes*, 11(4), 1986: 14–24.

Booch, G., *Object-Oriented Analysis and Design*, Benjamin/Cummings Publishing Company, 1994.

———, J. Rumbaugh, and I. Jacobson, *The Unified Modeling Language User Guide*, Reading, Mass.: Addison-Wesley, 1999.

Brooks, F., *The Mythical Man-Month*, Reading, Mass.: Addison-Wesley, 1995.

Brown, W., R. "Skip" Malveau, H. McCormick III, and T. Mowbray, *Anti Patterns: Refactoring Software, Architectures, and Projects in Crisis*, John Wiley & Sons, Inc., 1998.

Cantor, M., *Object-Oriented Project Management with UML*, Wiley, 1998.

Card D. and E. Comer, "Why Do So Many Reuse Programs Fail?" *IEEE Software*, 11(5), September 1994: 114–115.

Cheng, M.J., "My words are very easy to understand," *Lectures on the Tao The Ching* (translated from the Chinese by T.C. Gibbs), Richmond, CA: North Atlantic Books, 1981.

Constantine, L., *Constantine on Peopleware,* Yourdon Press Computing Series, Upper Saddle River, N.J.: Prentice Hall, 1995.

——, L. Lockwood, *Software for Use: A Practical Guide to the Models and Methods of Usage-centered Design,* Reading Mass.: Addison-Wesley, 1999. (see also *www.foruse.com.*)

Coplien, J.O., "Generative Pattern Languages," *C++ Report,* 6(6), (July–August 1994): 18–22, 66–67.

——, "The Column without a Name: Setting the Stage," *C++ Report,* 6(8), (October 1994): 8–16.

DeMarco, T., and T. Lister, *Peopleware: Productive Projects and Teams,* Dorset House Publishing Company, 1987.

Eriksson, H., and M. Penkar, *Business Modeling with UML; Business Patterns at Work,* OMG Press, 2000.

Eykholt, E., (ed.), *Best of Booch,* SIGS Books & Multimedia, New York: 1996.

Fowler, M., "A Survey of Object-Oriented Analysis and Design Methods," *OOPSLA'96* Tutorial No. 45, (October 1996): 6–10.

——, *Analysis Patterns: Reusable Object Models,* Reading Mass.: Addison-Wesley, 1997.

——, with K. Scott, *UML Distilled* 2d ed., Boston: Addison-Wesley, 2000.

Frakes, W.B., and S. Isoda, "Success Factors of Systematic Reuse," *IEEE Software,* 11(5), (September 1994): 15–19.

Beizer, B., *System Testing and Quality Assurance,* New York: Van Nostrand Reinhold, 1984.

Gabriel, R., "The Quality without a Name," *Journal of Object-Oriented Programming,* 6(5), (September 1993): 86–89.

Gamma, E., R. Helm, R. Johnson, and J. Vlissides, *Design Patterns: Elements of Reusable Object-Oriented Software,* Reading, Mass.: Addison-Wesley, 1995.

Gardner, K., A. Rush, M. Crist, R. Konitzer, and B. Teegarden, *Cognitive Patterns: Problem-solving Frameworks for Object Technology,* Cambridge University Press: 1998.

Gates, B., *Business @ The Speed of Thought,* Viking, 1999.

Glass, R., *Software Runaways: Monumental Software Disasters,* Upper Saddle River, N.J.: Prentice Hall, 1997.

Glenford, M., *The Art of Software Testing,* John Wiley and Sons, 1979.

Goldberg, A., and K. Rubin, *Succeeding with Objects: Decision Frameworks for Project Management*, Reading, Mass.: Addison-Wesley, 1995.

Graham, I., *Migrating to Object Technology*, Reading, Mass.: Addison-Wesley, 1994.

Greatrex, C. (KPMG Director), "Achieving Excellence through Effective Management of your IT project," *Proceedings of ITProject Management by AIC Conferences*, (April 1996).

Hammer, M. and J. Champy, *Reengineering the Corporation*, Allen and Unwin, 1994.

Henderson-Sellers, B., *Book of Object-Oriented Knowledge*, 2d ed., Upper Saddle River, N.J.: Prentice Hall, 1997.

———, and J. Edwards, *Book Two of Object-Oriented Knowledge, The Working Object*, Prentice Hall, 1994.

———, and A. Bulthuis, *"Object-Oriented Metamethods,"* New York: Springer, 1997.

———, and M. Serour, "Creating a process for transitioning to object technology," *IEEE 2000*, 436–440, 00896731; Also presented at *TOOLS USA 2001*.

———, and Unhelkar, B., *OPEN Modeling with the UML*, U.K.: Addison-Wesley, 2000.

Henninger S., "Using Iterative Refinement to Find Reusable Software," *IEEE Software*, 11(5), (September, 1994): 48–59.

Hudson, William, "A User-centered UML Method," in *Object Modeling and User Interface Design: Designing Interactive Systems*, M. Van Harmelen (ed.), Boston: Addison-Wesley, 2001.

Humphrey, W., *A Discipline for Software Engineering*, Reading, Mass.: Addison-Wesley, 1995.

Hutt, A., *Object Analysis and Design, Description of Methods*, OMG/Wiley, 1994.

Jacobson, I., "Time for a Cease-Fire in the Methods War," *Journal of Object-Oriented Programming*, July/August, 1993.

Jacobson, I., M. Christerson, P. Jonsson, and G. Overgaard, *Object-Oriented Software Engineering: A Use Case Driven Approach*, Reading, Mass.: Addison-Wesley, 1992.

Jacobson, I., G. Booch, J. Rumbaugh, *The Unified Software Development Process*, Reading, Mass.: Addison-Wesley, 1999.

Jacobson, I., M. Griss, P. Jonsson, *Software Reuse*, Reading, Mass.: Addison-Wesley, 1997.

Jalote, P., *CMM in Practice: Process for Executing Software Projects at Infosys*, Boston: Addison-Wesley, 2000.

Jones, C., *Applied Software Measurement: Assuring Productivity and Quality*, New York: McGraw-Hill, 1991.

Kimball, R., L. Reeves, M. Ross, and W. Thornthwaite, *The Data Warehouse Lifecycle Toolkit*, Wiley, 1998.

Kriendler, J., "Cultural Change and Object-Oriented Technology," *Journal of Object-Oriented Programming*, 5(9), (February 1993): 6–8.

Lanier, J., "The Frontier between Us," *Communications of the ACM*, 40(2), (February 1997), 55–56, Special Anniversary issue on 50 years of computing.

Lauder, A., and S. Kent, "Two-Level Modeling" *Technology of OO Languages and Systems, (TOOLS 31)*, Nanjing, China, IEEE Computer Society, J. Chen, J. Lu, B. Meyer (eds.), 108–117, 1999.

Lorenz, M., and J. Kidd, *Object-Oriented Software Metrics*, New Jersey: Prentice Hall, 1994.

Martin, R., "Patterns: PloP, PLoP, fizz, fizz," *Journal of Object-Oriented Programming*, 7(8), (January 1995): 7–12.

McGregor, J. and D. Sykes, *A Practical Guide to Testing Object-Oriented Software*, Boston: Addison-Wesley, 2001.

Meyer, B., *Object Success*, Prentice Hall, 1995.

———, *Object-Oriented Software Construction*, 2d ed., "The Importance of Being Humble," Upper Saddle River, N.J.: Prentice Hall, PTR, 2000.

Perry, W., *Quality Assurance for Information Systems*, QED Information Sciences, Wellesley, Mass.: 1991.

Rosenberg, D., and K. Scott, *Use Case Driven Object Modeling with the UML*, Reading, Mass.: Addison-Wesley, 1999.

Rumbaugh, J., I. Jacobson, and G. Booch, *The Unified Modeling Language Reference Manual*, Reading, Mass.: Addison Wesley, 1999.

Shaw, M. and D. Garlan, *Software Architecture: Perspectives on an Emerging Discipline*, Prentice Hall, 1996.

Sommerville, I., *Software Engineering*, Reading, Mass.: Addison-Wesley, 1989.

Thomas, D., and I. Jacobson, Managing Object-oriented Software Engineering Tutorial, TOOLS '89, Paris, 13–15 November 1989. This has been further developed by B. Henderson-Sellers, 1993, "The Economics of Reusing Library Classes," *Journal of Object-Oriented Programming*, 6(4), 43–50.

Unhelkar, B., 1995, "The MOSES Experience," *Object Magazine* (June 1995): p. 51.

————, and B. Henderson-Sellers, "The Role of Granularity in the Reuse of Object-Oriented Systems," *Proceedings of ACOSM'93 First Australian Conference on Software Metrics*, Sydney, Australia, J. Verner (ed.), Australian Software Metrics Association, Nov. 18–19 1993, pp. 51–66.

————, and B. Henderson-Sellers, "Evaluating the Role of Reuse in Object-Oriented Systems," *Proceedings of the First Australian Conference on Software Metrics, ACOSM'93*, Nov. 1993, J. Verner (ed.).

————, and G. Mamdapur, "Practical Aspects of Using a Methodology: A Road Map Approach," *Report on Object Analysis and Design (ROAD)*, 2(2), (July–August 1995): 34–36, 54.

————, "Developing a Financial Market Analysis Product: A MOSES Case Study," *Developing Business Objects*, A. Carmichael, (ed.), SIGS, (1997): 113–140.

————, *Effect of Granularity of Object-Oriented Design on Modeling an Enterprise and its Application to Financial Risk Management*, Ph.D. Thesis, University of Technology, Sydney: 1997–8.

————, *After the Y2K Fireworks: Business and Technology Strategies*, CRC Press, 1999.

————, "Transactional Analysis (TA) as applied to the Human Factor in Object-Oriented Projects," *Handbook of Object Technology*, S. Zamir (ed.), CRC Press, Boca Raton, Fla.: 1999, 42–1 to 42–12.

Van Harmelen, M., (ed.), *Object Modeling and User Interface Design: Designing Interactive Systems*, Addison-Wesley, 2001.

Wohlin, C., and M. Ahlgren, "Soft factors and their impact on time to market," *Software Quality Journal*, 4(3), (September 1995): 189–205.

www.MethodScience.com

www.omg.org

Younessi, H. and B. Henderson-Sellers, *Object Magazine*, 7(8), 1997: 38–42.

Yourdon, (ed.), *The Rise and Resurrection of the American Programmer*, Yourdon Press Computing Series, Upper Saddle River, N.J.: Prentice Hall, 1998.

Some additional recent and relevant titles:

- *UML and the Unified Process: Practical Object-Oriented Analysis and Design*, Boston: Addison-Wesley, 2002; ISBN: 0201770601

- *The Unified Process Explained*, Boston: Addison-Wesley, 2001; ISBN: 0201742047

- *The Unified Process Transition and Production Phases: Best Practices in Implementing the UP*, CMP Books, 2001; ISBN: 157820092X

- *The Unified Process Construction Phase: Best Practices in Implementing the UP,* CMP Books, 2000; ISBN: 192962901X

- *The Unified Process Inception Phase: Best Practices for Implementing the UP,* CMP Books, 2000; ISBN: 1929629109

- *The Unified Process Elaboration Phase: Best Practices in Implementing the UP,* CMP Books, 2000; ISBN: 1929629052

- *Applying UML and Patterns: An Introduction to Object-Oriented Analysis and Design and the Unified Process,* Prentice Hall PTR, 2001; ISBN: 0130925691

UML CASE Tools

Following are the tools I come across in my work; most I have evaluated, and some I have used in practice. It is difficult to come up with a spreadsheet comparison of UML-based CASE tools because the value of the tools depends on the context—the project, people, and purpose for using the tool. I recommend that you conduct your own research and comparison exercise.

Relevance of Modeling CASE Tools

With the application of any tool, it is always worth remembering the age-old advice, "Tools are a means to an end." The ideal starting tools for modeling (whether it is a house, a car, or a software solution) are still pencils and paper (and today, whiteboards and marker pens). Even if the project eventually changes from a small to a medium or a large project and requires more sophisticated CASE tools, from my point of view, the preferred starting point for any modeling exercise is still a whiteboard.

The only additional technology I prefer to use at this stage is an electronic whiteboard to help me print the models I have drawn. Many of my practical modeling workshops, or intense training sessions, start on a flipchart. And I am no longer surprised to walk into the project a few weeks later, to find those hand-sketched flipcharts placed as a reference on a side wall, and discussions on a use case diagram or a sequence diagram taking place based on that model. It is not uncommon for many of my clients and trainees to return to the rather unkempt use case or class diagrams a few months later, just to clarify a point!

Having said that, let me also emphasize that having good CASE tools provides phenomenal help not only in drawing neat-looking diagrams, but also in providing many additional features that a good model must have, and that may not be achievable with a simple whiteboard and marker pen. For example, it is difficult to provide inter-diagram dependencies (where we want to ensure that a message shown in a sequence diagram is indeed implementable, by virtue of being available in a class on a corresponding class diagram) on a whiteboard, but they are easily provided in a UML CASE tool.

Finally, the CASE tools discussed here only provide the mechanism to document UML-based diagrams. They do *not* provide the process steps to arrive at these diagrams. In other words, if you want to rely only on these UML-based CASE tools in your project, then the "how to" of drawing these diagrams is left up to you. Alternatively, you may want to consider process-based CASE tools, such as RUP and eTrack, to accompany the UML-based CASE tools. They are a topic of separate discussion (see page 365).

Criteria for Evaluating UML-Based CASE Tools

So, what are the things one should look for in terms of UML CASE tools that can help practical projects? Here is a brief discussion of some of these points. Following this discussion on the criteria is a list of UML-based CASE tools that I have seen, evaluated, or used. The list is restricted to my practical experience; I am sure there are other tools that have escaped my attention.

Compliance with UML

Many tools tend to add their own features to the OMG-standard UML. Thus, while they may contain some rich features, these features are not necessarily compliant with the *www.omg.org* list. This does *not* imply that the tools should be deemed negative for their noncompliance. However, I consider it important to highlight the fact that some tools have extended the UML to be, perhaps, more expressive.

Support of the Development Environment

Development environments of practical projects, while including many technologies, may still be bent toward one language or other. For example, some development environments are predominantly Java based and others are full of Visual Basic. Therefore, it is essential that the CASE tool that is selected is compliant with the language of choice. This compliance implies that the UML tool is able to represent correctly what will eventually become code of that language. This representation primarily revolves around class diagrams, sequence diagrams, and component diagrams.

Support of Multiple Users (Team Work)

A tool that works well with a single user and supports all the required UML features still runs into problems when thrust into a real-life team environment. Tools which are known to have extensive UML background and a good interface have failed when a team of five business analysts or designers has tried to work on them simultaneously. In checking this criterion, check the concurrency of use (developers using different diagrams at the same time) by evaluating the tool under simultaneous use. This also leads to identifying the number of people who will use the tool and is helpful with regard to licensing.

Information Generation (Document and Web Publishing)

It is important, especially in the business analysis/requirements engineering activity, that what is inputted by many people in the tool is also made visible to a large number of interested parties, especially the users. Users, still new to the concept of UML, usually find it difficult to navigate through diagrams put in a tool. Furthermore, they may not have the tools or the organization may not have sufficient user licenses. In such scenarios, it is important that the UML tool of choice is able to provide relevant feedback by means other than simply their soft files or direct printouts of the diagrams. Both these means are unsatisfactory in practice and better feedback mechanisms are required through the document-generation capability of the tool. Almost all contemporary tools have the ability to generate an intranet Web site, enabling end users and other interested parties to view, understand, comment, and track the work progressing within the UML tool.

Support of Reusability (Patterns)

UML tools are expected to come with either the ability to store and retrieve with ease reusable patterns, or patterns of their own. It is possible to derive significant reuse benefits with a good tool that understands and supports the concepts of reuse, as directed by a process.

Integration with Other Products

UML tools must understand configuration management, testing, project management, document management, and so forth. Therefore, the tools must be compliant with other tools that perform configuration management and testing.

It is worth mentioning the tight integration of Rational's ROSE with the rest of the Rational suite of tools. Also worth considering is the integration of TogetherSoft's integration with ClearCase and related tools. UML CASE tool evaluators should also check Windows and Linux file compatibilities and XML and XMI support capabilities.

User Friendliness of the Tool

Earlier UML tools focused more on developers and hence tended to ignore the usability aspect. However, in a large-scale and full lifecycle development environment, many nontechnical personnel use UML tools. These include end users, business analysts, quality-assurance personnel, and even senior program directors. Therefore, the user friendliness of the tool, including the ease with which new users can start using it, is important.

Costs of Licensing and Deployment

This criterion includes licensing costs, maintenance costs, deployment costs, and upgrade costs as new releases appear. These costs have to be ascertained from their respective vendors, but are more likely to be influenced by how many licenses are required by the organization. Arriving at the number of licenses required is crucial in ascertaining the costs of licensing and deploying tools. This also relates to the support of multiple users discussed earlier.

Ability to Suit a Process

UML is considered strictly as a technique and should not be confused with a process. While the process continues to direct the software activities, it is important that the tool is able to produce all the relevant deliverables, or to produce material that can be put in the deliverables. Furthermore, it is important that in an IIP process, the tool is able to adapt itself to suit the approach of the process.

Tool Support in the Region

With the exception of one or two, almost all popular UML-based CASE tools that are used in countries such as Australia and New Zealand are developed in the U.S. Therefore, while this may not be a vital criterion for American users, for others it is still important to note if the tool has a local vendor and local support. This is important in terms of receiving initial queries on installation and tool usage, corresponding training and consulting support, and frequent and timely upgrades.

Performance

By loading the tool with a number of users or by inserting a large number of classes and use cases in the case tool, we can figure out how the tool responds, *as the project progresses.* This is the equivalent of a stress or volume test of the modeling tool.

Compatibility

Is the UML tool compatible with Jbuilder, Jdeveloper, Visual Age for Java, and so forth? This is important information when a tool is considered for a full development environment, especially in the MOSS and MOBS modeling spaces, rather than just as a business analysis tool in MOPS.

References

How many other sites have used the tool, and for how long? These are crucial questions, as practical experiences with tools often turn out to be quite different from what vendors promise. Furthermore, check regarding the type of project (data warehousing versus integration) to ensure that the comments they are making are relevant to what you are trying to do.

Tool Friction Factor

The difference between what we are trying to accomplish, in terms of creating the models in the problem, solution, and background spaces, and what the tool provides is called the "friction factor" between the conceptual modeling and the models documented in the CASE tool. Furthermore, the conversion of the models into the final software product is also fraught with friction. Many good CASE tools try to reduce this friction by enabling as smooth a transition as possible between various models and between models and code. The key to reducing the friction factor is interaction. If a tool is able to provide continuous interaction between the various parties involved in modeling (the business analysts, system designers, system architects, and users) and the developers, then the CASE tool is said to have minimum friction.

Ensure that the tool complies with what you are trying to do, and not the other way around. CASE tool limitations should not limit the thinking of the modelers. For example, creating the MOPS, MOSS, and MOBS is an exercise that, when documented in a CASE tool, may have to become a single model. The differentiation between the modeling spaces is crucial, and the closeness of the three models is also important for a good quality modeling exercise. However, creating the three modeling spaces may not always be possible in CASE tool-based modeling. Ideally, CASE tools should enable the creation of as many modeling spaces as necessary, and then enable reduced or zero friction between the modeling spaces.

Disclaimer: Please note that I am a user and adviser but not a reseller of any of these UML-based CASE tools and I do not have any vested interest in recommending one tool over the other. My priority is always what is in the best interest of my client. The order of presentation of these tools is random.

Tau UML v 4.2 from Telelogic

Information	www.telelogic.com
Comments	Of the many products offered by Telelogic, I have had the opportunity to investigate Tau UML, particularly with DOORS. Although their latest release is v4.3, I have used the slightly earlier version 4.2. I found Tau UML extremely valuable in quality UML-based modeling but, more importantly, I was impressed with its ability to handle third-party integrations. This product can be very helpful in medium to large integration projects discussed in Chapter 1. Furthermore, because of its integration with DOORS (particularly for requirements management), Tau UML provides excellent requirements traceability.

Together v5.0 from TogetherSoft

Information	www.togethersoft.com
Comments	I have used TogetherSoft ControlCenter and I find its architecture and its sleek user interface excellent. It is aimed at the high end of the market, and does an excellent job in large projects with multiple teams. The availability of patterns within the tool helps with reuse and quality. Furthermore, as well-known author Peter Coad's tool, it has the necessary personality blessings that help it challenge other UML-based tools that enjoy a similar personality aura.

ROSE 2001 from Rational

Information	www.rational.com
Comments	Rational's Object Software Engineering (ROSE) remains the most well-known tool in the UML modeling arena. In addition to the awesome influence of the "three amigos" (Jacobson, Booch, and Rumbaugh) on this CASE tool, it is also important to note the comprehensive suite of other tools that go with ROSE (configuration management, testing, and process).

ParadigmPlus v4.0 from Computer Associates

Information	www.ca.com
Comments	I had the opportunity to evaluate and use ParadigmPlus v3.7.; however, CA has since released v4.0. The configurability of this tool to suit the needs of the modelers is excellent.

COOL Suite from Computer Associates

Information	www.ca.com
Comments	The COOL suite of products (COOL:Plex, COOL:Joe, COOL:Gen, and others) cannot be called UML modeling tools, but they do use the UML notations for their development work. The suite is worth investigating for UML-based projects.

ArgoUML 0.9 from Tigris

Information	www.tigris.org
Comments	I have not had the opportunity to investigate this product in great detail. However, many of my colleagues have and they recommend that I include it here. (Note the .org in the Web site.)

VisualUML 2.70 from Visual Object Modelers

Information	www.visualuml.com
Comments	VisualUML is aimed at the medium to low end of the market. It is ideal for small to medium projects. However, the tool can scale up and relates to various development environments. I have used this product and I find it excellent for the purposes mentioned here.

SimplyObjects v3.2.3 from Adaptive-Arts

Information	www.adaptive-arts.com
Comments	SimplyObjects by Adaptive-Arts is a "techie" UML product that goes directly to the heart of architecture and design. This is a definite advantage when starting your modeling work in the background space (creating MOBS). Integration with other products enables the creation of code. This is the only tool I am familiar with that has been designed and developed in Sydney, Australia.

Magicdraw v4.1 from NoMagic

Information	www.nomagic.com
Comments	MagicDraw UML is the product by NoMagic. NoMagic is not a tool vendor but more of a technology partner. MagicDraw also provides excellent support for UML-based modeling, particularly in the problem space (creation of MOPS).

Ectoset Modeller

Information	www.ectoset.com
Comments	Simplicity and affordability are the hallmarks of this tool. It is extremely valuable to small projects or pilot projects that are trying to inculcate the methods discipline. There is no reason why this tool should not scale up to large projects either, but I do not have that direct experience.

Visio

Comments	Occasionally, modelers have used Visio, but the general impression Visio gives is that it is more of a UML (and other) documentation tool rather than a design tool.

Process Tools
Using UML

Investigation and study of process tools helps to customize the process to enable the best use of the tool or customize the tool to ensure it best fits the project requirements. Process tools have the additional responsibility of facilitating and helping the project manager in her measurement and estimation efforts.

Disclaimer: Please note that I am a user but not a reseller of any of these tools and I do not have any vested interest in recommending one tool over the other. My priority is always what is in the best interest of my client. The order of presentation of these tools is random.

Rational Unified Process (RUP)

Information	www.rational.com
Comments	Rational's RUP is a process tool that is tightly integrated with ROSE. RUP also has the robust research background provided by Jacobson's earlier process work in objectory. Object Oriented Process Environment and Notation (OPEN)

Object Oriented Process Environment and Notation (OPEN)

Information	www.open.org.au
Comments	Original work on the OPEN process was done by Graham, Henderson-Sellers, and Younessi, followed by several other methodologists. However, OPEN needs to be configured within another tool of your choice, because OPEN itself is not a process tool but rather an extremely well-researched process framework.

MeNtOR

Information	*www.processmentor.com* and *www.oopl.com.au*
Comments	Object Oriented Pty. Ltd. (OOPL) Process Mentor is a fairly extensive, detailed, and extremely well-documented process that can help in any UML-based development. Its major strength is requirements modeling, although other areas of process are also well supported.

Catalysis

Information	D'Souza, D., and A. Wills, *Objects, Components and Frameworks with UML: The Catalysis Approach*, Reading, Mass.: Addison-Wesley, 1999.
Comments	A comprehensive process, together with the UML notations and diagrams.

ICONIX

Information	Rosenberg, D., with K. Scott, *Use Case Driven Object Modeling with UML: A Practical Approach*, Addison-Wesley, 1999. *www.iconixsw.com*
Comments	A UML-based process that, for most part, I like and agree with.

ETrack

Information	www.eTrack.com
Comments	A uniquely architected process tool that allows you to create a genuine iterative and incremental process plan. Due to its integration with Microsoft Project, it is easier for project managers to create an IIP plan and then translate it into a linear project plan.

Process Continuum

Information	www.ca.com
Comments	Process Continuum is a high-end process tool that needs to be configured to support your process. This could include configuring the tool to a suite of process-components described in Chapter 3.

"Lightweight" or Agile Methodologies

Following is a list of some contemporary "Lightweight" or Agile Methodologies that may be of interest to readers.

Agile Methodology	Information
Extreme Programming	*www.extremeprogramming.org; www.xprogramming.com*
Adaptive	*www.adaptivesd.com*
Crystal	*http://crystalmethodologies.org*
Dynamic Systems Development Method	*www.dsdm.org*
Scrum	www.controlchaos.com
Feature-Driven Development	Coad et. al., *Java Modeling Color with UML: Enterprise Components and Process*, Prentice Hall PTR, 1999

CD-ROM Contents

The training course based on the figures in the book is put together by *www.MethodScience.com*.

MeNtOR is the copyright of Object Oriented Pty. Ltd., Sydney (*www.processmentor.com, www.oopl.com.au*).

CBEADS is owned by the University of Western Sydney's CBEAD project team (*www.cbeads.org*).

1.1   Case Study: Lucky Insurance

This case study of Lucky Insurance is derived from work by *www.MethodScience.com* in a real insurance organization. It is provided here in full detail for readers to create additional workshop exercises based on the process quality checks discussed in the book.

1.2   Process-Components Activities and Tasks (based on Chapter 3)

The process-components described in Chapter 3 are described here, in tabular form. These activities and tasks, from the tables, can be easily inserted in a project task plan and are provided here for that precise purpose.

1.3   Quality Checklist for UML-Based Models of Problem Space, Solution Space, and Background Space

A checklist for the various model checks is provided here for additional help in checking the quality of the models produced during a project. Needless to say, these checks require more modeling-specific discussion than has been provided in this book. For detailed a discussion on the model quality, see the forthcoming *Model Quality Assurance for UML-Based Projects*.

1.4   Test Case Template

Electronic copy of a test case template is provided to enable readers to use it as a starting point for creating their own test cases.

1.5   Training Course Presentation Files

The PowerPoint presentation file contains all the chapters in "ready to go" presentation format. The idea is that with some modification, these presentation slides will be a valuable companion for a presenter in an industrial course, or for a subject (or part thereof) in a senior academic environment. If copies of the slides are made and modified to suit the reader's needs, a humble request is made to acknowledge the originator of the slides (Bhuvan Unhelkar).

1.6   MeNtOR Lite

This directory contains the product MeNtOR Lite by Object Oriented Pty. Ltd. (www.oopl.com.au). MeNtOR is a process-based tool that enables UML-based software projects to follow a software process. Readers are encouraged to try and place the process quality steps within MeNtOR Lite and evaluate the importance of a process quality.

1.7   CBEADS (Component Based E Application Development Shell)

The CBEADS directory contains a static process, configured within CBEADS, that demonstrates the various process-components of the software quality process described in this book (particularly Chapter 3). While this is only a demo of the product, it is provided here as a means of appreciating how a process can be configured in a tool. Notice how the total flexibility of configuring the process can be used even in an "Agile Methodology" environment.

Epilogue

Out of the plains of western India, in the dusty town of Baroda,[1] rises a structure of exquisite beauty called Laxmi Vilas Palace. With the backdrop of a diffused, red glow emanating from the setting sun in this part of the world, this tall and majestic stone palace takes on the personality of a mystique *every* night. Booch et al., in the opening discussion on architecture,[2] ask us to "think about the most beautiful building you've ever seen—perhaps the Taj Mahal or Notre Dame. . . . Both structures are architecturally simple, yet they are also profoundly deep." The palace in Baroda not only exudes the music in stone that the Taj Mahal does, it is also the epitome of strength and quality. For years I have almost religiously climbed on top of my home terrace in the evenings and serenaded this tower in silence.

Major Charles Mant, an officer of the Royal Engineers of the British Raj in India, was the original architect of this palace in the 1860s; it took a decade to build. It is profoundly deep, because apart from amalgamating Victorian style with Italian gothic and Roman designs, the palace intertwines the religious, social, and cultural diversity of India.[3] To add to its aura, this building provided residence to the erstwhile rulers of the state,

---

[1] The town is now called Vadodara.

[2] Booch, G., Rumbaugh, J., Jacobson, I., *The Unified Modeling Language User Guide*, Boston: Addison-Wesley, 1999, Chapter 27, p. 369.

[3] Gaekwad, Fathehsingrao, *SayajiRao of Baroda, The Prince and the Man*, Mumbai: Popular Prakashan, 1989, p 77.

and occasionally housed their grand durbars with more than 1,000 courtiers comfortably seated within one hall.

Major Mant went stark raving mad! He believed that all his architectural calculations on the palace were wrong. He had gone through his architectural and design calculations again, and again, and again. He could not successfully measure the immeasurable quality of what he had produced. Barely had the foundation of the palace been laid when he lost control of his senses. Even now, to my humble eye, the palace appears to be too tall for its width, and relatively wider at the top—almost like a water maid standing with an earthen pot over her head. It's a fine balancing act for both. Major Mant died at the early age of 40, convinced that his palace was out of balance and would soon collapse!

On January 26, 2001, I was on my home terrace, continuing my tryst with this stone structure, when the ground beneath me shook violently. The state of Gujarat in western India was hit by one of the worst earthquakes in the past 100 years, measuring over 7 on the Richter scale. Brick houses, mud houses, and many tall modern buildings less than 50 miles from where I stood looking at the palace collapsed. Luckily, my terrace stood. So did the palace, nonchalant in its demeanor.

I wish Major Mant knew! The quality of his architecture encompasses the dichotomy of beauty and utility, strength and subtlety, grandeur and functionality—just what we expect from quality, even in a software system. "Look harder and you will see details that are themselves beautiful and that work together to produce a beauty and functionality that's greater than the individual parts." Booch et al. could not have been more prophetic. Times change, viewers change, developers change, users change, and "the system" still holds strong! This happens when the sum of individual parts is *greater* than the parts. This *greater* bit, the one that is more than the sum of individual parts, is probably where the charisma of quality lies hidden. And such is its mystique that sometimes in stone, and more often in software, it eludes perception even from its creators.

Index

CD-ROM Warranty

Addison-Wesley warrants the enclosed disc to be free of defects in materials and faulty workmanship under normal use for a period of ninety days after purchase. If a defect is discovered in the disc during this warranty period, a replacement disc can be obtained at no charge by sending the defective disc, postage prepaid, with proof of purchase to:

Editorial Department
Addison-Wesley Professional
Pearson Technology Group
75 Arlington Street, Suite 300
Boston, MA 02116
Email: AWPro@awl.com

Addison-Wesley makes no warranty or representation, either expressed or implied, with respect to this software, its quality, performance, merchantability, or fitness for a particular purpose. In no event will Addison-Wesley, its distributors, or dealers be liable for direct, indirect, special, incidental, or consequential damages arising out of the use or inability to use the software. The exclusion of implied warranties is not permitted in some states. Therefore, the above exclusion may not apply to you. This warranty provides you with specific legal rights. There may be other rights that you may have that vary from state to state. The contents of this CD-ROM are intended for personal use only.

More information and updates are available at:
http://www.awprofessional.com